ORAL
HISTORY
A HANDBOOK

KEN HOWARTH

SUTTON PUBLISHING

07700235

First published in the United Kingdom in 1998 by
Sutton Publishing Limited · Phoenix Mill
Thrupp · Stroud · Gloucestershire · GL5 2BU

British Library Cataloguing in Publication Data
A catalogue record for this book is available from the British Library

ISBN 0 7509 1756 3

^{TM} ALAN SUTTON^{TM} and SUTTON^{TM} are the
trade marks of Sutton Publishing Limited

Typeset in 10.5/13pt Bembo.
Typesetting and origination by
Sutton Publishing Limited.
Printed in Great Britain by
WBC Ltd, Bridgend.

CONTENTS

INTRODUCTION

The rise of oral history has been dramatic. There can now be only a few countries that have not had some kind of oral history work taking place, and sound archive collections now exist in most of the developed world. Scandinavia, the United Kingdom, the USA, Canada and Australia have tended to lead the way, each respectively taking slightly differing routes. The approach, by and large, has been that of recording life histories of individuals – the backbone of oral history work – but as this publication reveals, there are other approaches too, such as using oral history interview skills in awareness work with disorientated patients in care.

A great deal of work in oral history has been conducted under the banner of social history research. The *Oral History Journal* has devoted issues to specific subjects over the years such as political lives, women's lives, ethnicity and so on as appropriate, sensible subjects to cover but very much in the academic pursuance of social history.

This publication, however, explores other uses of oral history by widening the scope of the subject to include the heritage world and, for the first time, oral history as a corporate tool. Nevertheless, the book has been intentionally written to provide a good solid introduction to the principles of oral history and to encourage the adoption of high professional standards. It is therefore particularly suited to those discovering oral history for the first time, whether they are professionals or amateurs seeking a professional approach.

Oral history (especially with projected funding by the UK Lottery under its community involvement policy and the pledged six-figure project for the Millennium Dome) will attract many new potential recorders and users, and will offer oral history a much-needed boost.

Much of the oral history recording accumulated over the years has been preserved in museums, archives and public libraries yet on the whole there has been a strangely ambivalent attitude towards it. The value of recording memories and reminiscences is clear and acknowledged yet the practical application of the technique, particularly in the understanding and interpretation of existing public collections, has been patchy and piecemeal. There are, of course, notable exceptions – such as the Department of Sound Records at the Imperial War Museum in London, The People's Story in Edinburgh, Birmingham Museum's inner city collections, Kirklees Museum Service, the Welsh Folk Museum at St Fagans and others – but on the whole many collections, especially photographic collections, remain unexplained and out of context.

Oral history in some ways is 'coming of age' and is growing in popularity around the globe. It is offering a voice to the unheard and unseen. The established traditional (and sometimes less than adequate) approaches adopted over the years are now being effectively challenged by new ideas and techniques. These new approaches apply particularly to interviewing skills, subject matter and the application of recorded oral history material. One such approach is the practical application of tried-and-tested interview techniques in the training of carers in sensitive non-patronizing communication with the elderly. New areas for study are also emerging, such as popular music, cinema and film production and the theatre.[1]

Oral history can be roughly classified into the following approaches and standards:

Professional. The primary aim is an accurate lasting record or statement made to the highest standards possible or available – both technically and in terms of content. In this approach, it is implicit that high standards are employed throughout, including clearance with informants on responsible use and access, moral and ethical considerations, and the deposit of the recordings with a recognized archive or other suitable repository.

A further consideration should be (within the agreed restrictions and closures imposed by interviewees or the law) that in either the short or longer term recorded material should, whenever possible, be made accessible to the community from whence it came – as loan copies, educational packs, exhibitions, publication, etc. In practice this last objective is sometimes difficult to achieve.

Dialectologists, for example, sometimes record samples of language and dialect in a naturally occurring situation so as not to influence the language form or structure by revealing the presence of a tape-recorder. After the tapes have been analysed they are erased.

Equally, in remote rural areas of the developing world where literacy is low, filling in clearance notes might be culturally unacceptable or straightforwardly impractical. The onus of responsibility in such circumstances for any subsequent use of the interviews is placed firmly on the interviewer or on the patron of the recording programme. Only the most principled standards in such circumstances are acceptable.

The emphasis throughout this book will be towards producing the highest quality oral history recordings while employing the most rigid ethical and moral standards. It is recognized that many important amateur recordings have been made over the years, often reaching very high standards, and it is certainly not intended to be dismissive of the contribution those recordings have made to understanding history.

Edited. This may be defined as oral history not meeting the highest standards required in professional oral history work as defined in the previous section. There are literally tens of thousands of such recordings in existence offering tantalizing but often inaccurate glimpses into the past. Generically, they come under the heading of oral history although many such recordings are often poorly researched, and involve suspect question techniques and answer-suggestion. Material is edited arbitrarily or published as 'authoritative', but often lacks even basic information about context, informants, date of recording, place, etc.

Most recordings in this category are edited and should be regarded as secondary source material. This less important status for edited material means considerable care should be taken to assess its reliability before use in exhibitions, publications, etc.

Although edited material should not be seen as accurate primary source material, somewhat paradoxically, it can reveal information by its very repetition. If every farmer interviewed in an area talks about making hay at a particular time of year and in a particular way, then it is likely that is how it was to a large extent. There are dangers, of course: every cotton power-loom weaver in Lancashire wore clogs – didn't they? Every weaver will tell you about clogs, but the truth is that not everyone did wear them.

In addition large accumulations of recordings and associated archival or printed matter accumulated by a particular person or organization become important as distinct collections in their own right. A good example is BBC local radio tapes.

Sometimes the exceptional and unique nature of a sole surviving recorded memory warrants serious attention. A good example might be a unique wax cylinder recording of Florence Nightingale. It is not so much the 'oral history content' that matters as the character, nature and quality of her voice: the fact that it really was – is – Florence Nightingale.

Reminiscence work generally. Here, as will be described in more detail in the section on Reminiscence work, the objectives are different. It is concerned with 'raising the quality of life' for individuals, with accuracy being a bonus rather than a fundamental requirement.

Having made such clear-cut distinctions in approaches to oral history recording, the way forward over the years – even for professionals – has been, to say the least, uncertain and at times faltering. The lack of adequate funding of oral history posts and oral history recording is very evident in the UK. Oral history has, as a result, been a product of enthusiasm in an experimental, fragmentary manner, often lacking structure, training and project co-ordination.

This situation is at last showing signs of improvement and fortunately, as something of a counterbalance, there are many examples of outstanding oral history work in the UK and elsewhere. However, in general the low availability of good quality training and inadequate resources still remain fundamental weaknesses.

Although some projects in the past can be criticized for their lack of scholarship and poor technical expertise, management and application, the availability of the unemployed in the 1970s and 1980s under Manpower Service schemes, STEP and others gave rise to a sudden flourish of oral history recording. Some schemes were highly successful – indeed a number of museums owe their very existence to such projects; others were disastrous. The team members on one scheme, recording the day-to-day operation of a textile mill, appropriated the cassettes at the end of the year, and copied computer games on to them, so that the information was lost forever. On the other hand Suffolk County Council's Information and Library Service brought together over 5,000 hours of recorded material featuring the memories of Suffolk people. The originals are housed in Suffolk Record Office, the project being a direct result of a well-managed two-year Manpower Services Commission team.

Where appropriate, examples and ideas have been given or suggested for as wide a range of interest as possible, especially for professional groups including librarians, archivists, museum curators, educationalists, planners, conservation officers, heritage interpreters and others. Non-professional groups might include local history societies, civic societies, community groups, ethnic minority groups, church groups, the Women's Institute, University of the Third Age, the Workers' Educational Association, etc. From what has been written it might be construed that individuals can offer little on their own. This is far from the truth. Many important oral history recordings have been made by individuals keen to record before it is too late and memories lost forever.

Those trained in museum and archive practice know full well the importance of good documentation detailing information about objects and manuscripts in their care. The provenance, legal ownership, physical description, copyright, conservation, location and other information is all carefully recorded and stored away. Yet, although this is almost instinctive training in museums and archives, the formal use of oral history as part of that initial information-gathering process has been almost totally ignored.

Oral history should be given a far higher priority than it has at present. It should be seen as a vital tool in collection research about almost any object or document. It is perhaps a process of re-evaluation and re-education. Oral history in one of its many guises should be considered as an *essential* part of the recording process and included in any forward plan. It is fundamental in assessing and understanding the use, social context and cultural worth of objects and documents. Oral history should be an accepted part of any formal acquisition process and/or collecting policy.

The strength of oral history lies in the fact that it complements written, printed and visual sources and can often clearly call into question those other sources. It can be, and often is, a fundamental method of acquiring information that cannot be obtained in any other way. For the heritage professional to ignore oral history would be like a general under enemy fire deciding not to use tanks because they are a little time-consuming and somewhat noisy. His lack of appropriate action will be judged by posterity.

Admittedly, there is always a question mark over the reliability of memory. Yet despite its inadequacies – such as the convenience of memory to enhance the individual in a social situation or the possibility of so-called phantom memories acquired from outside sources such as television or books – its track record in terms of accuracy is as good as the printed word and is usually far, far better. At least you can ask your informant questions: typefaces do not tend to answer back.[2]

Oral history and education has been examined in some detail. I have avoided looking just at the UK and the requirements of the National Curriculum. The application of oral history in developing nations is extremely important whatever the age of the student.

Also included for the first time is the application of oral history techniques to business management, public relations, and town and country planning. In the rush by oral historians to use oral history to research social history, these areas have been neglected.

The choice of case studies and examples has been very difficult. In the main, I have used examples from the British Isles, and in some fields, such as planning, I have deliberately cited pilot projects in the north of England in which I have been personally involved. In other areas such as tourism management, business management training, and public relations I have put forward a number of untried suggestions in an attempt to illustrate just how versatile and useful oral history can be.

If I were to offer a single piece of advice about oral history recording it would be 'have a go'. Not only is it rewarding, it is also enjoyable and very enlightening. The modification of pre-conceived ideas is one of its major attributes. Perhaps its greatest strength at an individual level is its innate ability to create lasting personal friendships.

Finally, I would like to acknowledge the considerable help and support given to me by my wife Jean, my son David, and my friends and colleagues over the years, especially Andrew Schofield of the North West Sound Archive, Peter Makin of RTS Audio, Arthur Shaw for his kindness in offering unlimited access to the Internet, BBC Regional Centre (Manchester), Granada TV news, BBC Radio Lancashire, David Lee (Wessex Film & Sound Archive), Dr Rob Perks (National Sound Archive), Alan Ward (National Sound Archive), Katherine Towsey (formerly of Kirklees Sound Archive), Katey Logan (Boots plc), Bridget Williams (Sainsbury's Archives), Charles Pugh (National Trust for Wales), Olivia Bennett (The Panos Institute), and also Allan Redfern for his extremely valuable comments on Chapter Five, Angela Fussell (Croydon Museum Service) and Dr Elizabeth Roberts (Centre for North West Regional Studies, University of Lancaster). I would also like to acknowledge the support received from Lancaster Maritime Museum, Oldham Museum Service, Bolton Museum Service, English Heritage, Lancashire Library Service, the British Empire & Commonwealth Museum and London Transport Museum.

Ken Howarth
Pendle Hill, England, 1998

CHAPTER ONE

WHAT IS ORAL HISTORY?

THE ORIGIN OF LANGUAGE

The transmission of information by word of mouth is obviously very old. There appears to be little certainty about how language originally developed, but there is a general consensus of opinion that the earliest known language systems go back at least six thousand years. It is likely that spoken language has its origins in 'grunts, barks and hoots copied by pre-human figures', so-called onomatopoeic sounds.[1]

Language development both spoken and pictorial is primary in mankind. Perhaps language was an effective aid for survival, but as humans advanced and speech-based language became more and more sophisticated this seems to have led generally to a desire to pass on 'useful' information from one generation to the next.

Some cultures painted cave walls or rock faces with images, unwittingly creating a pictorial language 'archive' for future generations. Illustration is just one way of transmitting information; objects are another. Writing, in the form of clay tablets, chiselled rock, or papyrus, guaranteed the continuity of collective wisdom, religious belief and memory for others.

COLLECTIVE MEMORY

The written word, and much later the printed word, gained dominance over oral tradition in the west, especially among the educated. This is not to say that many former societies, particularly those having so-called language deaths, such as recently extinct tribes in Amazonia, did not have a rich and sophisticated communication structure. The fact that there was an absence of a written legacy in no way negates the significance and importance of those lost languages. Today, in many parts of the world, speech is still the everyday method of communication – official and otherwise – while the West tends to insist on literacy as a priority over native language skills.

The powerful and disturbing images of television and other media have supplanted the spoken word to an alarming degree. Will these be the legacy by which the future will judge us? Alongside the moving image remains the still picture. Drawings, paintings and, of course, still photography have their role to play in this bizarre exercise in 'memory and emotional representation' preservation.

Are museums, libraries and archives an extension of this process? Are they perhaps a kind of collective memory bank? Could the Internet be the common link? People still feel a need to preserve and pass on what is deemed 'useful' or regarded as enjoyable and of seemingly good taste. Are our libraries, archives and museums part of a common conscience? Is part of their function the capability to preserve what is regarded as important by the society at that time? *Good* implies quality and taste, and high moral and ethical standards; *bad* survives as a lesson or warning to future generations.

The process of oral history recording and preservation is simply a refinement of this. Like an encyclopedia, it is a way of passing on important memories for posterity. A colleague, a social anthropologist, put it slightly differently: 'it is a way of ensuring that important knowledge essential and useful to the survival and evolution of mankind is carried forward'.

The development of technology such as printing, photography and television preserves a history of sorts. The oral tradition is still alive in many societies and cultures, although it is now under serious threat from change, particularly from television, and in developing nations from Westernization. Television, and to a lesser extent radio, literature, and the greater movement of people as a result of wars and migration, and the availability of affordable air transport have resulted in exposure to different values, cultures and practices.

In some ways this is helpful to an established culture, if that culture is wise enough to select what is useful and reject the rest. Sadly, other less resourceful cultures are simply swamped and lose many of their traditional values.

THE ORAL TRADITION

It is a common assumption that story-telling is reserved for the very young. Story-telling is, however, not just for children. How many people tune in to *Coronation Street*, *Eastenders*, *Star Trek* and all the others? How popular are the books of Catherine Cookson, Barbara

The continuity of oral tradition is well illustrated by the Bacup Britannia Coconut Dancers whose annual dance on Easter Saturday has been passed down through oral tradition and performance. (Author)

Children's play songs being recorded. The recording of what may seem pointless children's play songs is vitally important. The songs, rhymes and games contain clues to past events in the form of parodies, words, language and actions forming part of a vibrant oral tradition. (Lancashire Evening Post)

Cartland, Jeffrey Archer, Ian Fleming and others? Drama and opera are also ultimately part of the human need to tell a good story.

Story-telling within the community, as a social event or part of a family tradition, has been severely eroded in western society – with some exceptions. Yet despite the influence of modern media there are memories handed down from generation to generation within the family: the steel worker who passes down secret ingredients for a melt to his son or the woman who picks comfrey to soothe an injured limb because her mother said it was good and called it knitbone. They both rely on good oral tradition. Some secret societies, such as the Freemasons, also rely heavily on oral tradition and ritual to preserve their secrets.

It is always worth asking people for their earliest memories and for any memories, tales or reminiscences handed down by their parents and grandparents. In my own experience I have recorded family memories of the Peterloo Massacre in Manchester in 1819 and the Rainhill Locomotive Trials of 1829; and in the Survey of English Dialects recordings, a seventeenth-century story of murderers and brigands is recounted in detail.

One fascinating area of surviving oral tradition is children's street songs and games. Preserved in the seemingly meaningless rhymes are traces of bygone language, tradition and culture. The children's rhyme 'Ring-a-ring-a-roses' relates quite clearly the symptoms of pneumonic plague, a disease which affects the lungs and is invariably fatal within a few days. Traditional stories are passed down by oral custom and it is important to record the stories in all their varieties and forms.

Oral history and oral tradition overlap. Oral history is both a subject and a methodology, a way of finding out more by careful, thoughtful interviewing and listening. Interviewing is perhaps the wrong word, for successful sessions involve a high degree of empathy and are often more closely related to informal conversations or neighbourly exchanges between trusting friends.

In some countries the oral tradition is often still very strong and relevant to everyday life. As an example, in Trinidad a project was started by the University of the West Indies in St Augustine. Their work includes an investigation into the strong oral traditions of the Portuguese community, which includes an important Indo-Caribbean folk tale handed down in the oral tradition as part of the East Indian folk theatre.[2]

The importance of oral culture is also recognized by many ethnic groups now re-established away from their places of origin. Although this will be examined in more detail as part of community oral history, it is a tacit recognition of the significance of the unwritten record and the capturing of memories taking place not in the original countries but in the host countries, often among first or second generation surviving immigrants.

A Ukrainian man is interviewed in his home as part of Bradford Heritage Recording Unit's Oral History Project, recording the experiences of eastern Europeans. (Tim Smith, Bradford Heritage Recording Unit)

As an example, some of Liverpool's sizeable Chinese community were recorded by Maria Lin Wong. Described as 'an invisible group' with 'few contacts with Liverpool's wider society', their recollections resulted in a book on Chinese Liverpudlians which was published in 1991.[3]

Oral history has been recorded for many generations. Professor Paul Thompson in his book *The Voice of the Past* makes out not just an overwhelming case for oral history as a serious information source, but also outlines in detail how oral sources have been recorded and used effectively over many centuries. The opportunity to record oral sources and actually preserve the sound of the human voice had to await the arrival of appropriate technology.

ORAL HISTORY AND TECHNOLOGY

In June 1878, just one year after patenting his invention of the phonograph, Thomas

Alva Edison realised the great potential for recording of the human voice. Although he did not actually suggest the recording of 'family memories' or oral history, he certainly came close. In a list of ten possible uses he included 'the family record: preserving the sayings, the voices, and the last words of the dying members of the family, as of great men'. In another section he identifies 'educational purposes', and 'the preservation of language' – albeit as he saw it at the time – 'through our Washingtons, our Lincolns, and our Gladstones'.[4]

Many technical improvements in sound recording followed, but machines were bulky, expensive and largely confined to commercial record companies, broadcasters and the military. Running times were severely limited and it was not until the Second World War and the introduction of magnetic wire and tape-recording for propaganda purposes that this was really remedied. The die had, however, been cast for post-war development, although for some considerable time recording machines remained heavy and expensive. It was not until the 1960s and the advent of the cheap portable cassette recorder that the recording of the human voice, and therefore oral history, began to take off. The 1960s, therefore, made it possible for everyone to record simply and cheaply. Philips launched the compact cassette and this led gradually to a rising interest in the possibilities of oral history.

It is true that the BBC recorded and preserved programme interviews in their pioneer sound archive department, but those interviews, while providing irreplaceable glimpses into the past, are frustrating because of their incompleteness, editing and the particular social stance adopted by the BBC. Paradoxically, the BBC's sound archive collection offers a glimpse of what might have been if the climate had been right for systematic oral history recording in a broadcast environment.

The establishment of local radio throughout the UK gave ordinary people access to equipment and some basic interview training. Local radio recorded and broadcast – in the same frustrating way as their predecessors – 'bits of oral history'; these were heavily edited but at least they were recorded and an awareness of the value of human memory crept in.

The Manpower Service groups established to provide training for the unemployed gave impetus to oral history work which by then was seen as a community ideal. The formation of the Oral History Society with its publication *Oral History* and the publication of Paul Thompson's milestone publication, *The Voice of the Past*, further added to the movement.

There were other major steps forward such as Rob Perk's oral history and photographic project chronicling the lives of immigrants in the Bradford area; and indeed his appointment at the National Sound Archive as Keeper of Oral History was a tremendous fillip to oral history.

Another important project (in which I was involved) was the establishment of the North West Sound Archive in Lancashire to 'record and preserve the oral traditions and culture of north-west England'. New areas and methods of recording oral history have been explored, including work in prisons, hospitals, community arts, dialect societies and, of course, with museums, archives and libraries. Many of these approaches are described later.

WHAT IS ORAL HISTORY?

However, the question of what oral history is still remains unanswered. The validity of using the oral tradition as source material alongside other sources is apparent. Oral history interview techniques and skills allow access to those areas where the printed or official source is sparse or non-existent. Many memories are personal and not thought of by the individual as being important. The oral historian is able to cross-examine people about their often very personal experiences and memories.

Oral history is not just a way of allowing the 'working class' or 'deprived' a voice: it is far more than that. Official written or printed versions of events, or history, tend to recall the battles, the famous and the good. The official record often represents the interests, aspirations, bias, opinions and cultural values of the educated classes or the state. The official records, if produced within active living memory, ought be understood or 'interpreted' using oral history techniques as one of the approaches. Archives are not always the definitive record – someone wrote or compiled them and there were reasons for doing so.

Oral history then is a subject in its own right and its interview technique enables researchers to investigate memories and reminiscences on particular themes or subjects and to record them for posterity, usually on a tape-recorder but increasingly on video or, as a last resort, like Charles Dickens, with a pen.

Overseas oral history is gaining importance particularly in nations whose cultures and traditions have been repressed, such as the Ukraine. In Canada there have been numerous oral history community-based recording projects, where the function of oral history extends to bringing a community closer together with a sense of common identity. In Africa, India and China oral history has yet to play its full role of recording the history of the many.

It has its dangers too: 'official' oral histories can be selective and create the wrong image. (I hesitate to use the word propaganda, but the thesaurus is unable to supply a better one.) Even in the UK there is a feeling that oral history recording must be about 'ordinary people' or 'the working class' or 'disadvantaged' groups in society.

Oral history does not covet favour with any particular stratum of society or political conviction. There are numerous possibilities for other projects, such as country estate management, the House of Lords, upper-class life, space exploration, natural history collectors, local government, musicians, opera singers, television, royalty, banking and finance, and many more.[5]

SOUNDSCAPES AND ORAL HISTORY

Strictly speaking, sounds are not part of oral history methodology, yet relevant sounds should be recorded. How was the deafness of a former shipyard riveter acquired? How useful would it be to have a recording (along with decibel levels) and perhaps photographs of riveting taking place? At the other extreme of soundscape, an interview with an opera singer about her interpretation of a particular aria (a form of soundscape?) would be far more meaningful if a recorded copy of that piece of music and her specific performance were available. Soundscapes are very important in all societies and to a large extent can, and do, complement the oral history and photographic record.

The recording using oral history methods of what geographers call sense-of-place – the elements that make up the uniqueness or distinctiveness of a place – is just beginning to develop. Soundscape is part of that sense-of-place. The issues are complex and recording work in this area is still in its infancy. More of this new use of oral history is detailed in Chapter Three.

LANGUAGE AND DIALECT

Dialectologists have their own special way of interviewing and recording. The Survey of English Dialects recorded by the University of Leeds School of English from the 1930s to the 1970s contains much that might be defined as oral history and oral tradition, yet its main purpose was the recording of remaining rural language and dialect and its subsequent analysis. Ideally the dialectologist needs natural unhindered speech, but interviews can also provide linguistic clues if some information is recorded about the background of the informant. Such information would include details of his or her parents' origins, social status, and geographical and other influences, such as military service overseas.

The value of such information is clearly shown in the work of Dr Elizabeth Gordon, of the University of Canterbury, New Zealand, who was able to use recorded interviews of people born in the middle of the nineteenth century. These interviews, originally made by a broadcasting organization, are now valued as a 'linguistic treasure trove' illustrating the origins of the New Zealand accent and New Zealand English.[6]

ORAL HISTORY – ITS PLACE IN RECORDING HISTORY

Academics, particularly in the UK, have on the whole been slow to endorse oral history. In my own experience I recall being informed in no uncertain terms by the head of a university history department that I was wasting my time and I would be well advised to 'go and study proper history'. Such extreme prejudices are rare but they do still exist. No amount of reasoning or debate would ever convince such dissenters that oral history can have a place in the scheme of things. Yet there is a readiness to accept written material because it is written. It has been established earlier that written material is subject to the same types of prejudice, cultural contamination and inaccuracies as material derived from oral history sources, and should be subject to the same checks, scrutiny and interpretation. The concept of propaganda is far from new, as is censorship. The social context or the context in which documents were prepared is highly significant, as often is the intention of the writer.

Nor should the modern media be exempted from this scrutiny. Some newspapers are notorious for their lack of accuracy. In an experiment during the 1977 firemen's strike I recorded a great deal of information not only on the picket lines but also with serving

Picket line at a fire station during the national firemen's strike, December 1977. The various strikers in the photograph were interviewed as part of a contemporary oral history programme. (Author)

soldiers who were fighting fires and with others involved. During a particular night's recording session there was a fire-call. The soldiers ran for the Green Goddess fire-engines and set off to fight the fire. I followed in a police car. The blaze was not particularly spectacular – a small wooden garage was burnt to the ground – but a newspaper report issued just a short time afterwards bore no relationship to what had happened, concentrating instead on the alleged instability of the Green Goddess fire-engines in the wake of one crashing elsewhere in the region killing a soldier.

Film and television must undergo the same scrutiny. The visual image in western society is accepted as the 'truth' by the general public almost without question, yet film and television offer mere glimpses of reality and are edited at the whim of producers to provide maximum visual impact, often intended to boost audience ratings. In other words, it is the picture that dominates, the picture that tells the story.

TELEVISION AND ORAL HISTORY

One contentious area is oral history on television. There have been many successful television programmes featuring interviews with people who give detailed recollections of events or individual personalities. Fly-on-the-wall techniques have been described as oral history in the raw. But, as always, the sequences are edited, and shortened and intercut with other material and thus should not, in the author's view, be viewed as true primary source oral history.

Oral history interviews should be seen as the creation of an original document or artefact. Historians would not be pleased, on discovering an important written document for the first time, to find that pieces had been physically and irretrievably removed – so why accept unqualified edited testimony?

An uninterrupted session, or a series of interviews covering a wide range of issues, will deliver far more than popularist television ever could. There are personal moments, many of them not televisual – some, dare I suggest, might even be tele-boring, but to a serious researcher the information could be priceless.

The case I am making is for an understanding of the validity of oral history, its need for completeness, its overall context and relationship to other information sources – particularly archival, printed, photographic, artistic, object, etc., and for the preservation and eventual release (legal and agreed restrictions allowing) of the whole.

This does not mean that television programmes purporting to contain oral history are less enjoyable or meaningful. They can offer a useful but unavoidably selective viewpoint. They can uncover events and people who would otherwise never have been recorded, and offer a quick introduction to complex areas of study. But they are not direct substitutes for detailed audio oral history interviewing.

Having thus created a forceful statement about television and oral history, there are, of course, exceptions to the general rule. In 1989 in São Paulo, Brazil, a project was developed by the Museum of Image and Sound using video as a favoured tool for recording the memories and reminiscences of 'cultural workers and artists' including film-makers, musicians, actors and artists.[7] Their approach was unusual in oral history terms in employing, in the first instance, a researcher to 'study primary and secondary sources about each interviewee's life'. The researcher then collaborated with the interviewer to produce an acceptable question sheet. It is claimed that 'artists and intellectuals are not inhibited by video' and, although that may well be true, what is not stated is to what extent the interview scripts were sub-edited, or the interview tapes post-edited, which clearly are major considerations.

An undoubted strength of video is the capture of body language and in particular facial expression. To what extent could the video principle be applied to interviewing people unused to video and its attendant paraphernalia? The latest camcorders (including digital) may well offer at least a partial solution. Modern camcorders can operate in very low light levels and effective indoor lighting can often be obtained by careful positioning of reading lamps and similar illumination.

In the context of the previous argument about bias and editing, it means that any production is seriously devalued as a historical or factual record the moment editing takes place. Editing in this context would include the selective use of the camera during the actual recording session. Following the purist argument, the only acceptable interview is a long continuous and uninterrupted take. The preservation of that tape should be seen as paramount in the same way as an audio tape and regarded as sacrosanct. A work copy or edited version is probably a clearer objective for most people using video, but the primary exercise should be the preservation of the original along with notes, copyright clearance and other important contextual information exactly as though it were an audio interview. (See Chapter Nine for a detailed analysis of the subject along with a suggested methodology.)

ORAL HISTORY AND EDITING

A strong case has already been presented for television oral history recordings to be accepted as primary source material only if the originals are unedited and preferably continuous takes, accompanied by notes and information. This is also a fundamental requirement for serious oral history work whether audio or video based.

However, more and more material is being recorded under the generic name of oral history, material which is often post-edited, extremely biased or used to support popular themes and ideas rather than exploring them. Answers are supplied or implied within questions, and I have personally witnessed radio interviewers actually telling interviewees what to say for 'completeness'.

Once a professional interview has been recorded then that should be regarded as a unique priceless original from which other recordings or copies can be made for a wide variety of purposes. Whether it is by economical targeted questioning, cutting tape physically with a razor blade or electronic editing on a computer screen, any copy editing, whether to produce extracts for publication, selections for use in reminiscence work or sound bites for broadcasting, means the recording is no longer true primary source oral history and must be treated with appropriate suspicion.

SPONTANEITY OF RESPONSE

Many oral historians are concerned with the question of to what extent the immediacy and spontaneity of a reply is changed if the interviewee knows the nature of the questions in advance. Considered answers are not necessarily accurate answers, especially among those who will use their education and experience to check or present facts, and produce what their peers regard as a satisfactory answer. The spontaneous reply is often from the heart and can reveal far more about the person, providing the kind of information that is unlikely to be uncovered by conventional research. The accuracy of information contained in spontaneous replies can always be checked later.

CHAPTER TWO

ORAL HISTORY FOR THE ARCHIVE, LIBRARY AND MUSEUM PROFESSIONAL

ORAL HISTORY AND MUSEUMS

The application of oral history investigative techniques in social history and folklore is well established, and many Scandinavian museums have used tape-recording methods for many years. Oral history can, however, be demonstrated to be of great value right across the board in museum work, and in some cases it is glaringly obvious that the work should be undertaken as soon as possible.

How can museum professionals use oral history as a tool? Some ideas have been included in the section dealing with types of interview, but it is worth examining that potential a little more closely here. No better account of the role of oral history and museums has been given in recent times than that by Stuart Davies in his paper 'Falling on Deaf Ears? Oral history and strategy in museums', published in the *Oral History Journal* in autumn 1994. In his account he draws together ways in which museum professionals can apply oral history to their work, notably in collection research, interpretation of objects and collections, educational resource and links with the community.*

These important applications and objectives, generally accepted by the museum world, should and easily can apply to other heritage professionals. Collection research is a case in point. Some archivists and librarians (and indeed some curators), although almost obsessively proud of their professionalism, do little to encourage the understanding of the significance or social context of collections in their care. In a way they are simply warehousing for the future – but they are only warehousing part of the story.

Oral history can allow the investigator to explore the social significance and/or context of an object or document; the environment in which it was created; how, physically or technically, it was created; when and by whom. This information is not just useful in gallery displays and exhibitions, but fundamental to the understanding of an object or document – affecting collecting policies, financial forward planning, conservation, academic publication and research opportunities.

---

* These headings and other related issues are dealt with comprehensively later in this section and in Chapters Four and Ten.

The academic value of oral history is now well established. Investigation by interview is a technique of discovery, delving into areas where the written word is sparse or simply does not exist. The range of possibilities in museums is tremendous.

ARCHAEOLOGY[1]

As a subject that places such a strong reliance on physical evidence, this would seem a most unlikely choice for oral history. Yet oral history does have a place. In Egyptology it would, admittedly, be difficult now to record a Pharaoh, but there are other important areas which have been missed or, at best, scantily treated. For example, Nile boatmen still sing songs and tell tales passed down to them from the time of the Pharaohs. How does this relate to the archaeology? Perhaps there is a great deal waiting to be learned. While on the subject of Egyptology, has anyone interviewed the people who actually worked on excavations? Those still living or their immediate families have stories to tell.

Official reports are presumed to capture the factual detail of a dig. The human side – the story of how it came about, the uncertainties and difficulties – is rarely told. How were early objects conserved? What was used to repair them? Where have some of the objects gone? What do certain accession marks mean? What are we looking at in the record photo?

Nor is oral history methodology confined to exotic archaeology. Archaeologists investigating sites in Britain need to know local background information before committing their sparse resources to excavating potential sites. The local farmer might have knowledge of old field boundaries, or have from time to time excavated for field drains and come across pottery or other artefacts. Local people often have folk memories about places. Field and feature names are not necessarily recorded on maps or plans, yet can give vital clues to archaeologists. Similarly, older residents may well be able to recall the occurrence of local plants, sometimes a useful method of identifying geological and archaeological boundaries.

It is not just the early memories and reminiscences that are significant; it is important to know about more recent activity on or near a site. How did the local brickworks affect the Iron Age fort site? Were those bell-pits used for mining coal or could they be bomb craters following a wartime air-raid? When was the site robbed for building materials? Who put the drainage ditch across the site? What did they find? Has anyone excavated the site before?

Full-scale interviewing using a tape-recorder is not always necessary nor indeed appropriate, but good question preparation and the use of correct and effective interviewing technique is worth employing.

INDUSTRIAL ARCHAEOLOGY

Dr Arthur Raistrick is best remembered for his work as a writer on life in the Yorkshire Dales; indeed he was a founder member of the important *Dales Magazine*. He was also a pioneer industrial archaeologist and geologist with a particular interest in lead mining. He

Dr Arthur Raistrick, the pioneer industrial archaeologist, advocated oral history as a fundamental method of recording industrial archaeology. The photograph was taken immediately following an interview with the author. (Author)

was a pioneer of industrial archaeological research and was present at the original meeting when the term industrial archaeology was suggested. His concept of what industrial archaeology is about is today more readily accepted and understood. He took the view that it is not just concerned with the physical remains of the industrial revolution, as originally suggested by Kenneth Hudson, but with the remains of industry, science and technology since man first used tools. Implicit in this definition is the need to record these features in detail: not just their physical characteristics, but documentary and oral sources.

All this is recorded in a unique oral history interview I made with Dr Raistrick many years ago, in which he agreed to record his own contribution to assist in the very understanding of the need to use oral history. He himself contributed and became part of that recording process.[2]

Industrial archaeology is a subject where oral history techniques work particularly well, especially if combined with the complementary approaches of photography, film and video.

The Textile Industry

One of the finest early examples of recording industrial archaeology using oral history and photography as a basis was undertaken some years ago by Stanley Graham for the Pendle Heritage Centre, near Nelson in Lancashire. The closure of a local cotton textile mill, Bancroft Shed at Barnoldswick, prompted him to photograph the mill before its closure.

The steam engine is all that is left of the Bancroft textile mill, Barnoldswick, recorded by Stanley Graham. (Author)

His interviews were then based on the photographs, and the results offer probably the best interpretation of weaving shed life ever undertaken. The weaving shed has now been demolished although the huge steam engine which once drove the mill remains as testament to a once-thriving industry.[3]

I too have recorded various aspects of the Lancashire textile industry, including interviews with spinners, carders, trade unionists, weavers, shuttle-makers, bleachers, dyers and calico printers. Soundscapes of textile mills have also been recorded, with sounds such as the mill hooter, mill engine, the turning of line-shafting, and the pulsation and din of a weaving shed in action. The noise in a weaving shed was often so great that many weavers have been left with a degree of deafness. In the weaving shed environment they were forced to lip-read, points brought out in a meaningful way during interviewing, where the relevance of recording contemporary soundscape with realistic sound levels becomes apparent.

Another very different kind of soundscape was commissioned by the British Wool Marketing Board, recording members of the Wool Exchange in Bradford as they shouted out their bids across the floor of the Exchange.[4]

Surprisingly, some medieval textile processes survived well into the twentieth century. Take the case of possibly the last woollen tenters at work in a factory. The factory specialized in manufacturing massive woollen blankets for use on paper-making machines. Special extra-wide looms were used and the woven woollen cloth after washing was spread vertically on to special racks with rows of sharp hooks holding the cloth in place. The hooks prevented the wool from shrinking as it dried. A series of black and white photographs were taken of all aspects of the process and in the subsequent interview the pictures were interpreted and explained by the process foreman. A 16mm mute film was also shot of the highly specialized wide-loom weaving needed to produce the cloth.

Rope-making is very closely related to the textile industry. Although, of course, it was not exclusive to the north of England two projects come to mind. One project recorded in Atherton near Manchester used both oral history and photographs to record a rope-works which specialized in producing rope for use on huge steam-driven mill engines where it was used to drive the main line shaftings in textile mills. Out in the countryside in the Rossendale Valley is a long corrugated tin-roofed structure, one of the country's last surviving rope-walks. The rope-works produced rope for industry but as the market declined it also produced skipping ropes, clothes lines and barrier ropes for museums. The works still had much of the original machinery and was recorded using a combination of oral history, photography and video.

In terms of illustration the bias has been very much towards Lancashire and Yorkshire which once supplied the world market. There are, of course, many other areas of the country where related industries such as tartan-weaving or carpet-weaving are also important. Extensive oral history recording has been undertaken on the silk industry of Cheshire and a museum was founded partly as a result of that research. Other examples include the hosiery industry of the Midlands, the lace trade around Nottingham, fustian cutting in Warrington and Cadishead, flax growing and production, and the jute trade of northern Ireland.

Glass Works

In a joint project with Pilkington's the glassmakers, I photographed a glass-works in operation when it was still using a process called flat-drawn glass in which a sheet of glass was drawn up from a tank of molten glass into a tower. Using colour photographs of the process, the shift foreman was interviewed about what was actually happening in the pictures. That particular glass-making process has now been superseded by the float-glass process and no physical remains of the original glass tank now exist above ground. The buildings have been demolished and a new factory built on the site.

Railways

There are literally thousands of recordings (and videos) of steam locomotives pounding over a particular piece of difficult railway with evocative locomotive sounds echoing around. The soundscape is there but where is the oral history? Where are the recordings of signalmen, clerks, firemen, plate-layers, carriage upholsterers, boilermen, apprentices, porters, foundrymen, ticket collectors, locomotive designers, timetable planners, inspectors, goodsmen, shunters, carriers, women workers and the rest? How were railway carriages built? By whom? For what purpose? The LNER locomotive *Mallard* is recognized as being the world's fastest steam locomotive. Is there a detailed technical interview with the crew? Why is it the fastest?

Railway locomotive no. 1000, a Midland Compound, being recorded for archives. (Author)

A great deal has been written about railways, including what might be called reminiscence. It has already been established that edited material should be regarded with extreme caution. Useful though reminiscence is in the written or printed form, it does not allow interrogation and an unhindered exploration into other parts of the interviewee's railway experience or life history. It is secondary, selective, edited material.

Much has already been missed and is now lost. It is right, of course, for preservation societies to have concentrated on stock and locomotives, but how far would they have got without using the unrecorded oral history and the experiences of others? My own recording work includes engine drivers, boiler cleaners, firemen, signalmen, and an account of a railway accident given by a passenger who survived crashing over a railway viaduct into a river.

An area rarely covered is railway operation during the Second World War. How did trains operate during an air-raid? How did an engine driver know if the track was still intact after an air-raid? What happened to railway passengers during an air-raid? How were troop trains organized?

There are tens of thousands of objects associated with railways, ranging from tickets through to full-size railway carriages, all of which could form a catalyst for interviewing. The interpretation of the object and its social use is one approach; another is its technical development and context.

Engineering

To what extent has engineering been recorded in detail? The days of belt-driven engineering shops have long gone, but there are still people who can recall a life in engineering from their earliest apprenticeship through to the most modern computer-driven equipment. There are boiler-makers, turners and milling machine operators, pattern-makers, tool-makers, moulders, fitters and many more involved in heavy engineering. How were early Whitworth belt-driven lathes used? How were tools sharpened? How dangerous was casting iron? How were moulds prepared? By whom? What kind of machines were made? How many survive? Many machines destined for the scrapheap need to be recorded before they are smashed up. Examples include colliery winding engines and stationary

Professor Dennis Stephenson Wood, nearest surviving relative to George Stephenson. He was interviewed in 1980 for his family memories of the Stephensons as railway and colliery engineers. (Author)

mill steam engines. In the new industries there are aerospace, electronics, car manufacture and weapons development to be considered.

Papermaking

One of the difficulties of recording and preserving material from the papermaking industry is the lack of suitable objects. Fourdrinier machines are huge continuous paper production machines the length of a mill. About all that can be reasonably preserved are paper samples and the occasional hand-tool. Good photography and oral history work well together in this instance, interviews being based on the pictures. A similar approach can be adopted for the production of hand-made paper, where video to record the continuous sequences associated with the process is useful.

Wallpaper Manufacture

There are many aspects worth recording such as design, additive colour printing, roller engraving and relief surface manufacture, drying and festooning wallpaper, packing and so on.

Wind Power

Apart from the obvious recording of a miller and his experiences, it is also important to record those who repaired mills and sails. The preparation of millstones is highly skilled and again needs interpretation. Modern wind farms too – their designers, maintenance crews, etc., should not be neglected. The distinctive soundscape of wind power is worth recording.

Industrial objects sometimes require interpretation using oral history techniques. In this case, the waterwheel was using borrowed steam engine technology (the beams) from an older engine once used in the nearby bleach works. Oral history revealed much about the operation and maintenance of this peculiar hybrid.

Water Power

Again, as for wind power, there is a need to record those who use water power and repair and maintain the equipment. Water-wheels are well known. Water turbines were also used quite extensively, often to generate electricity. How was such equipment installed? How was it maintained? Where was it made? In many cities and ports hydraulic water systems were used to operate equipment ranging from swing bridges to hauling railway wagons with chain and capstan. Distinctive hydraulic accumulation towers were built and survive in some cities such as Manchester. How did the capstan system work? How was a head of water maintained? What might go wrong? Again there are many questions to be asked, and the distinctive soundscape of water power should be recorded for completeness.

Coal

Coal-mining by its very nature presents problems for the museum and heritage professional. Although objects such as pit-lamps and tools survive, much of the actual physical evidence is underground. Apart from straightforward interviews with colliers and others recalling social history, there are many other aspects to be recorded that illustrate the underground environment, such as:

Objects are often brought to light as a result of an oral history interview. This wooden clog sole was modified by a coal miner, allowing him to sit and slide down steep tramway rails underground. He described in detail how the soles were made, and used, as well as the hazards of travelling in this particular way. (Author)

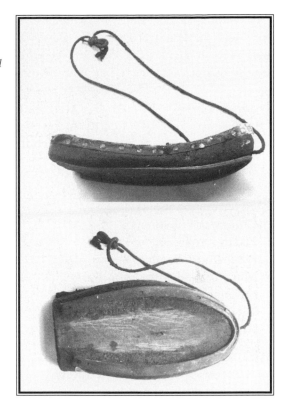

Belt conveyors – installation, maintenance, manufacture, etc.

Coal-cutting machines, shearers, ploughs, etc. Installation, maintenance, planning and design, power, etc.

Dust suppression systems

Electrical systems underground

Fan ventilation – maintenance, fan drift construction, etc.

Flooding and drainage. Submersible pumps, culverts, etc.

Geological exploration

Hand-getting of coal

Health and safety underground

Hydraulic props – manufacture and repair

Management

Mechanical haulage systems

Pit-ponies (care of underground, etc.)

Ripping of passageways – techniques

Screening of coal

Shaft maintenance

Training

Underground surveying

Winding gear. Erection, maintenance, rope-shortening, safety gear, signalling systems, etc.

Coal-mining in Lancashire and Cheshire, South Wales, Lanarkshire, parts of Yorkshire, Kent and the Forest of Dean have already been recorded to some extent and the results preserved in various collections. Nevertheless, there is still a considerable amount of recording, especially of a technical nature, that needs to be undertaken.

Iron and Steel

Oral history lends itself well to the interpretation of iron and steel work sites and the techniques that were once used. Examples of subjects include:

Blast furnace processes, such as the Bessemer converter
Blowing engines
Crucible steel making
Cutlery manufacture
Electric arc furnace operation
Forging and drop hammers operation
Moulding and casting processes
Open hearth processes
Puddling process
Rolling mill operation

Two men pour molten iron into moulds in an iron works casting machine parts for use in industry. Oral history allows the investigation of working practices, works layout, tricks of the trade, etc. (Author)

As an example, when Thomas Walmsley's Atlas iron works closed in Bolton in the 1980s it was one of the last firms in the UK still producing iron using the traditional puddling process. Much of the equipment was moved to Ironbridge Museum in Shropshire where it is now preserved. Oral history recordings were also made with the iron puddlers and a drop-hammer operator to complement the physical objects.[5]

Non-ferrous Metals, Lead, Silver and Tin, Copper and Gold

All these extractive industries are represented in the UK. Some recording of the lead-mining industry has been undertaken in the Peak District and in the Yorkshire Dales. Silver, which is often associated with lead and separated during purification, has not been covered to any great extent. In North Wales, where active extraction of lead, silver and gold continued until recently, little oral history work has been completed. Gold has been mined near Barmouth at Bontddu and other places for many years, yet the industry has not been systematically recorded using oral history techniques.

Other lines of oral history enquiry in North Wales include Parys Mountain on Anglesey and the Great Ormes Head at Llandudno – two well-known sites worked for copper within living memory. Tin has been extracted in Cornwall for centuries, the last mine closing only recently. The opportunity exists here to record the memories of old and new technologies.

Stone, Slate and Other Extractions

Slate and stone quarrying has occurred all over the British Isles. Some quarries, such as the Delabole slate quarry in Cornwall, are open to the sky, while others, such as Dorothea and

Oral history works particularly well with industrial archaeology subjects. This photograph of a slate truck, taken in 1969, shows the unusual double-flanged wheels and the quarry incline at Llechwedd slate quarry in North Wales. Its analysis could lead into many questions about underground haulage, track laying, truck manufacturers, man-riding, quarry operating, extracting and so on. (Author)

A workman in the 1960s at the Llechwedd slate quarry in north Wales splits a large lump of slate using the traditional method of a hammer and chisel. Although the technology of slate mining is well recorded there are many aspects of quarrying which should be recorded using oral history. (Author)

Llechwedd slate quarries in North Wales, are underground and spectacular in size. (Llechwedd is open to the public.)

How were they worked? How was the stone or slate removed? Where were the workshops, tramways, explosives store? How was slate split? In the Pennines there were numerous quarries in the gritstone and limestone areas. Many of the limestone quarries, such as Hope in the Peak District and Ribble Valley, are still operational and manufacture cement on-site in huge rotating kilns. The oral history of cement-making has never been recorded.

In Cornwall china clay extraction has been a major industry for many years. Again, to what extent have the social and technical aspects of this important industry been recorded using oral history?

Details of installations, tunnels, tramways, drainage culverts and other quarry features can be plotted on large-scale maps. An annotated base plan can be plotted during an actual interview by using overhead projector transparent overlays which are marked as the interviewee advises. The whole sequence should be recorded on tape as the analysis takes place. Each transparent cell is marked with grid lines and key features allowing accurate relocation over an Ordnance map at a later date.[6]

Oil and Gas Extraction

Oil and gas are arguably two of the most important industries today. Yet virtually no oral history work has been done on either their social history or the technical side except in Shetland. The whole story of exploration, rig construction, support services, disasters, etc., needs recording.

Oil was extracted from oil shales by heating in Lothian, Scotland, as late as 1963. The technique and technology of oil shale working is clearly an oral history recording priority.

Chemical Industries

Little seems to have been recorded in any depth on the chemical industry. My own work for the Catalyst Museum of the Chemical Industry at Widnes recorded working conditions in the chemical industry before the Second World War. Other tapes included an interview with a man whose specialized job was to smell. His ability to add precisely the right amount of enhancement to products in the food industry was extraordinary.

Other possibilities for Oral History recording include:

Artificial fertilizers
Chlorine manufacture
Electrochemical processes
Epoxy resins
Ink manufacture
Munitions
Nuclear chemical industry
Paint manufacture
Paper fillers
Perfumes and scents
Photographic chemicals and dyes
Plastics manufacture
Rubber industry
Silicon chip manufacture
Soap and detergent manufacture
Soda ash manufacture
Sulphuric acid manufacture
Wax production

The Salt Industry

Cheshire supplies most of Britain's salt. It was extracted from underground mainly in the form of brine. The brine was then heated in huge metal salt pans and the water evaporated. There are relatively few remains above ground except for the depressions caused by extraction, which are known as flashes. Salt pans and associated equipment still survive at the Lion Salt Museum at Northwich although little oral history has so far been attempted to interpret the site.

In a separate exercise, a series of interviews was recorded in the 1970s and 1980s to understand how the salt was prepared and to interpret many of the objects in the care of Cheshire County Salt Museum at London Road, Northwich.

Dyestuffs

Early dyestuffs were mixed in dye-works. Mixing a 'perfect black' was regarded as a great skill. Some years ago I recorded a dye-mixer who used to mix various blacks in the dye-house. He described in detail how the dye arrived at the works, and then, beneath a daylight colour temperature lamp, was graded and mixed. It was a Health and Safety officer's nightmare. In his own words: 'The black stuff just flew. It flew everywhere. It went in your eyes, your ears and your mouth. You were still spitting it out when you got home.'

As far as can be ascertained, dyestuff manufacture has not been covered at all using oral history.

Gunpowder Manufacture

The traditional manufacture of gunpowder took place in various parts of the country including the west country around Dartmoor and at Faversham in Kent. Oral history has been used at Faversham to record memories of the works before its closure in 1934. In the southern Lake District gunpowder was manufactured around Haverthwaite, relying to some extent on local coppice wood for the charcoal used in the process. Oral history was used by the author to interpret and understand the various buildings and production on the site.

Public Utilities

This is another vast and largely untapped area for oral historians, particularly in the interpretation and understanding of buildings and structures, along with any surviving objects. Examples include: water supply, reservoir construction, temporary villages for workers, engineering, quarrying, tramways, filtration, pumping, waste disposal, sewer construction, screening systems, public health issues, disposal of toxic wastes, pumping systems, waste collection and disposal, destructors, recycling, health risks, and rubbish collection vehicles and methods.

Gas Supply

The Gas Industry Museum has recorded some oral history on the gas industry. A great deal more can be achieved, especially using objects from the gas industry during interviews. Biggar gas works in Lanarkshire was one of the last gas works to use hand-fired retorts. Oral history interviews have been recorded by the local headmaster in the village as part of a wider project. Oral history interviews on gas exploration also need to be recorded.

Electricity Manufacture

The electricity industry is a changing one, not just because of privatization, but because of new methods and approaches to generating electricity, such as wind and wave power, and nuclear energy. Examples of topics that might be covered include:

Coal-fired stations: coal supplies, boiler maintenance, turbine operation, transformers, supply methods, cooling systems, cooling towers, transmission lines and networks, demand control, etc.

Nuclear power reactor design, new approaches to safety, research, handling of materials, etc.

Roads, Bridges and Tunnels

The road network has not been looked at in oral history terms, yet the construction of the motorways has changed almost everyone's life. How were they built? By whom? What problems were encountered? How are they used and maintained today? How were specific features, such as the Tyne, Conwy, Channel and Mersey Tunnels, constructed? How are they serviced?

Rivers and Canals

A national canal recording project has recently been established by the Boat Museum at Ellesmere Port. Many local recordings of rivers and canals already exist, but at the time of writing (1998) the proposed survey seems likely to be the most extensive ever undertaken. My own work on canals in the north-west of England has included material on the Manchester Ship Canal, Manchester Salford Junction Canal, Manchester, Bolton & Bury Canal and Leeds & Liverpool Canal.

A barge loaded with maize makes its way along the Bridgewater Canal near Trafford Park in 1967. The current national canal oral history project being organized by the Boat Museum at Ellesmere Port is the first major concerted effort to record canal workers. (Author)

The Sea

This is a vast subject, which lends itself particularly well to the oral history approach. The establishment of the Merseyside Maritime Museum relied a great deal in the early stages on oral history recollections of former dock workers and others. These memories were crucial when it came to reconstructing the interiors of buildings and in understanding just how the docks worked. In another example, at the National Fishing Heritage Museum at Grimsby oral history interviews were used to explore how fishing boats were utilized as mine-sweepers during the Second World War.

Across the Atlantic oral history was used at the Ellis Island Immigration Museum in New York. In a period of about sixty years over seventeen million immigrants passed through Ellis Island on their way to the United States. Interviews with immigrants, replayed via telephone handsets in various parts of the museum, recount the awesome experiences of arrival by sea in the New World.[7]

Another good example is an oral history project by Donald Hyslop and Sheila Jemima of the Southampton Museum Oral History Archive who researched the liner *Titanic* and its association with Southampton. The story of the sinking of the *Titanic* in 1912 following a collision with an iceberg in the Atlantic is well known and well told. Most of the published material about the disaster concentrated on the sinking, the aftermath and the stories of treasure-hunting. The authors of this project argue that oral history is 'perhaps the most effective tool for looking at events like this from a different perspective . . . and in a wider context . . . the communities and individuals they touch'. Interviews were made with many people, including an employee of a local company who made the uniforms for the crew and two survivors; and the results also illustrate memories of the effect the dreadful news had on the people of Southampton, and the fate of the surviving crew on their eventual return to England.[8]

In many ways ships were closed communities on the move. In order to appreciate how a ship functioned, interviews should be made with captain and crew about daily routine, problems at sea, storms, sea-sickness, sleeping arrangements, food, leave, etc. Then there are fishing boats, trawlers, shrimpers, flats, and many other types of boat. How were they built? By whom? When? Where did they sail to? Why?

Relying heavily on ships and the sea were the ancillary industries such as barrel and cask making, binnacle manufacture, sail-makers, rope-makers, block-makers, boiler-makers and many more.

Ship-building is another large subject area in its own right. How were ships built? Where? By whom? When? What was involved in fitting them out? What about launches, tests, plate construction, rivetting, engine testing? The list is extensive. There are many good collections of manufacturers' glass negatives still surviving – how many of these have been used as a basis for interviews? Modern artefacts such as ships' bells, crockery or equipment can easily act as a catalyst to recollection in an interview situation.

There are other aspects of the shipping industry that should not be overlooked, such as on-shore installations – docks, light-houses, customs buildings, locks, cranes and bridges. Off-shore there are buoys, observation towers, oil rigs and even pirate radio stations!

The SS Aquitania *leaves the landing stage in Liverpool in 1919. The wealth of detail shown in this photograph — the ambulance, the motor vehicles of the wealthy, the porter, the horse-drawn vehicles — has great potential for interpretation by an informant. It illustrates well how a photograph can be used as a catalyst in oral history interviewing. (National Museums and Galleries on Merseyside, Maritime Museum)*

Oral history now has a role in maritime archaeology. Interest is growing in maritime history, particularly among sports divers who are keen to locate wrecks. Wreck information is also of considerable use to mariners and chart-makers as well as maritime archaeologists. Oral history is an important source of information on shipwrecks and disasters.

Although oral history does not seem to have been used much in any systematic way by maritime archaeologists to collect data it is, nevertheless, used widely in a casual way to obtain local information. At the present time there is a great deal of work being undertaken recording marine archaeological sites around the British coast. The definition of marine or maritime in this context has been interpreted to mean remains below the low water mark as far as the 12 miles international limit.

Surveys have been carried out in Orkney and Shetland and along much of the Scottish coast. Remains vary from Bronze Age settlements such as Jarlshof in Shetland to industrial remains on the coast of Fife. The priority among maritime archaeologists has been to record the physical remains for inclusion in regional and national databases.

Oral history has two roles to play. The first is in the acquisition of information about the location of physical remains and sites, whether land- or sea-based. Archaeologists have long known that the moment they start to excavate or survey, members of the public arrive asking questions. Some archaeologists regard these people frankly as pests as they can, on accessible shore sites, interfere with an excavation that may only be possible between tides or before it is infilled and buried again with sand and silt. Nevertheless, such people can be an invaluable source of information about other sites and should be harnessed to advantage. Names and addresses should be taken and followed up at a later date.

INFORMAL MEMORY SESSIONS

One way of capitalizing on public interest and recollections of potential maritime archaeological sites is to arrange an 'invitation only evening or afternoon' for visitors to see something of the work of the group or survey. This not only fulfils the need to inform and educate the public, the public relations role, but also encourages recollections and memories of sites and possible wrecks. The session can be recorded.

Although money is tight for large oral history projects, if cash for training and some basic equipment is included in the survey costs, it may well be possible to train a volunteer to actively record members of that initial group meeting, or if the enthusiasm grows, then the group itself might undertake the recording.

There is, however, a place for the professional oral historian working with the marine archaeologist to develop very specialized and specific question sheets to solicit information about key areas of interest. Careful question construction and cross-checking procedures ensure some degree of accuracy in the responses.

The second way that oral history can be used is in the interpretation and understanding of features such as former docks, boat yards, lighthouses and so on. Interviews should be recorded with surviving individuals concerned but also by using the survey approach, described in detail elsewhere. Survey interviewing might look at, for example, how a port actually worked and how buildings were used, and by whom. The information is then plotted on a base map.

So what kind of information can be retrieved using oral history methods? The list is surprisingly long. For example:

Abutments and other remains of bridges and causeways
Beacon sites
Buildings and footings
Caves, tunnels and caverns, including some below sea-level such as those in County
   Clare and at Berryhead, Torbay
Changes in coastal erosion patterns
Changes in marine deposition patterns
Changes in sea-level
Coves and landing places

Illegal dumping grounds at sea
Location and use of fish weirs
Location of ballast banks
Location of former excavated channels
Location of navigation aids such as markers and buoys
Location of old groins and baulks
Location of submerged forests, coal outcrops and peat beds
Martello Towers and similar structures
Memories of 'fishermen's fastenings' – articles brought up in nets or snagging nets on
    the sea floor
Quarry works by the sea
Remains of the leisure and tourism industry – piers, open-air swimming pools (on the
    Isle of Man there are the remains of a zoo in the cliff face!)
Salterns
Second World War ammunition dumps at sea
Second World War remains generally – pill boxes, gun locations, concrete landing
    craft blocks, forts, PoW camps, ammunition works, etc.
Semaphore signalling stations
Small on-shore boat yards
Telegraph stations
Wrecks and hulks

This list is far from exhaustive. Although the coastline of Britain has many fascinating features, it should not be assumed that most remains will be from the nineteenth or twentieth century. It is quite amazing what still survives from the distant past: recent excavation work in sand-dunes revealed a Bronze Age wooden causeway complete with what are probably casts in the hard silt of Bronze Age footprints.

HISTORIC REDUNDANT CHURCHES AND OTHER RELIGIOUS BUILDINGS AS PLACES OF WORSHIP AND MUSEUMS

One of the limitations of oral history recording is that material has to be largely recorded from within living memory. Churches, abbeys, monasteries and other religious buildings often have a history stretching back well beyond the reach of oral historians, yet there are still some possibilities. In closed communities such as monasteries the oral tradition can be very strong. This applies not just to knowledge of everyday events but also to a need to retain their own traditional form of devotion and way of life.

At a practical level, recordings can be made about, for example, flag and banner repair in order to determine which methods and materials have been used in the past and therefore help in planning future conservation requirements and resources. Similarly, there are other workers to be interviewed: vestment-makers and repairers, church furniture makers, stonemasons, craftsmen, bell-founders, architects, organ builders and repairers, stained-glass makers, organists, composers, choir, the clergy, helpers and friends, and, of course, members of the congregation and the community around.

Sound plays a very important part in church life. There is church music, prayers, bell-ringing and something only rarely recorded: complete church services including burials.

Taking a typical English church, there are many items that could form a basis for an oral history interview:

Flags and banners: questions about use and repair, materials, storage, age, damage, legends and stories, general recent history, interpretation of the religious or other symbols

Church registers: completeness of registers, repairs, storage, modern annotations, rebinding, present location of missing registers, etc.

Family and Church Bibles, hymn books, psalters, Sunday School prizes, etc.

Origins of Bibles, annotations, details of local families, repair work, rebinding, tooling of covers, craftsmen involved, etc., Sunday School prizes and other prizes, why they were offered and to whom

Church furniture and other accoutrements

Altars: construction, materials, use, history and origins

Pews and seating: type and style, origin of the wood, maker, repairs, characteristics and special marks including graffiti; woodworming and conservation methods

Baptismal fonts: origin, artist, materials, repairs, etc.

Candles: why they are used, when, how; who makes them? Where? Who lights them? Origins of candle holders, materials, repairs, etc.; accidental fires

Incense burners: where are they used and how; materials, oils and incense; suppliers of burners and incense; repairs, etc.

Holy Relics: origins of, stories and legends attached to, establishment of long-term storage conditions, provenance or authenticity; examination of storage cases, style of glass and other decoration, materials, extent of interference and repairs

Communion silver and plate: use and origins; distinguishing features and marks, maker, repairs and conservation; cleaning practice

Stained glass: explanation of the narratives and images in glass; makers, replacement work and repair works; interview with contemporary restorers working on the glass to chronicle their activities; use of colour photography to illustrate the glass (for example, transparencies printed to permanent Cibachrome)

Interior decoration: explanation of symbols, carvings, etc.

Pictures: origins and provenance; re-framing and other conservation and restoration work; explanation of the picture and its meaning; establishing a possible artist; current 'cleaning' practice

Statuary: origins and provenance; materials, annotations, history and origins, conservation and restoration work, current 'cleaning' practice

Bells: origin, numbers, ringing use, damage; handbells and their uses, makers, materials, provenance, symbols, etc. (If possible, record the bells and ringers)

Church brasses: types, origins, 'cleaning' practice, repairs, etc.

Tombs and vaults: individual histories, artists, materials, damage and restoration, current 'cleaning' practice; occasional opening of vaults, their contents; meaning of various symbols, pictures and cryptic wording

Carvings, misericords, mosaics, etc.: origins of carvings, their meanings, age, restoration work, etc.

Organ: type of organ, number of pipes, organ builder, changes in design, organists, restoration work, electrification of bellows and console, historical background; record organ music if possible; music manuscripts

Vestments: origins, making repairs, types of textile used, explanation of images and symbols, current storage and religious usage and significance

Church archives: repairs, completeness; photographs

Building tour: possibility of tour-style interview in a church or other religious building involving the identification and interpretation of architectural or historical features

Some religious oral history work has been done on the origins of the Methodist Church, but it has tended to lean towards personal experience and life history rather than being interpretative. A project at Englesea Brook Primitive Methodist Chapel and Museum in south Cheshire is currently recording early memories of people partly for interpretive use in their museum. The original hand-pumped wooden pipe organ has also been recorded playing Primitive Methodist hymns as part of the re-creation of soundscape for visitors.

The Mormons have even established a department of oral history at Brigham Young University in Salt Lake City, Utah. Within their religion still lies the opportunity to record family memories of the hardship of the treks across America, the foundation of a major Church and the establishment of a new social order and city. Doubtless many other religious groups across the world could use oral history successfully as a way of maintaining their past and presenting it to the present, thus strengthening conviction and belief.

The potential for using oral history within other religious denominations is considerable, but very little recording has taken place. The present writing is deliberately object-orientated, but oral history could readily be extended to include interviews with believers, religious leaders, scholars and others, including aspects such as education, spread of belief and perpetuation of traditional stories and texts.

At least one religious museum was actually founded as a result of an oral history project. The work undertaken by Bill Williams and others in Manchester led to the acquisition of the former Portuguese Synagogue in the city as the Manchester Jewish Museum. This museum now has excellent oral collections and uses oral history interviews in the display galleries of the former synagogue.

COSTUME COLLECTIONS

Costume is inextricably linked to social history, and oral history offers considerable potential for curators charged with the care of costume (and most museums will have some costume or costume accessories in their collections). Very early costume is outside direct human memory, but a great deal of costume is not. There are many avenues though in which oral history methods can be used, for example:

Everyday clothing. How was it bought or acquired? By whom? Who repaired it? How? When? Where was it made? What textiles were used? How much did it cost? How was it washed or cleaned? Where was it stored? What was used to keep moths at bay?

Hats. Who made them? What did they cost? How were hats made? (Hat block-making, mercury and felts, etc.) How were they stored when not in use? How were men measured for their hats? Where did ladies acquire hats? How were hats kept in place on a windy day? What effect did fashion magazines have on hat purchase?

Night-wear. What was worn in bed? Who made the night-wear? What materials were used?

Fashion wear. Who wore fashion wear? Where was it obtained from? How was it copied? By whom? Who made it? What were they paid? What materials were used? Who repaired it?

Under-clothing. Where was it obtained from? What textiles were used? Was fashion important? How were corsets fastened? How comfortable were feminine under-garments? How taboo was it to wear certain types of clothes? How were they repaired? How were they stored?

Leisure wear. What materials were used? Determine dye-fastness, in the case of bathing costumes – acceptancy. Walking and cycling attire – how were they used?

Work clothes. What treatment were clothes subjected to, what materials were used, who made them, cost, repairs, frequency of use, how they were used, etc. Protective work clothing such as a butcher's apron could lead into related areas such as the meat trade or simply the question of how the butcher's wife removed blood from his workclothes.

Footwear. How were the items worn? What was used between the foot and the shoe? Who made them? Who repaired boots, shoes, clogs, etc. How were they cleaned? What tools were used in the making? How was highly specialized footwear used and by whom? What problems were there wearing socks or stockings? How were early nylon stockings regarded by women? Types of footwear (shoes, slippers, clogs, boots, etc.), shoe-shops, assistants, X-ray machines, shoe horns, price, repairs, colour, materials, advertising, practicality, when worn, etc.

Clothing for special social occasions.

Weddings. How were wedding dresses made? Who made them, why, from what, what happened to them following the wedding day? Accessories such as gloves, jewellery, headdresses, clothing worn by bridegroom, best man, etc.

Christenings. Christening robes: traditions, materials, storage, makers, etc.

'Sunday best'. Best clothes for weekend – why, how they were kept, repaired, purchased, materials, etc. Accessories such as watches, handbags and jewellery.

Formal dress. Dress suit or dinner jackets. Why they were used. Who purchased them? How were food stains removed? Formal dinners, food, servants, etc.

Funerals. Type of clothing, traditions at funerals, armbands, etc.

Folk dress. Types of traditional folk dress, dyeing, spinning, weaving techniques. Knitting patterns, organization of labour, etc.

Ceremonial – civic. Mayoral dress, type of materials. Civic ceremonies, traditions and customs, civic objects such as the Mace or mayoral chain.

Church. Liturgical or religious vestments. How they were used, their significance, makers, storage, materials, etc.

Legal. Dress for court-room, how it is used and why.

Uniforms: nurses, nannies, military, public service (police, fire, ambulance). Use of the uniforms, the material used, and accessories including insignia.

Accessories. These range from costume jewellery through to hats, fur stoles, silk gloves and wigs. The questions are likely to revolve around how the objects were used, made, acquired, stored, altered, repaired or conserved. It could also lead into interviews with fashion accessory designers and fashion designers generally and easily overlap into the field of decorative art.

STATELY HOMES AND COUNTRY HOUSES

Nowhere near enough quality oral history work has been carried out in Britain's stately homes and country houses. The National Trust in England has encouraged people to record oral history at their various properties with varying degrees of success. At the time of writing (1998) the National Trust for Wales is undertaking a similar exercise but extending oral history to include contemporary property and land management. (See Chapter Three)

Stately homes and large country houses with land should be seen not as single buildings, but rather as economic units with strong social links. This means that if recordings are to be made about a particular family and their occupancy of a hall or country house, then it soon becomes apparent that it is also essential to examine the local community in detail, for they were often reliant on the economy generated by the local squire and he, in turn, on their loyalty, skills and services.

English Heritage has recently acquired for the nation Brodsworth Hall near Doncaster. Oral history was seen as a possible way of acquiring information about the hall and its contents. Interviews have been recorded with gardeners, servants, villagers and members of the family in order to illustrate a cross-section of life at Brodsworth. As well as recording general reminiscences about the hall,

Staff of the National Trust for Wales practise interviewing in front of Erddig, a property near Wrexham. (Author)

another important approach has been room by room interpretation. A series of colour photographs formed the basis of interviews, and informants were asked specific questions about individual rooms. For example: can you recall how this room was used in your time at the hall? How were the statues cleaned? What was used? How did the chairs become damaged?

The questionnaires used at Brodsworth are long and detailed and cover many subjects from works of art to gardening and from dinner parties to heating arrangements. The answers reveal much about the hall and its use, some of the information being particularly relevant to conservators and those involved in the longer-term interpretive process for visitors.[9]

OTHER BUILDINGS

Stately homes and country houses form a special category, but there are many other buildings which can also be interpreted using oral history and photography in tandem. Although by no means an exhaustive list, buildings might include: railway stations, signal-boxes, dock warehouses, windmills, former military installations, domestic houses, shops, schools, theatres, etc.

ART[10]

Modern and contemporary art works are excellent areas in which to use oral history methods. Older works, too, should not be completely relegated from the process. It may be no longer possible to interview Rembrandt, but oral history still has its place.

FINE ART

Interviews with art curators, patrons and collectors can often reveal information about a picture's history and provenance. Conservators are also important people to interview, indeed anyone who can add to the history or interpretation of the painting or sculpture should be involved.

Portraiture is a case in point. Much additional background information can be obtained simply by talking to the family of the subject in the painting, assuming that a link still exists. If the artist is living then an interview on tape is the first stage, followed perhaps by video or photography combination as the situation permits. It would also be interesting to talk to the sitter and obtain his or her genuine feelings about the portrait.

When a picture, sculpture or other piece of work is commissioned a small sum could be included to record an interview about the work. This would allow the artist another channel of expression, permitting a deeper understanding of what the artist felt or was trying to achieve. In addition, questions should be asked about the technique and technical aspects of a work. Such information will be invaluable to restorers and conservators in years to come.

A number of galleries already record artists. At the Yorkshire Sculpture Park it has long been the practice to record artists and sculptors about their work in order to create a better climate of understanding and as an educational resource. Also the National Sound Archive in association with the Tate Gallery has recorded over eighty interviews with artists recalling their feelings and lives.[11]

In addition to the audio oral history interview, video can work well but, as has already been established, it is not a substitute for fundamental oral history research, merely complementary. (See Chapter Nine)

DECORATIVE ART

Decorative art includes everything from wall-coverings to teapots and from stained glass to seaside knick-knacks. Interviews can be tackled in a number of different ways, such as examining the creative side of decorative production with designers, potters and artists. Then, of course, there are the people who actually work in the factory, painting, preparing and checking the work. For example, a short series of interviews was conducted in the 1960s by the late Frank Mullineux of Manchester who recorded the memories of potters, artists and finishers at the Royal Lancastrian Pottery in Swinton.

Individual potters might talk about their work and the materials they use. In 1996, at a conference held in Aberystwyth entitled 'Telling tales with technology', it was revealed that oral historians/art historians had tended to lean towards recording life stories in order to explore 'formative influences (that) led someone to embrace a career in ceramics' and also, presumably, to explore future aspirations.[12]

Glass and stained-glass artists should also be interviewed about their approach, design and other work they have completed. In textiles there are weavers and dyers to be interviewed, and in Scotland and other places knitters still working traditional patterns such as Fair Isle. The opportunity still exists to record.

Turkish and Persian carpets and coverings have featured in a number of important exhibitions in Europe, yet to my knowledge, other than for the immediate requirements of exhibition labels, weavers and others were never properly interviewed. The sweeping changes taking place throughout the world make oral history recording exceedingly important to cultures under threat.

So-called ethno-art is often bought and sold without any true understanding or recognition of the religious or cultural significance of the artefact in question. The lack of adequate recording is certainly not confined to the ethno-art trade. In many respectable museums, opportunities are missed simply to record information about the social and cultural context in which 'modern' objects had their origins.

Traditional clock and watch-making has been hit hard by quartz watch and clock manufacturing, but there are still some traditional makers in Europe producing high-quality mechanical time-pieces. Have they been recorded? Then there are the retired watch-makers and repairers once found in every high street; there are also scientific instrument makers, so essential to academic research.

Little, if any, work has been done to record the jewellery trade. Although Birmingham City Museum has recorded information about the city's involvement, other recording is rare. At the top end of the market there is a great deal of confidentiality involved between studio, production house and client which might present interviewing difficulties, but other opportunities to record exist such as with retired jewellers, assemblers and designers about their work. How was quality jewellery, and for that matter costume jewellery, worn and by whom? How was it kept? Has it ever been altered? Is it original? What is the history and provenance of a piece? Where was it made? Are the original sketches still in existence? Did it stay in one particular family?

MUSEUM COLLECTIONS

Ethnic Collections

Many museums have ethnological collections of material which have been accumulated over the years. The understanding, cultural value, appreciation (especially of religious significance) of ethnic collections should be high on the museum's list of priorities. It may well be too late or simply impractical to use oral history methods to find out about, say, the ceremonial significance of mid-African spears or the shrunken head of a Jivaro woman. But it is always worth a try. The original anthropologist or collector may have died many years ago, but there could still be good family recollections which, in turn, might give new leads to documentary or photographic evidence or further artefacts hitherto unknown to the curator. Modern anthropologists record in great detail, often using the latest technology to capture such aspects as language, traditions, stories and everyday life. Can museum curators afford to ignore collections in their own care that have not had that kind of systematic recording? The realization in many emerging nations that artefacts from their own cultures are preserved in western museums and art galleries should at least give an impetus to recording even at this late stage.

In the UK ethnic art and related artefacts are nowadays actively collected by museums based in areas with strong local ethnic representation. A pioneer in the use of oral history and minority ethnic groups was the Bradford Heritage Recording Unit in West Yorkshire. Although specifically established to retrieve objects, the unit encouraged unemployed people from Bradford's many ethnic minority groups to record their own experiences on tape. In addition, a photographer chronicled the communities for posterity, capturing scenes from everyday lives.

In Blackburn, with its strong Asian grouping, the museum has a gallery of South Asian Art which actively encourages local Asians to become involved in oral history recording. The recording has been encouraged not just in Blackburn but also, as a logical development, in Gujurat state in India. The extended project will ensure that the traditional oral culture is recorded and preserved for the benefit of those in India, and also that Blackburn's Asian community will be able to understand and preserve its own culture before it is lost. Coupled with this project is a photographic survey and the preservation of appropriate cultural artefacts.

There have been many other community-based projects chronicling ethnic, minority and socially disadvantaged groups. I have deliberately not included a great deal of detail about the oral history work undertaken with these minority groups, as many have little direct relevance to objects per se, but more towards community-based oral history which is dealt with more thoroughly in Chapter Four.

Agriculture

Agricultural collections and farming museums are another important area for oral historians. Today a surprisingly large number of people simply do not understand the countryside, let alone farming methods and techniques. The recording of old farm workers contributes greatly to overall understanding of the objects and how they were once used. One of the early pioneers in recording oral history in the countryside was George Ewart Evans who recorded and wrote about East Anglian farm labourers and their way of life. He often took along to an interview session an old tool, such as a sickle, primarily as a catalyst for talk. The understanding of the object itself, its manufacture, social context and significance, is extremely important for the museum curator. Interviews based around objects can be particularly rewarding, not just in the explanation of how items like ploughs were actually used, but also in how they were repaired, dismantled or maintained. Embodied within the recording is the dialect and language of farm workers and farmers, and the technical terms they used every day without them realizing.

So what else can be recorded? Agriculture has been called 'the quiet revolution' and there is much that needs to be recorded before it is too late. A simple list of subjects will suffice to whet the appetite:

Animal husbandry
Beef cattle
BSE and its effect
Buildings – construction, need, materials, changes
Clipping/shearing
Clothing and dress
Common Agricultural Policy
Dairy products – cheese, butter, etc.
Dialect, language – special terms used
Ditch or dike clearing
Farmhouses
Farm machinery
Game and game protection
Harvest
Hiring-fairs, etc.
Horses – uses, numbers, tasks, shoeing, etc.
Irish labourers
Lambing
Marts and selling stock
Milking
Pig-killing and curing
Ploughing
Seeding
Set-aside land
Tractors

Vets

Wall–building

Winter feed

World wars – effect on farming, crop changes, labour, etc.

The recent concern in the UK about possible huge social changes in the countryside must make Oral History a priority in recording this changing scene.

Miscellaneous Collections

Medical collections. How were surgical instruments designed, made and used? The identification of individual instruments. How does an operating theatre work? What 'objects' are used? Who is present? What goes on? Changes in drug and medicines, anaesthesia, hospital care, the patient's view, etc. What did wards and operating theatres used to look like? What photographs survive? Early X-ray problems.

A good example is Beamish Museum, which reconstructed a 1920s dental surgery using oral history to 'provide detail and social historical facts, to locate and identify objects, to obtain details about the interior and appropriate ambience, and to position the dental equipment in the surgery and workroom'.[13]

The dentist's surgery reconstructed using oral history at Beamish Museum. (Beamish, North of England Open Air Museum, Stanley, County Durham)

Museum, archive and library histories. Official organizations such as museums, libraries and record offices over a period of time generate their own history. Oral history techniques can be used to interview former curators, archivists, librarians or other members of staff about a wide variety of items such as accessions, provenances, changes in display technique, missing artefacts/archives, early attempts at conservation, field collecting and, of course, personalities.

Musical instrument museums. Recorded sound is used more and more in illustrating how musical instruments were played and how music can be interpreted. Cassettes, compact discs and records of such music are widely available, but where are the recordings with contemporary musicians, composers, performers, etc.? The classical musical instrument is only one aspect. How were accordions used, or polyphons, flutes or musical boxes, and perhaps, stretching the definition of 'musical instrument' rather too far, early cylinder recorders, pianola rolls and gramophones.

Open-air museums. Beamish Museum in the north-east of England has already been mentioned in connection with its pioneering use of oral history to recreate a 1920s dentist surgery. It has also used oral history techniques in other ways, such as researching into the social history background when reconstructing the site's Co-operative store.

Photographic museums. The use of photographs as a catalyst for interviews has been discussed elsewhere, but scope remains to record interviews with individual photographers, including photo-journalists, artists, fashion photographers, high street portrait photographers and, of course, amateur photographers. Camera manufacturers also need recording. Where are the interviews with pioneers such as Victor Hasselblad, or the numerous other camera designers and manufacturers from Leica to Nikon? Tremendous technical innovation has led to greatly improved lens performance. Has the technical side of lens manufacture been recorded? Film may soon be dated as digital technology makes its mark. Are there interviews with the pioneers from Kodak, AGFA, Perutz, Ilford and Fuji?

Law and order, police museums, prisons, etc. Scotland Yard's Black Museum has many gruesome artefacts in its collections, each with its own story. The official record (when publicly available) will reveal only part of the story. Away from televisual crime, the true story is often of painstaking, boring, repetitive labour and it is a story that is rarely told. How does a police investigation actually work? Are there recordings of the old style of copper of pre-war days? What was it like to live in a police station? What was discipline like? What was it like being in the police during the war?

How did a court operate? Who was on the Bench? How were they selected? What was it like going to prison for the first time? How did the criminals feel? Why do they commit crime? The list is endless, ranging from the interpretation of how, say, a birching stool was used, through to re-creating a court of bygone days using retired court officials and others.

Science and technology collections. Scientific papers rarely recount the sleepless nights and struggles involved in developing a technology or in discovering some new technique or process. The personal stories of scientists need to be recorded just as much as their inventions or discoveries. There are still family memories worth recording. As an example, some years ago an old lady told me of how when she was a child, her father, a then famous scientist, used to invite distinguished visitors to stay at their home. Her most vivid memory was of Hans Geiger (of Geiger counter fame) who, she assured me, had duelling scars on his face, and 'was a most pleasant man to talk to'.

There are others, too, again from my own experience. I recorded the feelings of the scientist who successfully ran the world's first stored computer program, and on another occasion the very human excitement at the Jodrell Bank Radio Telescope when they received, for the very first time, space signals from Sputnik.

Folk museums. The Scandinavians were among the first to understand the need to record memories and reminiscences as part of their folk museum movement, albeit with pen and paper rather than cassette recorder. To operate a folk museum without the inter-action of people and the recording of their memories is surely absurd.

Some folk museums have, however, led the way for years systematically recording information on tape as well as with pen and paper. Geraint Jenkins at St Fagan's Folk Museum (National Museum of Wales) recognized over twenty years ago the significance of collecting and recording associated information using oral history. As a result, sound recordings of Welsh life, industry and culture have been made over many years, chronicling not just artefacts and buildings in the museum's care but also preserving, on tape, the Welsh language and dialects.[14]

The Defence Medal – a typical medal preserved in a military museum collection. The story behind the medal is often best revealed using oral history. (Author)

It is therefore reasonable to argue that oral history recording must be considered a fundamental part of any folk museum's collecting and recording process. To collect an object in isolation, however desirable it may be, demeans the object to posterity if the oral history background and social history are ignored.

Military and regimental museums. It is not always easy to define how to understand and interpret military museum collections. What perspective should be taken? Should the recording of experiences of former prisoners of war be made simply to interpret existing objects? Should part of the active collecting also include the impassive recording of recollections of 'active' conflicts, like the military observer of old? Some recording seems inevitable and obvious, such as the personal memories of battles, campaigns, people, places, etc. This approach has particular significance in the interpretation of objects and events because of the imposition of wartime censorship regulations and imperfect communications at the time.

Military museum collections contain a wide variety of military artefacts from campaign medals to ration books and from tanks to full-size flightworthy planes. The scope for oral history recording is again considerable and cannot be neglected by the museum professional if the collections are to be understood both now and in the future.

One of the dangers of oral history recording in the military sphere, particularly in respect of regimental oral histories, is the insistence by some curators on what has been described as glory and gore. Conflict is a fact of life. There is nothing glorious about war and the oral historian should adopt as dispassionate an approach as possible during interviewing. Notes kept with the completed tape must explain the context and perceived bias of the interview, thus giving future generations an insight into the thoughts of the interviewee at that time.

The Department of Sound Records at the Imperial War Museum is a pioneer in the oral history recording of wartime memories and experience relevant to its collections. Its recordings have international significance and are an excellent example of how oral history can, and should, be used by the museum professional.

Natural history and natural history collections. Admittedly Charles Darwin is a little too far back for oral history recording but there are many natural historians around who should be recorded. Some will already have deposited important reference collections of material into our museums and libraries and their recollections are vital in the overall understanding and possible future scientific appraisal of their work.

Natural history, naturally enough, includes the earth sciences and a considerable effort has been made by such people as the Geological Curators Group (UK), resulting in a better understanding of scattered, and sometimes obscure, nineteenth-century mineral and fossil collections. Perhaps now is also the time to collect the memories and reminiscences of geologists and palaeontologists before it is too late?

Has anyone ever done a professional oral history interview – as opposed to a much-edited, much-shortened, selective broadcast interview – with, say, Sir David Attenborough? Detrimental environmental pressure on the planet's biosphere will undoubtedly make zoological information increasingly important in the years to come. Field notes, whether written, verbal or audio, should be preserved alongside existing collections of material.

Social history collections. So fundamental is oral history recording in the understanding of an object and its social context that it is perhaps not too surprising that most work in museums using oral history has been associated with social history. Some curators believe that social history is a quite separate subject, and that curatorship is solely about collection management. This could not be further from the truth. Throughout, the emphasis has been to record as much as possible about the object, whether that recording (in all its forms) is at the time of its original collection or later.

An entire book could be written on oral history and social history collections, but perhaps a few examples will suffice to whet the appetite.

Example A. The Harris Museum and Art Gallery in Preston recognized a gap in their collecting, namely of contemporary teenage material. After considerable thought, teenagers were invited to the museum and during recorded interviews were asked about their likes and dislikes, and about objects they use and why, thus building up contemporary information to complement active collecting and help plan an appropriate collecting policy.

Example B. A museum was planning an exhibition on 'Christmas past'. The collections held only a relatively small amount of material on Christmas: a few Christmas cards, decorations,

Road transport. Where was this charabanc going? Who were the people? Where was it taken? By whom? (Author)

toys and similar things. Missing – because at the time they were not thought worth preserving – were Christmas trees, lights, labels from presents, advertisements, and home-made toys and dolls.

The Friends of the Museum arranged an informal 'Christmas Remembered' evening with carols and mince pies, to which they invited older people from the community. During the evening session, they were not only able to identify older people whose memories of Christmas were worth recording, but many of them were also willing to lend or donate old treasured presents, wrapping paper, labels, dolls and other toys for the exhibition. Subsequent local press coverage brought in more objects and eventually recordings were also made and preserved for future years.

Transport collections. Great efforts have been made to preserve transport history, not just by museum professionals but largely by volunteers and private preservation groups. A great deal of time and effort has been spent in restoring and preserving historic vehicles – and rightly so – but echoing back to the previous section on industrial archaeology it is equally important to record the memories and reminiscences of those who worked with, repaired, drove, owned and indeed built these vehicles.

Subjects might include buses, tramcars, taxis, private cars, rally cars, aircraft, etc.

ORAL HISTORY AND ARCHIVES

A minority of professional archivists in the UK still hold the opinion that oral history has little or nothing to do directly with archives. However, in general most record offices now embrace the requirements of modern record preservation. The Society of Archivists, for example, has recently been recording interviews with fellow archivists about their work for the Society's 50th anniversary. However, relatively few archivists see themselves directly as field workers or collectors of oral history but rather as preservers or custodians of recorded materials.[15]

Awareness of the possibilities of oral history and archives could lead to new approaches in the care and use of archives. There are lessons to be learned from the museum world on aspects such as collection research, interpretation of collections, and their use as an educational resource and as a way of forming links into the community. Local councillors in charge of funding are increasingly demanding that archives – indeed all services – are more accountable and accessible. Oral history is one way of achieving a link between the desires of councillors and their committees and the public at large.

Oral history investigation might reveal how the accumulation of archival material came about, when it was deposited and by whom. Examining the archives themselves, there are many perplexing questions that can be answered using oral history techniques. For example, a study of church archives might include aspects such as the completeness of registers, repairs, their storage, modern annotations, rebinding and seals. Then there are family and church Bibles, hymn books, psalters, Sunday School prizes. Questions can be asked regarding the origins of Bibles, annotations, details of local families, repair work, rebinding, tooling of covers, craftsmen involved, etc. Other archive material might include church music manuscripts. When was the music written, and by whom? Was it ever published? Where was it played? Why was it written?

Similar detailed projects could be made of the following:

Canal company records
Driving licence applications
Electricity supply records
Estate documents and plans
Implementation of Acts of Parliament
Local authority gas records
Music scores
New town development committee meetings and minutes
Personal letters and diaries
Photographs
Private company records
Railway company records
School day-book records
Second World War notebooks and diaries
Town planning records
Tramway records
Wills

ORAL HISTORY AND THE INTERPRETATION OF DOCUMENTS

Oral history is an important way to understand and interpret some documents. In one particular case a former squadron leader in the Second World War wrote a journal of his experiences in the Far East. The oral history interview was based directly on his hand-written accounts. He simply opened the journal at page one and began to relive his experiences. So thorough was the enhancement of the written work using oral history that it took several sessions, providing in all over six hours of sound recording. The interviews describe in great detail how he escaped by sea immediately before the fall of Singapore to the Japanese, how his boat was sunk at sea, and his subsequent capture and horrific experiences as a prisoner of war on Sumatra.

Documents, just like objects, can also be used successfully in the interview situation. It may not necessarily lead to an interpretation or explanation of the document but it can act as a catalyst in reviving other memories. Sainsbury's Archive in London has successfully used documents such as old advertisements or price lists as a catalyst in their oral history programme about the company.

THE OFFICIAL COLONIAL RECORD AND ORAL HISTORY

Developing nations are discovering that oral history gives them access to information inadequately covered or even excluded from the official record. For example, in India oral history has been used to investigate social attitudes to leprosy in rural communities to aid the national leprosy eradication programme. The official colonial records referred largely to cities where leprosy was seen as 'a threat to the well-being . . . of both Europeans and the native elite of India'.[16] The Lepers Act of 1898 had such a profound effect on how people perceived leprosy that it still maintains its unfortunate implications to this day. Apart from official records there is also what is described as 'missionary literature': leaflets, books and journals which tended to view the sufferer as a 'sinner ready to receive Christ'.

The use of oral history to fill in the gaps left by the official record has led to an effective treatment programme for sufferers, as well as the potential for establishing a rehabilitation programme. There will be, presumably, a recorded legacy to co-exist with other sources of information.

ORAL HISTORY AND THE INTERPRETATION OF PHOTOGRAPHS

Huge numbers of photographs have been preserved, yet few have actually been studied and interpreted using oral history. The technique offers a unique opportunity to study and understand the context, particularly of recent images. That can vary from the identification of individuals in a school photograph through to identifying people, shops and buildings in a typical commercial postcard street scene. Every photograph has a story behind it. Each was taken for a reason and the maxim 'every picture tells a story' is very true.

Nowhere is the value of using oral history to interpret photographs more clearly illustrated than in the following example. In 1937 Humphrey Spender was commissioned as a photographer to record life in the then mill town of Bolton as part of Mass Observation, an exercise in chronicling contemporary life. He produced many outstanding photographs and in 1997 he came back to Bolton to be interviewed about his work.

All the available photographs were systematically worked through during the interview, Humphrey Spender explaining in detail how, when and why each photograph was taken. Among his many outstanding photographs is one taken in a local public house. This

Humphrey Spender's often misinterpreted photograph of life in a Bolton public house in the late 1930s. Oral history revealed what actually happened. (Bolton Museum & Art Gallery)

photograph in particular illustrates why it is necessary to obtain complementary oral evidence and not simply rely on the impact of the image.

Examine the photograph carefully. Notice the friendly wave given by the man at the bar to the right of the picture. Spender's ideal was to 'photograph the natural thing' and that is by and large exactly what he did, often concealing his camera under his coat, the photograph being a point-and-shoot operation. He now takes up the story.

HS: There is a photograph . . . of a man doing that to me.

KH: His hand raised.

HS: Yes. People tend to think that was a greeting. It wasn't. It was a keep-out sign and by this time I knew that half my intentions were defeated anyway – because he had drawn everybody's attention to my presence. And I thought I would just snatch a picture and get out.[17]

ORAL HISTORY AND LIBRARIES

Libraries have tended to use their basis of a long association with the borrowing public to encourage use of local history stock for community outreach work and as an educational resource for schools and colleges. Public libraries on the whole have not taken on the responsibility of collection research and management like their cousins in museums and archives. There is some encouraging evidence, especially where museums, libraries and archives work cheek by jowl, that traditional barriers over collection management are breaking down and joint projects are emerging to the benefit of all participants. Librarians were among the first to exploit the government's Manpower Service programme and apply oral history to their area. Oddly, this was often not as collection research – although photographs were used from local collections as a basis for interviews – but rather to collect local memories before they disappeared. Some public libraries have undertaken extraordinary initiatives in oral history work, especially in recording.

My own introduction to oral history came via the library world. It was soon evident that the books had serious limitations when it came to preserving local memories. In the library in which I first worked there were no books at all about the local coal-mines. Then, by coincidence, an old collier came into the library and started talking about his lifelong passion for 'gals'. Assuming, incorrectly, he had a passion for young ladies, I questioned him further, only to discover that he was actually talking about the Galloway pit ponies used in the mines. After that first interview came another person talking about the local canal and soon after that a group of librarians, museum curators, archivists and others was set up to establish the North West Sound Archive, to which I eventually became archivist.

Some libraries have gone even further. Birmingham City Libraries actually had a mobile van and invited people to come in and record their memories and allow the library staff to copy their old photographs on the spot. In the United States there have even been 'oral history buses' touring country areas in an attempt to capture rural oral history before it is too late.

Some libraries have also held competitions to promote oral history. Tameside Libraries in 1995 ran a competition for the best oral history interview which shared the experience of becoming an immigrant to Tameside.

There have also been coordinated cooperative ventures between libraries, record offices and museums, such as the project at Oldham where, although the recordings are carried out by the museum staff, the library staff operate a listening station where local people can hear the tapes.

CHAPTER THREE

ORAL HISTORY FOR BUSINESS, MANAGEMENT AND ENVIRONMENTAL PLANNING

ORAL HISTORY AND BUSINESS

Little has been written about the possibilities of using oral history as a business tool. It has been extremely difficult to find good examples of how the technique has been applied. In the UK the very idea of using oral history techniques to make money has been described as anathema by some oral historians. It therefore comes as no great surprise that the business potential of oral history has been neglected by traditional oral historians. In addition, commercial companies and businesses, and indeed other organizations – such as local government – have failed to recognize oral history as an effective public relations tool or management training aid or as a method of retaining useful expertise.

COMPANY HISTORIES

Even the *Oral History Journal*, usually the oracle on all matters concerning oral history, has little to say on corporate or institutionalized uses (or abuses) of oral history. In a report from South America it was claimed that 'State-owned companies and state institutions are commissioning histories as an assertion of legitimacy against privatisation; conversely new private companies seek to legitimize their roles by creating a history.'[1]

The accuracy of the statement is not important to this discussion. What is important is the perceived view that there is a systematic move towards using oral history as a persuader. Creative oral history is at one level both worrying and quite unacceptable to oral historians. That said, oral historians throughout the world record, and then produce, edited publications or similar. So what is the difference as long as master tapes are kept for posterity? It has to be recognized by businesses and institutions that it is important to record systematically all aspects, including the unsavoury parts of corporate or institutional history. These recordings must, as part of the package, be preserved intact in a public record archive, possibly with closures or restrictions placed on their immediate use. That at least allows the survival of the original record for comparison with the usage it is put to by the company or institution.

Irresponsible companies or bodies will always exploit oral history or anything else that can be used to their advantage. An argument against the application of oral history methodology in business as a persuader or image-maker would therefore be meaningless. The adoption of established professional guidelines in oral history work will help, however, and there are, of course, more positive and responsible approaches to corporate oral history work. Many companies are proud of their long history and when a suitable occasion such as a centenary is reached it may offer an appropriate occasion to recall, preserve and publish something of their past.

In the United States one company, Terra Firma Design of Fort Collins, offers 'Corporate storytelling' as a service. They record 'stories of your company' with 'life-encompassing interviews with the founders'. The interviews are then used as a basis for 'a corporate identity, a marketing strategy, insight into a customer's needs or to preserve the company's unique history'. They have produced, for example, for their client Wetsel-Oviat, a 10 CD audio archive, a 2 CD photo archive, and a 'single listening CD'.[2]

Another firm listed on the Internet is History Enterprises, which claims to have been set up by professional historians and archivists 'expert in writing history, building and maintaining archives and oral history interviews'. Their clients include Lincoln Electric Co., Pitney Bowes, and AT&T for whom they have produced company histories, mainly in book form.[3]

In the UK, as far as I am aware, my own company, Heritage Recording Services, is the only one offering an even remotely similar service. Oral history has, however, a far wider application in business than has been so far identified or developed by our US cousins.

SKILL LOSS

Many of the older established industries have been laying people off, 'downsizing', or offering early retirement and generally slimming down their workforce. Some of these workers have been loyal to the company for many years and the break from the company is felt very keenly. I am not aware of any company taking the initiative to assist their retired workers (and themselves in the process) by suggesting they record, or be recorded on, some aspect of the company's oral history other than for a corporate history. There could be pitfalls, of course, especially if the company doesn't have a good track record, say, on safety, but even that can be used to advantage in a company trying to reorganize and change, as will be discussed later. In my experience even recently retired people need a sense of connection and continuity, and recording an oral history is one way of attaining that.

There are definite advantages to the company, too. When people take early retirement or are made redundant they take with them skills, expertise and knowledge of the company, its products and, of course, its working history. Older workers may well recall the day the firm supplied XYZ to the Queen or completed some complex order for a foreign customer, but others will recall more up-to-date activities of practical use to the company. All this is good PR even long after the event. It shows the company has a good track record and a caring attitude towards its workers.

How does this work in reality? Most managers in the British style of management tend to see this approach as irrelevant to making a profit rather than as a way of retaining expertise and streamlining the company for relatively little cost.

THE ASSOCIATES CLUB

On leaving a company on a redundancy or retirement basis, part of the package would be free membership of the 'Associates Club'. A newsletter would keep people in touch with what is happening and associates would be invited to the usual run of Christmas parties and other social events. However, the essential difference between a traditional Benevolent club and an Associates Club would be the level of direct involvement in the company. The cultural framework for active cooperation and inclusion in the company's activities would be maintained, the Associates Club offering many advantages to the company, such as:

- A recognized pool of expertise on various topics from technical information to staff relations
- Access to the expertise quickly and cheaply via a database and telephone
- Involvement in management and shop-floor training using retrospective oral history interview techniques
- Consultancy and research as the occasion demands, and possibly even a short-term contract if that is warranted
- A social group with no barriers
- A social group that could involve itself directly in producing the newsletter within the company thus retaining the link
- Creating a good public image
- A cheap and effective tool to maximize available resources

The catalyst would be oral history but the concept of an Associates Club goes far beyond that. The retrieval of information in the first instance using oral history would then need to be formed into training programmes of various kinds, whether management or shopfloor. The Associates should have access to all ages, sexes and levels within the company. An essential part of the Associate Club would be the passing on of knowledge and wisdom to younger people. It would have the effect of raising awareness and respect among younger people for older people and would create a better workplace culture.

The concept as suggested here is very much my own and needs further thought to fully develop the idea.

INDUSTRIAL ARCHAEOLOGY AND MODERN BUSINESS

Again this may seem an odd combination. Yet understanding past technology can be crucial to present-day companies. Take a theoretical case of, say, one of the newly formed water companies who wish to find out about pipework at a very old reservoir site. The nineteenth-century engineering drawings have long since disappeared so they approach the now retired former engineer for the site. He is able to sketch out plans and point to features on the ground of direct interest to the water company. Oral history in this instance has been used as an effective information retrieval tool. A specially constructed interview is a cost-effective way to achieve that goal and is a great deal cheaper than excavating the site in search of lost pipework.

Oral history as a basis for essential research can be taken even further. Maintenance and assembly manuals have been created using oral history by one company that uses special steam-driven printing machines for producing patterned textiles. The machines were old, temperamental and always breaking down, and oral history was used to talk to older fitters and mechanics who suggested ways to improve reliability through regular maintenance procedures, drawing up schedules, parts lists, and disassembly/assembly instructions.

Oral history and industrial archaeology in its broadest sense will become increasingly important in the future. Less and less information is permanently stored on paper, the less certain electronic storage techniques becoming the norm. Industries where this approach could potentially be very useful include the nuclear industry, aerospace, aircraft and helicopter production, and the computer industry itself.

Food for thought? Perhaps on the periphery of industrial archaeology is the retail grocery trade. Recently, large supermarket chains have been exploring the possibility of incorporating so-called traditional high street skills into their stores. The role oral history could play in staff training is unmistakable.

THE PUBLIC RELATIONS ROLE

The intention of such an Associates Club or Group would principally be that it should retain and develop a pool of expertise among retired or former employees while serving the

An early aircraft at Ringway, now Manchester International Airport. The airport established an important archive some years ago and recorded many early memories of Ringway as a parachute training centre, as well as interviews with pilots, flight engineers, cabin crews and representatives from the many airlines using the airport. Although conceived as an extension of Public Relations, like many archives it has a much wider role to play and is now indispensable. (Manchester Airport Archive)

social need of providing active involvement in the future of the company. Not everyone in an Associate Club would wish to become involved in the formal advising of the company but they might wish to take part in social and community projects. In local government the concept of outreach into the community is well established, but in industry it is less so. Some firms do encourage retired employees to visit clubs and other outside organizations to talk about their employer, show slides and generally promote the right image. However, the outreach concept allows children in school, for example, to interview – using oral history techniques – retired members of our theoretical business as part of the National Curriculum. The construction of a company history based on the memories of both current and retired employees would be a way of bringing in front of the local community the company and its responsible attitude towards local people and its employees. Children have parents and so the information would be spread around.

There are many other ideas that can be cribbed from the local government sector not directly to do with oral history, such as drama presentations, publications, arts events, reminiscence work support, storytelling – all relatively cheap and effective public relations tools.

LONDON TRANSPORT MUSEUM – PUBLIC RELATIONS ROLE

Some large companies have taken great pains to preserve their past. Often the motive for such effort was pride in the work they were doing or awareness of its historical significance; for example, Cable & Wireless in its early days encouraged employees to keep diaries which now form part of the company's archive. Other companies, such as London Transport, played such an integral part in the life of the capital both in peace and during wartime that the creation of a museum was in many ways a natural extension of their everyday work. That the museum has a major public relations role to play is clear, but the staff have gone much further and used oral history to enhance the museum's role. They have an active oral history programme recording present and former members of staff. These interviews include tram-drivers, B-type bus drivers, inspectors, poster artists, and train drivers, including the first woman train driver. The biggest

The biggest single oral history project undertaken by the London Transport Museum has been the recording of staff originally recruited from the Caribbean in the 1950s and 1960s. (London Transport Museum)

single project to date has been the recording of staff originally recruited from the Caribbean in the 1950s and '60s.

The interviews are collected to add to the unwritten social history and to help understand the provenance of artefacts acquired by the museum. There is also an occasional programme of outreach reminiscence work with the retired and elderly using objects such as bell-punch ticket machines, slides and photographs. The museum also provides educational services, and has a library and archive.[4]

ADVERTISING AND DESIGN

The creation of an appropriate image for a company often depends on its earlier history for inspiration. Oral history recorded at the Levi Strauss Company in San Francisco has also been used in its current brochures, press releases and annual reports. Similar work at the Louis Matini Winery, St Helena, California, has resulted in the use of oral history in its advertising, establishing the image of an 'old, traditional family business', reinforcing the quality of their wine.[5]

Many UK companies have far older bases than American companies and therefore the prospect of reaching back into history to influence the present is a very real and potentially rich option. Some companies have invested in company archives though few, if any, have actively applied the archives as a resource to develop and use to influence other parts of their operation.

One exception to this is Sainsbury's Archive in London which has made both audio and video oral history recordings of employees. The material is seen not just as a purist archive but also as a resource for the company. One use has been to reinforce corporate identity by including 'reminiscence pieces' in an internal magazine programme. Many of the video-tapes have been based on earlier oral history recordings, but, as the archivist Bridget Williams explained, video has a wider range of uses and is more easily accepted than audio as a resource.

MARKET RESEARCH

The area of well-tried market research question techniques might seem an inappropriate place to think of oral history. Yet the skills applied to oral history interviewing can also be applied to some aspects of market research, such as monitoring product reliability and customer service quality.

Car manufacturers might, for example, commission a number of independently recorded interviews with car owners. As the interviews are in depth and do not simply rely on a fairly indifferent interviewer ticking off items on a list the results are much more likely to be honest about the performance of the car. This is particularly true if the interviews are recorded on an anonymous basis by an independent oral historian working for the company but whose objectives are clearly stated as being for market research, company archives, or an education programme with copies eventually being deposited under a closure agreement at the local record office.

Cost-wise, although interviews are longer and more thorough, fewer would be required and as oral historians are cheaper to employ than statisticians or market researchers there could be a net saving overall.

Other services and products which could benefit from this approach include drug manufacturers, perhaps with specially commissioned interviews with users of their products. Much more of the social background and realistic use of the drug treatment would be revealed. Honest answers about side-effects could be determined. Anonymity of interviewees and independent oral history interviewing would be the key to its success.

Customer care is a major concern for many organizations, such as railway companies and airlines. The application of oral history to establish personal views on an anonymous basis could be very revealing. Someone travelling on a plane or train and asking passengers for their true feelings, perhaps at the very moment they are delayed, will be more revealing than straightforward questionnaires after the event.

An actual example from the United States concerns a robotics company that has been using 'stories' gathered from teachers and children to evaluate the success (or otherwise) of their products in the classroom, presumably to improve design, manufacture and effective marketing.

Focused Discussion Research Groups

Market researchers use focused group discussion to investigate attitudes and changes among customers and consumers – effectively, group interviewing. Such groups often consist of specific categories of people, such as young mothers, or a cross-section of middle-income earners or whatever mix is appropriate. Plainly, many of the techniques developed by oral historians pertaining to group interviewing could be safely and usefully, applied.

The Role of Market Research in Developing Countries

Elsewhere in this book it is demonstrated how, by using oral history techniques, knowledge can be obtained from remote, low literacy groups in developing countries which can have a marked effect on the application of Aid and Health programmes. The principle, taking into account the feelings and experiences of sufferers, clinical and social, is also potentially important in a commercial sense. The opportunity exists to use oral history primarily to benefit the target group, but also as a very personal form of market research. It also raises new issues for oral historians which need to be carefully addressed.

A theoretical international drug company might fund an oral history project into the impact of a particular disease in a particular area or country simply to gain a trading advantage with the country's regime by being seen in the right light. After the work has been completed the regime may still not accept the company and people will have been interviewed in vain. Hopes will have been raised and then dashed. There are clear moral issues involved. However, on the positive side, such projects could place responsible companies into major potential markets and also enhance internationally their 'humanitarian' image. This low-cost approach to public relations and market research certainly deserves further consideration.

Another permutation of this would be for a company to offer to record and preserve a region's or district's heritage using professional oral historians and heritage recorders, seen to be independent of the company. The gathered information would then be returned to the people to help them retain their heritage and enhance their own status through an educational programme or cultural resource.

Imagine yet another theoretical company that was pitching for a contract to build a new factory in a developing nation. The factory, with its hydro-electric scheme and dam, would change for ever the local way of life. The inclusion in the proposition-for-contract of the involvement of local people in recording and preserving their common heritage as part of the overall deal could give the company the edge it needed to gain the contract. This would be especially true if the recording programme led to the creation of a cultural resource. That information, in association with some simple business management skills training, could lead to the creation of sustainable development linked to traditional cultural values.

Competitor Research

Firms spend large amounts of money trying to establish just how their competitor operates so successfully, or what the future plans of the company are likely to be. Interviews with former employees and others in the industry could be very revealing. There is often little employer loyalty after a worker has left or been dismissed from a company. As long as the interviewee's anonymity is maintained then it would be a reasonable method of approach. The counter-action of this would be, of course, for competitors to take on board the idea and question your company's ex-workers! Whether or not informants were paid for the interview is largely a commercial matter, although it would raise eyebrows among oral historians who traditionally do not pay interviewees. A key figure with expert knowledge might, however, insist on receiving payment.

It is recognized that this is a controversial area. Are the interviewers oral historians or industrial spies? What ethics and morals are involved? Whatever the moral implications for oral historians contracted by industry, it is apparent that interviewing skills could be used to great advantage both for companies and posterity. If the interviews were undertaken by an oral historian not directly associated with the company the task in some ways becomes easier. The oral historian would be seen as separate to the company, independent to a certain degree and professional in attitude over clearance and deposit. That professionalism would need also to extend to promises of confidentiality (both to the company and the interviewee) and ensure that pledges concerning commercial usage of the information were clear and recorded as part of the clearance agreement which all parties might sign.

Although the primary commercial aim would be information about competitors, it would double as an effective and cheap public relations tool, as well as an eventual historical source.

RESEARCH AND DEVELOPMENT

Oral history has been applied by a number of companies and organizations, mainly in the USA to research and development (R&D). For example:

Case one: A drug and chemical company was concerned at the amount being spent on R&D and its relationship to the introduction of new products. An oral historian was employed under a commercial confidentiality contract to discuss with R&D staff experiments they had conducted over the years. Some of the early experiments, especially during wartime, were unrecorded and retired employees felt free to talk about their work for the first time. In addition, failures were re-evaluated and near-miss products re-assessed. Some experiments had been regarded as dangerous or too expensive to develop, but with time and new technology, a number of products which had failed in the test-tube – so-called near-miss products – were revived and became commercial successes.

Case two: A fire protection firm was researching into causes of fire, how materials are consumed, and the toxic gases emitted. While valuable information was obtained from fire-fighters and post-fire inspection it was recognized that research information might also be obtainable from survivors of fires. Oral history was used to interview a cross-section of survivors to explore various themes relevant to design and use in emergency situations. These themes included:

Their ability to recognize potential fire hazards and accelerants
What action they took on realizing their situation
What action they took to control the fire
To what extent were those actions effective
How the actions of others related to their own actions
What difficulties they encountered with equipment
What difficulties they encountered during the escape
What thoughts went through the minds of those trapped

Analysis of the answers to these and many other questions helped to build up a profile of different types of people which led to a better understanding of the psychology of people in such extreme situations. As a result products were modified to make their use easier and simpler – and therefore more effective – in such emergencies.

An unexpected by-product of the research was the enormous relief shown by survivors that they were able to tell their story and the hope that their experience might help to save someone else's life. All of this provided good-will towards the company, its products and its reputation.

Other authentic examples of commercial information retrieval where oral history techniques have been applied include:

Aircraft production: crash investigation
Brewery: retired workers revealed the 'secret' ingredients of a former brewer's successful beer
Coal-mining: location of natural methane gas vents in relationship to buildings, leading to assessment of liability and recourse

Chemical company: unorthodox and unofficial technique of brick-lining a rotary kiln which resulted in the lining remaining intact for longer, thus reducing costs

Oil exploration industry: deep sea submersible rescue, oral debriefing both personal and technical. A detailed interview with the crew revealed different stages of adjustment and ability resulting in better design and surface-to-submersible communication. The ships attending the incident were not well coordinated in their endeavours, rescue equipment was in the wrong place and so on. Interview revealed why this was so and how it could be rectified

Oil exploration industry: location of wrecks and other hazards

Factory fire: explanation and assessment of extent of unusual features and foundations uncovered during the re-building work, the extent of which affected the duration and cost of reconstruction

Glassworks: examination of flues beneath a nearby nineteenth-century glass cone looking for an unrecorded type of flue control system mentioned by former workers during interviews with oral historians. The flue construction could have an economic value in the design of new glass tanks

Nuclear industry: examination of non-standard and unofficial methods of working. Unreported accidents and near-miss incidents and their effect

Steel works: anonymous recording of unorthodox practices of dealing with hot metal and spills, handling practice, etc., as part of an overall contribution to health and safety and therefore, by implication, costs as a result of fewer lost man-hours, etc.

PERSONNEL

Personnel interviewing has its own well-established techniques and practices. Some of the basic techniques of oral history interviewing, such as asking Why, When, What, Where, Who, Which, How, can still be applied. For senior posts the technique is capable of considerable development and application. In some organizations it is customary for an informal interview to take place. Here again, the techniques still apply and searching questions can be asked in an informal and non-threatening way.

The techniques used in personnel interviewing are so well established that it may well be perceived that oral history has little, if anything, to offer. In my own experience of asking the questions of a potential employee I have found the oral history approach extremely useful and revealing.

Staff Debriefing

In some ways this is closely related to competitor research. If a new member of staff joins a company from a competitor, oral history techniques can be used to solicit information about that competitor. The interviews in such a case need not be formal or even recorded.

A similar role is taken when a person leaves or is moved to another part of the company. So-called exit interviews based again on oral history interviewing principles can be very revealing and useful to both company and employee.

BUSINESS MANAGEMENT AND ETHICS

This may seem a surprising heading in a book on oral history. In the USA Professor Walter Bennett, a distinguished lawyer, former court judge and director of the Intergenerational Legal Ethics Programme, has used oral history as a 'model for teaching ethics'. Although his model is aimed primarily at lawyers going through law school, his approach could certainly be applied to business management ethics as well.[6]

The University of North Carolina School of Law developed a new model known as the Intergenerational Legal Ethics Project. The project has two parts: the Oral History of Lawyers and Judges Seminar (1992) and a Model Mentoring Programme. The underlying theme is that 'the teaching of professionalism must engage students in open inquiry and discussion of values – not just rules of conduct'.

There was a general unwillingness among students to discuss moral issues and oral history helped explore ways to do so in a non-competitive environment. The process 'forced students to look at their future in moral terms . . . and their reasons for becoming lawyers and their own moral stance in relation to the person they interviewed . . . and to take a pride in their work'.

The mentoring part of the course paired off students with practitioners such as senior judges, who guided them and allowed some shadowing of their professional activities. The mentoring process meant that professional and ethical values and experience at the highest level were available to students.

Could business schools, Training and Enterprise Councils, trade unions, the Industrial Society, and some service organizations be involved in oral history and mentoring? Are the principles of the American project too distant to introduce in the associate clubs suggested earlier?

Management – Decision Making

There is a strong case for using oral history to explore how and why decisions are made and the effects of those decisions on others and the performance of the company or service. The introduction of oral history interview techniques as part of management training may seem fanciful but it has already been tried successfully by a number of companies and corporations both in Britain and in the United States. The results were revealing and useful. In London a major merchant bank has been analysing 'wrong decisions' among its senior management, using the skills of an oral historian, to discover the circumstances surrounding each decision. No recordings are made but the information is used to ensure such errors are not repeated by the bank.

In another project trainee managers were asked to look at specific decisions made by their colleagues during the preceding year. The groups then constructed detailed question sheets based on established oral history techniques and selected an interviewer, each member of the group interviewing different interviewees in turn. (It would be interesting for, say, two different interviews to be recorded with the same interviewee. Two different interviewers would produce different results.)

The interviews were then recorded in a relaxed atmosphere and on audio-tape to retain informality and spontaneity. Interviews lasted up to an hour, and sometimes several interviews together with accompanying papers and other documents were provided to understand complex decision-making procedures. The results were then analysed and discussed by the group. A number of things became clear:

- Decisions which at the time had seemed illogical or irrational were often made for good sound reasons, taking into account issues about which perhaps the trainees were largely unaware
- When wrong decisions were made it was possible to look at the way those decisions affected others and identify monitoring points within the management and workforce that would give an indication of what was really happening
- The transparency of the decision-making process benefited all taking part, and the tapes were kept for other sessions
- The process allowed access to areas of senior management which had hitherto not been accessible
- The interviewing process reinforced the loyalty of trainee management
- The process allowed senior managers to identify weaknesses in their own performance and in the performance of others and make recommendations and implementations as appropriate
- The improvement in interpersonal skill development was considerable among all the members of the core groups taking part

Local Government Management

The technique could be employed by many organizations, for example, local government or Health Care Trusts. In local government the decision-making process is convoluted, with professional officers advising committees of lay councillors – elected members. In recent times there have been a number of very public cases where the political aspirations of some elected members have interfered with the democratic process. In some authorities dangerous precedents have been set with chief officers taking decisions with minimal reference to elected members. There may be many reasons for this, such as the technical or specialist nature of the material, political interference, infrequency of meeting cycles, straightforward poor advice from consultants, etc. In a democracy, decision-making should be transparent and obvious. There is a real case for incorporating within officer training the kind of oral history analysis package and mentoring discussed earlier. The tendency to run local councils on a business-like basis is not impeded by this process, but strengthened.

In the United States preliminary White House staff exit interviews are recorded and preserved at the Ronald Reagan Library. The information given on the Internet does not make it clear whether or not such interviewing still continues, or to what practical use the results may have been applied. However, the principle is there and it is a short step for someone to take the initiative and implement such information in staff training, resource management, and administrative forward-planning procedures.[7]

The Hostile Take-over Project

A series of interviews were recorded with top management in 1991 at the Goodyear Tire and Rubber Company, Microdot Inc., and Richardson-Vicks Inc., in the United States.

The project was developed by William Crowther, former director of Marketing Communications at Richardson-Vicks, in association with the Oral History Section of Columbia University, New York.

The interviewees describe their experiences of so-called hostile take-over attempts at their respective companies and discuss how this form of 'business practice' could affect the US economy. The project, which is on-going, raises interesting issues for the oral historian and business management. The information about the project supplied on the Internet does not mention how the recordings would be used, but their potential as a resource for management training is obvious.[8]

Health and Safety at Work

The technique is not simply confined to management and trainee management. One large organization in the United States has employed an oral historian to interview employees, both current and former, who were involved in or associated with accidents or near-misses. All the interviews retained the anonymity of the interviewee and explored the nature of the accident or near-miss and invited comment on how the health and safety at work record might be improved. The results were startling. There was some whistle-blowing and acrimony, but most informants were constructive in their suggestions, rather than destructive.

A surprising number of illegal work practices were uncovered, some of which actually laid the corporation open to prosecution. Needless to say, the situation was rectified rather quickly.

Small Business Development

Although the application of oral history to small businesses is limited it does have its place. The following are based on actual small firms, although for various reasons the details have been altered.

Example one: the button man. An old-established, old-fashioned manufacturing company in the Midlands had for many years made components for stiffening shirt collars. There had been very little imaginative expansion except for branching out into stiffeners for the shoe industry. However, when that industry came under threat from overseas competition things were looking bleak.

A chance meeting with an oral historian in the local library set the younger of the two partners thinking. First he went back to the library and discovered that his firm began not by manufacturing stiffening for shirt collars as he had always been told, but by making a wide variety of items ranging from whalebone corsets to bandages. Further research revealed the existence of an early catalogue of thousands of different kinds of button the firm had once made. The local museum also turned out to have hundreds of the buttons surviving in its collections. At first it was a matter of curiosity, then interest. The potential of the discoveries slowly began to dawn. The firm was almost a hundred years old and it had occurred to the partner that in some remote way there might be a business opportunity in celebrating that fact.

Again, it was a chance conversation about his discoveries with the works foreman that convinced the partner that oral history was the way ahead. The foreman had been there for many years and recalled the button-making machinery still being used for the odd production run – indeed he himself he had worked a little on it – and also that at least one of the smaller presses was still at the back of the warehouse.

Encouraged by this, the partner started to interview in his spare time some of the older members of staff, and then people who had once worked in the factory. He even had a go at interviewing one of the informants with his camcorder.

Eventually, he had collected enough material to form the basis of a plan, hardly a business plan as such but rather the first stage towards the revitalization of the company. A centenary exhibition was held at the works to which the press were invited. This in turn led to more information about the company being uncovered. Eventually, he discovered some of the moulds and templates and started making specialist buttons for the fashion industry. One of the television programmes featuring clothes and fashion gave him a three-minute spot about buttons and the company was moving in the right direction again.

Oral history

- allowed a useful retrospective view of the company
- provided ideas for change
- generated free publicity
- saved a company reliant on outmoded products
- provided a new lucrative outlet for an old product. Forward-planning ideas included other fashion accessories and a visitor centre which is, essentially, a direct sell shop
- improved its local image

Example two: the basket-maker. A family decided to move from London to south Wales. They bought an old mill with the vague intention of creating some kind of craft workshop and tea-room. On closer examination of the deeds it was discovered that the old mill was in fact a former basket-making workshop and not a corn mill as they had thought. With its water-wheel still intact, the site, although derelict, seemed an ideal place to bring up a young family and run a business.

The land nearby held rights of access to the lodgement where the water accumulated before being fed into the feeder channel for the water-wheel. Local enquiry soon revealed that the reeds used in basket-making were grown alongside the feeder channel in special allotted areas. During the restoration work machinery was uncovered and local people began talking about the old mill. Using a simple cassette-recorder local memories were recorded. After an appeal in the local paper several retired workers came forward and the family soon realized that, with some guidance from the old workers, making baskets at the mill might just be viable, as an attraction rather than a going-concern, to make ends meet. A great deal of oral history was recorded, not just memories but interpretative – how the mill was fitted out – as well as recordings made on video of the actual techniques involved.

Fortunately, the site had a good location with a car park and tourists came flocking in to see the basket-maker at work. The mill was split-level on a hillside and visitors entered on an upper floor and made their way down. On the floor beneath the demonstration area was an exhibition of local arts and crafts, and below that children's toys, down to the lower floor to the café and exit via the shop. The whole thing was kick-started by approaching a television company who included the site in their holiday programme.

Oral History

- helped to develop a clear theme for the attraction
- was essential to the understanding of how baskets were made
- introduced the product, and the family, into the local community
- attracted publicity through the novelty values, and local people once employed in the trade became unpaid supporters of the project
- helped to preserve a dying rural craft as well as an old building

Example three: the furniture man. A small antique business was looking for new ways to increase turnover. The proprietor enjoyed collecting and selling locally made furniture. Initially out of curiosity, he recorded the memories of a former worker. He then realized that oral history, although it would take a little time to complete, might help in the expansion of his business and reputation. Very little had been written about the furniture and so, largely in his spare time, he carried on researching and recording as many workers and owners as he could find. This led him to share his enthusiasm with others and gave the opportunity to see a wider range of furniture.

In effect this was personal contact market research. As he became better known, he became regarded as an authority on the subject. Now he was not only researching out of interest, but also applying direct selling of his services to those interested in furniture. Eventually he accumulated enough information to produce a book. This led to invitations to speak at conferences and thus effectively gave him a niche in a specialized market. An exhibition was launched and covered by radio and television. This had the effect of raising his credibility even further by making the general public aware of his interest. He became widely known as a specialist and produced a newsletter giving details of showroom prices and new information about his beloved chairs and tables. This rapidly spread and information was even placed on the Internet. His turnover and profit increased accordingly.

Oral History

- gave him the opportunity to meet other collectors
- gave him the opportunity to see what type of furniture was popular, or needed, to fill the gaps in a particular collection
- made him an expert
- gave him free and extensive publicity
- cost little to do over a period of time and did not affect his cash flow
- gave him enjoyment and satisfaction
- increased his turnover and profit as he would also buy and sell furniture for clients
- gave him a basis on which to plan the expansion of his business
- provided useful public relations: he was seen in a good light by the public who had seen him on TV or read his book

EMPLOYMENT AND TRAINING PROGRAMMES

An Introduction to Business

Students are required to understand not just the managerial aspects of businesses but also how they operate on a day-to-day basis.

Oral history can be used as a key to gain access to manufacturing or service industries in order to explore what there is on offer. Some larger companies offer work experience, which is valuable, although it is difficult in a short space of time to understand the range of possibilities, short-comings or advantages of a particular business. Oral history allows the interviewer to explore around the edges of an industry and not be reliant on work experience at a single firm. During the survey, if the right approach is made, oral history will open doors to key people and offer an insight into management and organization. This works two ways, of course, as management will be looking for employees with intelligence, communication skills and initiative. It will soon become apparent which firms are good employers and which are not, and indeed if there is any reasonable future with those firms. The industry may be found, on researching, to be moribund. Ask the workforce to talk about issues such as health and safety, wages, management, conditions, strikes and so on.

Site Research

I have worked for several developers and builders interested in the history of sites scheduled for proposed developments. Their interest was far from academic as the following examples illustrate.

Case one: oral history was used to determine the exact location of a mine shaft and out-buildings. The exercise involved using maps and photographs of the site prior to demolition and recording interviews, using oral history techniques, with former miners and others to establish the location of footings and other remains. The actual location of the seventeenth-century shaft had been buried under spoil. Interviewing local people on site allowed key features to be identified and then, by interpolation and measurement, the position of the shaft was located. This saved the builder the cost of drilling several sites to find the void.

Case two: a water company received reports of fish found floating in a river. There was no obvious source for the pollution but illegal dumping of refuse in quarries adjacent to the discharge area was thought to be responsible. Oral history interviews with local people revealed that there had been considerable illegal dumping of motor-car tyres (some of which were burned), unspecified chemicals and liquids. When a broad enough cross-section of knowledge was obtained the decision was taken to sink a borehole in the alleged culprit site. The borehole revealed extensive dumping which led to a series of prosecutions and an extensive clean-up operation.

Using an oral historian to investigate the matter had the advantage that the person was seen as independent. People are likely to talk to a historian far more freely than they would to a water company researcher.

Case three: research was carried out into the extent that land adjacent to a river had been flooded within living memory. The height and depth of such flooding were serious considerations in the development of luxury homes on the site. One informant recalled how, even though his cottage was never directly flooded, the river water would nevertheless back up in the drains and prevent land drainage from reaching the river, resulting in partial flooding well away from the river boundary. The developer, by slightly modifying his plans, was able to create a flood-prevention wall and include adequate separate land drainage. The sewage system was 'sealed' and pumped off site to a higher level discharge.

ORAL HISTORY OUTLETS

There are relatively few outlets for the direct sale of oral history material. Most oral history material is reprocessed into books, educational packs and other published forms. There is a market for oral history on radio and television, although at present it is a very limited one. The reason for this is not just cash, but attitude. Many broadcasters believe that modern audiences will not sit and listen to lengthy pieces of oral history – which is simply not true. Rolling programmes are also a feature of local radio and twenty- or thirty-minute pieces are difficult to fit into such schedules. It is also the day of the sound bite. However, not all local radio stations, especially state or BBC local radio, share this attitude. Sometimes joint projects between oral historians and broadcasters have been very successful and attracted large audiences. A good example is a series broadcast by the old Piccadilly Radio Ltd, in Manchester, on the memories and reminiscences of people who lived and worked in Trafford Park, an early industrial estate situated alongside the Manchester Ship Canal.

Television can offer more substantial financial rewards but for the reasons discussed earlier it can degrade the value of the oral history material through editing and picture selection. However, using original oral history research as a basis for television can be rewarding. The work of Rogan Taylor of the University of Liverpool on the oral history of football produced considerable revenue; first broadcast on local radio on Merseyside, it was later made into a major television series, *Kicking and Screaming*.

ORAL HISTORY AND THE PLANNING PROCESS

Oral history is playing an increasing role in contributing to the planning process. In the past, town and country planning has, understandably perhaps, paid little heed to 'the ramblings of old folk' as one planner succinctly put it. National and international awareness of green issues, the need for sustainable development and the direct needs of people – their quality of life – are all issues that directly or indirectly now have an influence on planning issues in the UK. The evidence for this is to be found in post-war planning practice – the rise of conservation areas, sites of special scientific interest, areas of outstanding natural beauty and, of course, the establishment of National Parks.

Growing populations in the cities meant greater pressure on the countryside, and the enlightened strategy of greenbelt land and the creation of local country parks provide a

Motorway under construction: oral history has a major role to play in chronicling environmental impact and change. (Author)

leisure and recreational facility for many city dwellers, as well as a refuge for wildlife. Strategies for the management and interpretation of these parks must include public access and also take into account the feelings of those living and working there. This is particularly true of National Parks. This new awareness of 'points of view' failed to take on board the potential of oral history as a method of acquiring knowledge and acquiring solid local support. Oral history has been seen as irrelevant to the planning process, as something the museum or local history society should be doing – certainly not planners.

This situation is now beginning to change. People want to know more about where they live. Often they want a historical focus for their community, to develop a pride in where they live. However, viewing oral history from the planning perspective rather than a community perspective, it has to have a different agenda from that of the local history or civic society, and possibly even a different style or approach to interviewing. In reality, though, 'partnership' or 'community cooperation' or 'participation' are all buzz phrases used to achieve specific objectives, usually resources. So how can oral history help in the planning process?

Soundscapes

Soundscapes are those characteristic sounds which make up the specific identity of a place or community and contribute significantly towards what geographers call a sense-of-place. Examples of modern soundscapes might include the noise and bustle of the promenade in Blackpool or the sounds of a cattle mart on market day.

The recording of soundscapes provides important evidence for the social historian, showing how societies have changed, or are changing; but more than that it provides important clues on how the quality of life might change for the communities involved – a matter of direct interest to planners. An obvious example would be a quiet rural community being suddenly and irrevocably changed by the presence of a motorway. Sensitive screening by earth embankments would help to reduce the undesirable soundscape to a minimum.

Many natural history sound recordists record in the same place year after year and it is possible to make general comparisons about the presence and survival trends of, for example, different birds. Town and city sounds also change; most modern cities have a traffic problem and aircraft roar overhead. Compare that with the sounds of 1900: the clip-clopping of horses' hooves and the rumble of wheels, sounds that would have been typical of many city centres at that time.

Recent work in the field of soundscapes by geographers is now suggesting that far more attention should be paid to the nature and effect of sound on people and the environment. The engineered reconstruction of soundscapes for the general betterment of communities (so-called soundscape composing) is being given a higher priority than ever before, and strong cases have been made to record – using oral history techniques – memories of former soundscapes as an aid to understanding and perhaps recreating worthwhile sounds of the past.

Sense-of-Place

Geographers, social historians, planners and others also need to identify and sustain what is known as sense-of-place, that is, the characteristics that make a place unique or distinctive. That could be, of course, physical, in the form of mountains, rivers, trees or buildings, factories and roads, even field patterns. For example, the limestone scenery of the Yorkshire Dales or the design, placing, structure, layout and organization of central New York. Could new farming methods or building on greenbelt land destroy Yorkshire's drystone walls? Once the walls have gone then so has, to a large extent, the sense-of-place.

Modern place and area names are often a political or administrative contrivance. The 1974 local government (UK) re-organization and creation of new county and metropolitan areas is an example of such a contrivance. People, however, still

'Sense of place' is the uniqueness of a place, that which makes it special – such as the limestone walls and scars of the Yorkshire Dales. (Author)

Oral history can also explain minor things – such as this disused spring, once of great importance to the community it served. (Author)

follow geographical and cultural boundaries rather than imaginary lines on a map. Taking this one stage further, different groups of people see sense-of-place in different ways. In Australia's Northern Territory Jan Bathgate has been working on a fascinating project using plans of a declining gold-mining town to plot cultural spatial awareness from oral history interviews. The town's inhabitants over the years have included Aborigines, Chinese and Europeans.[9]

Could this technique be applied in the UK? The answer must be yes, as part of an overall understanding of the nature of a particular community, sense-of-place, and the needs of community and society at large. Developments such as new roads or quarrying must undertake environmental impact surveys (EISs). To what extent does this European Union directive include the community in its definition of environment? How important is sense-of-place in this context? The possibility of examining, say, a village and viewing it in different ways in this context is exciting.

How do the farmer and the postman see the village? How different is it to the squire or *nouveau riche* second-home owner? How does the quarry owner see it? Even the seasons can affect the perception of sense-of-place. Seaside resorts in the winter are very different in summertime. The farmer struggling to make a living on poor soil curses the place, while the holiday-maker sees only its beauty. And so it goes on.

Public participation in the decision-making process is very laudable and public consultations are held before major changes, such as the creation of conservation areas. It is beginning to emerge that the survival of communities, whether rural or urban, must take into account the new way of thinking. Adjusting the 'layering on the sense-of-place map' to enhance or maintain sense-of-place might well be an important step forward.

Heritage Audits

The creation of conservation areas where particular features, especially buildings and structures, are preserved within tight planning regulations has been an important step forward in preserving 'oases of quality' in Britain where people want to live. However, all too often the 'conservation' process has been concerned specifically with the fabric of the environment, houses, roads and trees, and has not taken into account the whole. That is not to say that the views of local people have been ignored, but the opportunity often exists to record the memories and reminiscences of older people before they are lost forever, and perhaps, more importantly, before the community loses something of its cultural heritage forever. It is, of course, all very well to record such memories and reminiscences but of what practical value are they and who are they for?

Whether working in conservation areas, areas of outstanding natural beauty, or complete communities, planners and others need to make decisions on the degree of preservation required, what time period is represented, whether satellite dishes should be allowed, where tourists should park, whether it is reasonable to extend a local factory on to a green field site to ensure village employment, etc. This may seem to be getting away from oral history but it has its part to play.

How can a planner assess what should and should not be preserved or maintained in a particular way without first asking older residents? Some key features may be obvious, such as a windmill or a castle, but it is the smaller undistinguished items that the planner can never appreciate. Many such features have a significance well beyond their mundane appearance. Recent history is largely in the minds of individuals and should not be ignored. Take an actual case of a foreign company that set up on the banks of a river to produce sodium cyanide in secret for the war effort. The years went by and the factory closed down. The site was cleared and today little remains of the factory in what is now a country park. Yet, in all probability, not far below the surface lurks sodium cyanide in sealed drums. Fortunately an interview was conducted with someone who knew about the factory, and was able to describe the process and where it was carried out. A couple of photographs also exist.

In fairness, some local authority planning departments have taken the initiative to record local features or industries before they disappear, partly for permanent record and partly to understand the community they serve. Some years ago I was commissioned by a planning department to record an oral history of slipper-making in various factories in the area. Cultural, social and religious divisions became apparent during the interviews with workers and management – such factors are important in understanding how communities work and, of course, in the planning of future industrial strategy. One factory was recorded and photographed in considerable detail. It has since closed down and the building demolished. Although the initiative for the work came from a local authority planning department, its application is wider and it is worth relating it to a different perspective: that of the industrialist. The understanding of an established traditional workforce, how they lived, worked and even worshipped, could, arguably, assist in training, recruitment and expectation. It could assist in the basic research process in the siting of new factories or companies, or the creation of industrial parks or units.

A practical approach was used by National Park authority planners who exploited oral history techniques to locate hidden copper-mine shafts and drainage tunnels. A former miner was taken to the site and identified the surface remains that still existed and assessed the threat they might pose to public safety. An extreme example of the practical approach is the resiting of the small former coal-mining community of Arkwright in Derbyshire. The terraced housing, village school and other buildings were demolished and the site open-cast for coal. The community was moved a short distance and rehoused in a custom-built village in which all the villagers have had their say in design.

The impetus for some record of change actually came from the village school whose pupils wrote down older people's memories in a series of booklets. So much more could have been done, giving a lasting resource and historic base to that community. Perhaps there could even have been a virtual reality village on computer. Had the village removal occurred today it would have made an ideal study project for oral history recording, including photography, sense-of-place, spatial mapping and soundscape architecture.

Extending the principle one stage further the idea came about of communities working with professionals to produce 'heritage audits'. Planners and architects can readily identify buildings and structures worthy of preservation, but there is much more to a community, whether it is inner-city or in the countryside, that is worth preserving. A good 'heritage audit' document can assist with sympathetic planning, the management of tourists and other visitors, and countryside interpretation, as well as identifying what is of value to a community.

The direct involvement of the community is essential. Local people know, for example, where the wild orchids grow and the importance of keeping tourists away from the site. They know, too, why the meadow is important as a scene of a tragic event collectively recalled and important to those who live nearby but not formally or officially acknowledged. These are parochial features all too often missed or dismissed as unimportant by outsiders.

A heritage audit collects as much data as possible, initially using oral history interviews as a base. Older residents are interviewed about the community and their own lives. People can be taken to specific sites and easily missed items such as an old iron ring set in the wall take on new significance when it is revealed it was used for bull-baiting. Other information might include how buildings have been reused or altered over the years and the interpretation of building interiors, such as the local church. Older residents unable to walk can be interviewed using photographs or even video as *aide-mémoires*. This initial survey must be combined with high-quality photographic images of people and places. Such basic survey work is exactly the kind of task the local history civic society or Women's Institute can undertake. Children too, up to a certain point, can also be involved in practical classroom work.

However, such projects need a professional coordinator. Planners and others work closely with the community, providing large-scale maps and plans with which to work. Other professionals will also need to be involved, such as the local museum curator, local history librarian and archivist. Professional archaeologists, botanists and geologists should not be left out either, being brought in to identify those features important in the area covered by the audit.

When the audit is complete a document is produced which can then be used as a basis for conservation planning, heritage management, tourism control, interpretation, etc. The great plus for the community is that it has a value and worth that is formally recorded in a document in which local people have had a direct say. The fundamental recording element uses people's memories, and acknowledges their personal commitment to their community.

Finally, add to the heritage audit the results of a professionally recorded sense-of-place survey, soundscape recollection and cultural spatial awareness and there is a powerful base for action and forward-planning.

ESTATE, COUNTRYSIDE AND COUNTRY HOUSE MANAGEMENT

The responsibilities of an estate manager are considerable and rely to a surprisingly large extent on information from oral sources. Many estate offices have comprehensive maps and plans of estates, but these often are only able to tell part of the story. The memories of older tenants may prove invaluable in locating a lost well, or explaining an old land drainage system. Many estate managers see their responsibility in a broader way than simply the maintenance of property or the collection of rents from tenants. The efficient running of any organization (many estates today operate as companies) requires an efficient management sensitive to the needs of people as well as shareholders. Decisions should always be made using as much information as can be reasonably obtained. Admittedly this may not always work in the favour of heritage management, but at least if the estate manager knows there is a geologically important drumlin in his field, or that rare orchids grow in a particular ditch, then those quality items in the landscape can be taken into account.

There are, too, the historical traditions that occur in day-to-day estate management. One of the most interesting of these is the collection of rent from tenants. The practice varies from estate to estate but, for example, land rent on one estate was always collected after harvesting, on others it was always collected before. Rents are still collected in traditional ways; for example, in cash in a room at the local pub.

ENVIRONMENTAL SCIENCES

In the United States oral history has been used to research into past events that have had profound effects on climate change and land denudation. The recording of the oral history of climate and weather is still in its infancy, but could greatly enhance the understanding of climate and occasional cataclysmic weather events.

In Britain at least one oral history project has looked at local weather and meteorology. On 22 July 1907 there was a tremendous thunderstorm in the Honddu Valley in the Black Mountains of South Wales. At least 3 inches of rain fell in three hours. There were also huge hailstones which flattened crops and destroyed hedges. The downpour also resulted in considerable damage through flooding and active erosion. The oral historian was able to construct a storm damage map from all the available information and provide an important complementing record to the official weather statistics.[10] There are many so-called freak weather events in Great Britain – blizzards, tropical deluges in the summer, whirlwinds, and hurricane force winds, like the 'Great Storm' which hit the south of England in 1987.

In other parts of the world eye-witness accounts of other natural phenomena are recorded. The Pacific Tsunami Museum in Hawaii records the oral history of Tsunami breaking on the shores of Hawaii and the Pacific Basin. D.S. Allan and D.B. Delair used oral histories to chronicle 'scores of indigenous people who were probably eye-witnesses to a meteor-like bombardment'.[11] Although it has not been possible to trace any specific projects, other possibilities for recording natural events include eye-witness accounts of earthquakes, mud- and land-slides, and volcanic eruptions.

The Rio de Janeiro Conference on global warming, at which the developed nations pledged to reduce their emissions of CO_2 gases, also opened the need to identify and quantify effects and changes in the atmosphere and biosphere. Although scientific methodology is required for eventual action, much of the initial stage information could also be acquired from oral sources. Such oral sources are ready-made monitors who can indicate trends and changes offering additional information and initial pointers to scientific observers such as changes in river levels, fish catches, coral growth, iceberg migration, aridity, vegetation cover, crop growth, well water levels and so on.

I am not suggesting that oral history techniques will provide circumstantial evidence of global warming, but it will provide pointers to changes and identify places where research might never otherwise have taken place.

THE RECORDING AND PRESERVATION OF CRAFTS

Over the years many organizations have set out to record and, in some cases, preserve, particular rural craft skills. Many of these crafts are still relevant and in the changing, more affluent leisure-orientated society, skills such as those of the blacksmith are once again in demand. The bottom line in recording crafts, or any other process for that matter, is whether

Andrew Schofield of the North West Sound Archive interviews a basket maker about his work. (Author)

the craft can be recreated from the material evidence left behind in museums and archives after the craft has finally disappeared and there is no one left to show others how it was done.

There are many surviving photographs giving tantalizing glimpses of crafts and rural industries, but these are no substitute for good descriptive accounts of how things should be done. Oral history has a major role to play in the recording of rural crafts and skills, and although there may well be some problems of confidentiality and family honour over traditions and secrets, it is nevertheless an effective recording tool.

An example of using an oral history approach as the basis for a film record of an unusual craft is given in the *Oral History Journal*.[12] A succession of recordings about rope-making was made with women who worked in the spinning room at the former royal dockyard at Chatham. The dockyard closed in 1983 and a film was made of rope-spinning, a process which had never been recorded before because of the secrecy of the work. Oral history interviews were recorded with the workers and their reminiscences were used, in edited form, as background to the final film record.

Oral history can capture attitudes as well as factual statements. When Stott Park Bobbin Mill at Finsthwaite in the Lake District closed down it was the end of an era. For generations the firm had supplied wooden bobbins made from locally coppiced wood for

The Stott Park Bobbin Mill in the Lake District is now a museum open to visitors. Here, in 1988, a workman drills coppiced wood before turning it on a lathe. The owner of the mill was interviewed in depth, especially about the practice of coppicing. (Author)

This was an opportunity missed! A worker prepares fireclay in a mould ready for firing in 1968. He was one of few surviving chimney cowl makers – but no one thought to record him. (Author)

the textile industries of Lancashire and Yorkshire. It was an unusual kind of craft production, and almost personal in the way the business was run. This attitude is captured in an interview I recorded with the then owner. The interview reflects the character of the company and its unspoken philosophy. It also helps to interpret or understand the various processes involved, as well as the inter-relationship between bobbin-making and the coppicing practices. Stott Park Bobbin Mill has since reopened as a museum.

Some museums, notably the Welsh Folk Museum at St Fagan's, have been recording rural crafts and country life for many years. The Castle Museum in York has large collections of the relics of country life; others, such as the Weald and Downland Museum in West Sussex, provide practical demonstrations of rural crafts such as charcoal burning, the fabrication of thatching spars, blacksmithing, etc. The Weald and Downland Museum has recognized the importance of recording oral history, using all available sources, and is currently recording the last surviving thatching-spar maker. The emphasis is not so much on life history as craft technique, the objective being that others can learn to copy what he does.

Heritage and countryside interpreters: what is interpretation? Well, according to Interpret Britain, the professional body representing interpreters, 'Interpretation is the process of explaining to people the significance of a place or object they have come to see, so that they enjoy their visit more, understand their heritage and environment better, and develop a more caring attitude towards conservation.' So who are the interpreters? They come from all walks of life: there are local authority planning officers, museum curators, architects, countryside consultants, heritage attraction owners, geologists, naturalists, exhibition planners, tourist guides, teachers, countryside wardens, etc.

Oral history is a particularly valuable tool for interpreters; it enables them to explore local memories for information about sites and people, often from first-hand accounts.

Park and countryside rangers: in their everyday work park rangers meet and deal with a wide variety of people. Inevitably, they will meet people who want to talk about the area patrolled by the ranger service. One of the rangers' many responsibilities involves explaining, or interpreting, the designated area to visitors. Gone are the days when park rangers were only to be found in the National Parks; today they are present even in the inner cities. Ribbon parks have been created along river valleys and heritage parks along canals. One of the primary functions of a ranger is public relations in its broadest sense, and so oral history should be used at every opportunity before it is too late. Not only will it allow an active and real interpretation of site features, such as old buildings, but will assist in the identification of features that have long remained a mystery. Nor am I giving this an unfair industrial or architectural bias, for many rangers or wardens deal solely with natural history sites and oral history work with local people in these areas can be most revealing and rewarding. Knowledge of site evolution is paramount. Recordings about land management, drainage, flowers, trees, game, birds, and many other aspects are waiting to be recorded. Other people who can add important information about sites include local anglers, poachers, gardeners, naturalists, ornithologists, and visitors.

Rangers and guides taking local groups on guided walks can use the opportunity to quiz people about their knowledge in much the same way that group meetings are used to identify potential interviewees in more conventional oral history work. The recording sessions take place at a later date, either on site or indoors under more controlled or hospitable conditions. (See Chapters Six and Seven)

Although the interviews are recorded primarily for research, again there is scope for cooperation between professionals. Tapes can be made available via the local library as well as the Information or Interpretation Centre. Recordings can, of course, also be developed into a viable commercial product for on-site resale.

Tourism officers, tour operators and guides: oral history can be used in a number of different ways, such as finding out about the local area and identifying specific areas of historical interest. A popular and quick way of guiding tourists to points of interest, while at the same time accomplishing visitor management objectives, is the use of trails or self-guided walks. Such trails are easily set up using information from a variety of sources, including oral history. As an experiment, try walking round a local village or site with someone who was born there and has lived there for most of his or her life. Ask about the buildings, the people who owned them, particular features such as old advertising signs, the tradesmen of yesteryear and so on, and very soon a ready-made trail begins to emerge. The taped interviews can be used as a basis for information packs, audio-cassette car tours and so on.

Blue Badge Tourist Guides offer special guided walks in most principal tourist areas. Part of the basic research for such guided walks should include oral history reminiscence. One tour guide who regularly ran tours across the United States had snippets of oral history on tape which she played back whenever the coach reached a particular point in the journey where the oral history helped to interpret the site.

Staff Training

At the Beamish Open Air Museum in the north-east of England visitor guides and demonstrators are recruited, where possible, from those who have experience of the subject they are describing or demonstrating, such as a retired miner to talk about coal-mining. It has long been recognized, however, that the time will come when such people no longer exist, and in anticipation of this – and partly to ensure good staff training – guides and demonstrators with working experience are recorded both on video and audio. These tapes are then used for training new members of staff and demonstrators.

Clearly this training procedure, using oral history as a practical resource, could be employed by other groups including countryside rangers, interpreters, information officers, tourism officers and guides.

CHAPTER FOUR

ORAL HISTORY IN THE COMMUNITY

Oral history in the community is a huge subject. It is also, potentially, a major growth area for oral history work. Although the focus of this book has so far leaned towards the academic and historical worth of oral history, it would be quite wrong to assume that all oral history work has such a focus. Community work in oral history across the world reveals very different end objectives. Health care – including reminiscence work with the elderly – is one such focus, another is sport: the passing on of skills, technique and experience.

So what is a community? The dictionary defines it as 'a body of people in the same locality, a group having common interest, character or culture'. Accepting this as a working definition, the concept of community becomes widely applicable and could include, say, prisoners in a closed institution, trawler crews, people sharing common experience of war, villagers in the Yorkshire Dales, or the victims and perpetrators of violence in the inner cities. Industries such as ship-building or coal-mining brought groups of men into close everyday contact, in effect forming closed working communities. In mining and fishing particularly, men relied on comradeship in times of danger for their very lives. Such close-knit workplace communities still exist and are inextricably linked to the social communities where they live and bring up their families. Community means different things, however, to different people. It also changes according to circumstances and events.

A graphic example of the difficulty of defining 'community' accurately is illustrated in a series of recordings chronicling the Pretoria Colliery disaster in Lancashire in 1910, when 344 'men and boys' perished in an underground explosion. Not only were the colliers a tightly knit group below ground, they lived cheek by jowl in their local community above ground. The aftermath of the disaster was devastating for the communities of Chequerbent and Westhoughton where most of the men lived. Almost every household lost someone in the disaster. Normal life could not continue. In a series of interviews recorded in the 1960s and '70s, people recalled not only the bravery of the men but also the reaction of local people on the fringe of the mining community – those who were not directly employed in the industry yet felt a tremendous sense of empathy and belonging.

A local teacher was about to be married. She recalls:

We had a wedding coming off at Christmas [the disaster was on 21 December 1910], and you couldn't get ready you know. . . . The vicar said you can't be married that day – too many funerals – put it off. Two or three days he came and the last time he came he said would we be married at five o'clock in the morning.

Well we said yes.

Well I can see us now lighting the fire.

No happiness – no.

We went to church. He didn't want us to meet any funerals. We went at five o'clock in the morning. It was a lovely service but you couldn't rejoice at all.[1]

The effects on neighbouring communities are not recorded, but to get a picture of the whole, where should the focus on community be? With the surviving miners? With their families? In effect the study would be of events affecting several communities, including the larger national community. The disaster shocked the nation, especially as it happened so close to Christmas.

Similarly, on Clydebank, the great shipbuilding area of Scotland, local communities were found to be inextricably linked to the fortunes of the shipyards and their workers. The Clydebank Oral History Project discovered that 'family ties and contacts were of vital importance for Clydeside shipyard workers. Families formed the basis of the skilled boiler-making gangs and apprenticeship was typically a father's legacy to a son.'[2]

In his book *The Handbook of Oral History – Recording Life Stories* Stephen Humphries argues that essentially community history is to do with 'Life experience'. Indeed chapter one starts from the premise that 'life experience [is] the starting point' and that 'each individual, whatever their age and supposed ability, has interesting and important things to say and to share with others'. This is certainly something that can never be understated: everyone has a history and can be involved whether he or she is an affluent company director or the person who stokes the boiler.

Stephen Humphries also makes the point that much community oral history can be about perceived injustice or inequality, and provides a voice for those who would not normally speak or produce the written word. This is a fair comment, but urges the immediate note of caution that oral history is not just about those 'with a perceived justice or inequality in society' – it is far wider, as has been established elsewhere in this work.

Does this mean that a minority group or community with strong political views and loud voice can use oral history techniques as propaganda? Yes, unfortunately it does. There are certainly examples, both in the UK and abroad, where this has actually occurred. The checking of facts against official records and all other sources of information is paramount in situations where suspected fabricated propaganda, or exaggerated hearsay, is presented as honest oral history testimony.

Paradoxically perhaps, taking the viewpoint of the sound archivist rather than the scholar for a moment, the reactionary approach to recording oral history is perfectly valid as long as detailed notes are retained with the recording offering the historian the opportunity to at least understand and test the validity of statements thus presented.

ETHNICITY, NATIONAL IDENTITY AND RACE RELATIONS

The use of oral history as a way of establishing and focusing on national identity, and therefore ethnicity, is one the subject's great triumphs. Although considerable work has been undertaken in the UK and in the United States, other countries, particularly developing or politically oppressed nations, are also beginning to realize the potential of oral history.

Rob Perks, Keeper of Oral History at the National Sound Archive, writes in the *Oral History Journal* about his experiences in the former Soviet Union. His aim was to interview Crimean Tatar victims of Stalin's deportation programme in 1944, when hundreds of thousands of people were uprooted from their homes and moved to places as far away as Uzbekistan in Soviet Russia. Many were treated little better than animals. Families were displaced and communities destroyed. It is only now that there is a willingness to examine and face the past, to try to come to terms with what happened.

Rob Perks commented: 'The first thing you realize about oral history in the Soviet Union is that people never look askance at you when you say what you are doing. In a society where written documents have long been treated with suspicion and doubt, an oral tradition has flourished. People willingly retell their past with a concentration, enthusiasm and a sense of realization of the value of the oral record which I found unusual. . . . Soviet society is opening up for the first time in generations and I was constantly aware of a determination to put the record straight. . . . It brought home to me just how important oral history is in the Soviet Union in reconstructing not just the past but an identity.'[3]

In the United States there have been many projects relating to black history. One of them, described as 'an oral history of American race relations', paradoxically stated that it did not set out to seek answers but rather to chronicle experience. Its results have been published by Bob Blauner under the title *Black Lives, White Lives: Three decades of race relations in America* (University of California Press, 1990).

Blauner, with a small research team, interviewed a large sample of both black and white people from 1967 through to 1969. The assassination of the black civil rights campaigner Martin Luther King in Memphis, Tennessee, in 1968 gave a poignancy to the project at a time of both racial and social unrest in the United States. The work effectively charts black and white attitudes over a period of time, with further interviews being recorded in 1978 and 1986. The project allowed feelings to be vented and perceptions of what was happening – whether accurate or not – to be stated and recorded.

Ethnic does not, of course, mean black, as is apparent in the work of the London-based Ethnic Communities Oral History Project. Their oral history-based publications include the memories of Irish, Iranian, Greek-Cypriot, Asian, and Chinese immigrants.

THE HOLOCAUST

Over 12 million people died in Europe in Nazi death camps during the Second World War, of whom approximately 6 million were Jews. It is therefore perhaps not surprising to discover that a large amount of oral history recording has been undertaken with Holocaust survivors across the world.

The National Sound Archive in the UK has produced a special resource pack for schools entitled 'Voices of the Holocaust' featuring extracts from oral history interviews recorded with survivors.

PARTNERSHIPS

Not all community oral history work has been recorded or even initiated directly by communities themselves. In no way does this invalidate the work as outside research can often be to the direct benefit of the community in question. Outside agencies – such as institutes of higher education – can take a detached and objective view of events and offer expertise and facilities not normally available to communities. There are also many examples of combined projects – partnerships – where the community actively participates by undertaking recording on behalf of, or in association with, the initiator.

Such a partnership offers a gateway into the inner workings of a community and can be vital for the success of projects. Organizations such as museums, libraries, and archives offer useful long-term partnerships where local people know they can gain access to the recorded material at a later date and confidentiality will be maintained.

Involving community leaders directly in the recording programme has huge advantages. Leaders have contacts, they know the people, local language and traditions. Above all they have trust and respect in their neighbourhood.

A good early example is the work of Caroline Adams. Caroline was a youth and community worker in Tower Hamlets, London, in 1974 where she acted, somewhat unwittingly, as a catalyst in recording the experiences of Bangladeshi residents from Sylhet living in inner London. Caroline visited Bangladesh as an extension of her work and was surprised to discover memories – even in remote villages – of adventures in England in the 1920s from old men who had worked on ships sailing between Calcutta and the UK. She saw the possibility of recording the stories of the oldest of the Bangladeshi settlers in London and using it directly for the benefit of the community, particularly to counter racial propaganda.

Caroline's work soon began to blossom. 'I was at first very hesitant as a white person, to undertake an oral history project with Bangladeshi people. . . . It was only under pressure from the Bangladeshi community and because of the urgency of catching the stories . . . that I undertook the work.' Her work has resulted in a number of publications and exhibitions and has undoubtedly done much to create a climate of understanding and a sense of self-awareness among the Bangladeshi community.[4]

The use of oral history as a tool in the creation of racial understanding and tolerance clearly should not be underrated.

HEALTH CARE

Using oral history in health care may seem at first glance very unlikely, but advocates of oral history have proved beyond doubt the usefulness of the technique both at home and abroad. For example, Sanjiv Kakar describes how oral history has been used to the direct advantage of isolated communities in India.[5] This oral history project took place between 1991 and 1993 and was intended 'to provide essential data for any interventionist offensive' on leprosy in India. The reasoning behind such a strategy included the inadequacies of the old official records in dealing with social and other problems, and in communicating with ordinary people in remote country areas where illiteracy and ignorance are still commonplace.

With over two-and-half million people suffering from leprosy in the sub-continent, new effective multi-drug therapies have been introduced as part of a national leprosy eradication programme and time was seen to be of the essence. The interviewing of sufferers revealed much new information not just about the clinical aspects of the disease but also about the reaction of others – including their own families and villagers – towards the affliction. Many sufferers were forced to leave their homes and spend their days in leprosy asylums, so investigations into community attitude were therefore seen as essential if any effective rehabilitation programme were to be introduced.

The human cost cannot be underestimated. In a telling quote Kakar states: 'The oral narrative reveals . . . the trauma of the mother separated from her children or the condition of the wife who is discarded by her husband when he learns that she has leprosy. There are also numerous instances of healthy wives who remain with diseased husbands, even following them into exile.' The statement clearly illustrates the way that oral history complements official records and shows that oral history is able to provide information for workers which enables them to administer the drug programme in a cost-effective and humane manner.

Kakar goes on to hint at another intriguing use for oral history. AIDS in some parts of India is being interpreted in rural communities in much the same way as leprosy (in one village it was described as the rich man's leprosy) and individuals are being shunned and made into social outcasts. The experiences gathered, using oral history methodology, will provide a wealth of experience on the best way to tackle such ignorance and offer victims social contact, dignity, pain relief and a quality of life in their suffering.

The obvious question is how can the experiences of Sanjiv Kakar be applied in other areas of the world? Can the technique also be used in developed countries to counter ignorance and to provide knowledge for carers and sufferers? Can it be used to plan the effective use of limited financial resources in other developing nations? What useful non-patronizing approaches can be adopted?

Knowledge about the very nature of suffering, and the social stigma of some types of disease such as cancer or Aids, can help in the effective planning of treatment and care. In the UK the 1995 Disability Discrimination Act has placed new emphasis on the true meaning of disability. Oral history can reveal much about attitudes towards those with disabilities and how they might be better cared for in the community. It also offers a voice to those institutionalized or permanently in care for some perceived disability. There is no more vivid illustration of this than a recent interview I recorded.

Bert now lives in the local community but spent most of his life incarcerated in a sizeable mental hospital. He was there not because he was clinically insane and incurable, but because he was deaf. He was, as a child, unable to cope with his profound deafness and, frustrated, lashed out at those around him. He started to throw things and this resulted in a broken window. In keeping with the thinking and moral attitude of the time, he was taken to various institutions which, frankly, failed him. Now in his eighties he is totally without sight and still profoundly deaf. His current day-care workers, who keep a watchful eye on his health, thought his was a voice that should be heard. He had little malice against a system which had robbed him of so much normal life, and answered questions honestly and with a surprisingly dry wit. The carers pointed out that his was not a unique case: there were literally thousands of people in care with similar stories to tell, people the system had failed.[6]

Jan Walmsley of the School of Health and Social Welfare at the Open University recorded a number of life histories with people with learning disabilities. In her landmark article in the *Oral History Journal* she describes how by using 'life maps' – simple sketches with obvious symbols – she was able to examine their experiences, particularly in the care situation. She experienced (much as I have in my own work with people with learning disabilities) the problems of working through other agencies and the unintentional coercion of interviewees whose carers forced them to be recorded. Nevertheless the benefits to both interviewer and interviewees are considerable. Writing up the life stories of the individuals was a significant part of her work, a way of returning the history back to the informants for their appraisal.[7]

In the United States a recent publication, *Polio's Legacy: An Oral History* by Edmund J. Sass, is based on thirty-five interviews with polio survivors. The interviews relate personal experience, including hospitalization, and illustrate how relationships with friends and colleagues were affected. Those experiences could help others coming to terms with disabilities. How interesting it would be to interview sufferers in India and Pakistan and compare their experiences with those in the USA.[8] It would be inappropriate to conclude this section on polio without mentioning Tom Atkins. Born in north-east London he was a lifelong sufferer of polio until his death in 1992. His story was published in the *Oral History Journal* and is both revealing and poignant, underlining the need to record and give a voice to sufferers of social and physical disabilities.[9]

The recording of life experiences of sufferers, although fascinating, needs in a way a clear sense of purpose, a definite objective or objectives. The telling of experience has an important value over and above recording for posterity or academic study. The person recounting the memories has an opportunity to express feelings, ideas and opinions that have often been discounted, or lain dormant, for years. It creates a feeling of value and personal well-being, of being useful and wanted, and offers help to recent sufferers. It allows carers to understand their patients and their needs and feelings, not just their clinical symptoms and statistics.

'I am still here – a life with encephalitis lethargica' is an account by John Adams, a lecturer in nursing studies, of his work recording the experiences of sufferers of this unusual and debilitating disease. His approach echoes the need for the direction of oral history to be shifted away from clinical correctness towards the sufferers 'as people rather than as patients with a rare and strange pathology'.[10]

However, nowhere is the 'therapeutic' use of memory so actively employed as in reminiscence work.

REMINISCENCE WORK

There is much confusion among oral historians as to the validity and relevance of reminiscence work despite the fact that the *Oral History Journal* devoted an entire issue to the subject as long ago as 1989.[11] Most reminiscence work has been undertaken with the elderly, particularly with those suffering from the effects of various forms of dementia. The popular term 'reminiscence therapy' has been avoided here quite deliberately as it implies a 'curative power' and this is, in general, far from the case. Not all reminiscence work occurs in retirement homes: it is used in hospitals and as part of care-in-the-community, as well as in schools and in the home.

It is therefore important to differentiate between traditional oral history and reminiscence work: the objectives are quite different. Oral history recording generally sets out in a systematic way to record and preserve, as accurately as possible, memories and reminiscences and to relate those memories to other sources of information such as archives. Reminiscence work, or reminiscence therapy, sets out to enrich the quality of a person's life, if only for an hour or two. That does not mean that occasionally important oral history material may not emerge, or that oral history interview techniques might not be usefully applied, but the overall accuracy of the result is less important than the therapeutic effect on the patient or patients.

There is, however, a grey area here. In my own experience there have been times when the interview is plainly having a deep effect on the interviewee. Often the effect is surprisingly beneficial to the informant, even if memories are tragic or deeply personal. In this sense, oral history techniques can provide a 'safety valve for pent-up emotions'.

There is, however, a downside too. Some people may well not wish to relive past traumas and the oral historian or reminiscence worker must be prepared for such an eventuality. It is always a difficult judgement to make. The basic research necessary before commencing oral history or reminiscence work with sensitive subjects should offer a degree of awareness of the possibility of traumatic memories being released, although sometimes even the best preparation does not reveal very deep-seated emotions and the interviewer must make a difficult choice as to whether to continue, or terminate, the interview session. Often that decision can be made simply by asking the informant if he or she wishes to continue, with the tape-recorder on or off. Leave them a way out. If in doubt, stop the session, and ask for professional medical or psychological help before continuing.

In practice there are other interests in how reminiscence work should be conducted or recorded. Different partnership funding agencies have different objectives, and even the older people being interviewed might wish to set their own agenda. An example of this is perhaps the Photo-media Project established in 1988 at the Hertfordshire College of Art and Design in St Albans. Funding was derived from a variety of agencies including the Arts Council. The original objectives were to 'research and pioneer small-scale photography and media studies pilot projects across the educational spectrum from primary schools to the university of the third age' – an objective seemingly far removed from oral history and reminiscence activity.

A photo-history group was set up in Welwyn Garden City with cooperation from the local library, museum and archive service. A group of senior citizens elected to focus the work on the Second World War, to coincide with the 50th anniversary of the outbreak of hostilities. A wide range of old photographs were produced and members of the group were encouraged to bring their own photographs, including family albums.

Similar old photographs were used in outreach work by Warrington Museum Service. It proved possible to identify many of the people in this classroom photograph. (Warrington Museum and Art Gallery)

As an exercise in community involvement such projects are first class, but there can be difficulties. One of the commonest is peer levelling. People in a group tend to agree with other people in the group so as not to lose face. As an example, if one member of the group had a bitter relationship with the schoolmaster who is generally warmly remembered as a 'wonderful man' by the rest of the group, then it is likely that the unpleasant experience will simply be withheld and a substitute comment added which agrees with the general consensus. If there are regular meetings of such groups it may well emerge over time that our fictitious schoolmaster was not quite what he seemed. Once that has been established the peer levelling can then work the other way, with members of the group recalling, selectively, their own less than perfect memories of the schoolmaster.

The other huge weakness in group work is the editing, not just of completed tape and text, but with selectivity even at the question sheet preparation stage. In my own experience I have found groups basing entire projects on one or two dozen key questions arrived at from pre-conceived ideas democratically agreed (with all the dangers of peer levelling) without serious objective research. The agenda has been changed by consensus.

There is also the question of who is being educated in the most general sense? Good community projects should educate, or at least create awareness, not just among the participants but among all taking part whether they are interviewees or professional staff. Such 'education' is not formal. Each person gains from the experience in his or her own way – often without realizing that their established views and perceptions are changing. That effect transgresses the project, affecting other people they meet such as users of their taped interviews and publications, or visitors to the project exhibition.

REMINISCENCE WORK AS AN APPLIED TECHNIQUE

Much of the work has been developed not in the heritage world but by carers, particularly of the elderly. The range of memory-jogging activities has been enormous, from converting an entire hospital ward back to the time of the Coronation through to actually taking individuals back to their place of birth. All people reminiscence throughout their lives, but in older people the long-term memory tends to survive when short-term memory loss occurs.

The benefits to the patient are clear enough. For example by:

- Raising a person's self-esteem
- Highlighting lifetime achievements
- Sharing common experiences with others in a group
- Encouraging self-expression
- Re-establishing individual identity
- Forming new friendships in group situations
- Re-establishing of trust with others
- Indirect, unwitting learning
- Encouraging, where practicable, of simple co-ordination tasks
- Using reminiscence to return the attention back on everyday events. (For example, one recent topic of discussion was the national mourning after the untimely death of the Princess of Wales in 1997)
- Bridging the generation gap between children and older people: children will listen spellbound to older people and have a greater respect for them as individuals.

The effect on the individual can be profound. In their booklet Age Exchange make the point that a wide range of emotions can be released by individuals varying from grief, anger and frustration to relief and happiness. But reminiscence work is not one-sided. There are benefits for carers, too, by:

- Sharing of common feelings and experiences, such as childbirth or schooldays. This helps considerably in understanding the reactions of individuals
- Helping to develop and improve staff training programmes
- Using reminiscence techniques over a period to reduce the potential of trauma of admission to institutions

- Creating mutual trust
- Making repetitive daily work more interesting
- Identifying natural leaders and communicators
- Reminding carers (if they need reminding) that people who are confused or have other problems are still people with feelings and a story to tell.

Many techniques have been developed over the years to encourage recollection. It is not my intention to cover reminiscence work methodology in any great detail but some examples may be of general interest.

- A group of older people enjoy meeting regularly at a Blackpool day centre. Led by a day centre worker, they explore set themes. They have produced from recollection a simple exhibition, a booklet on Blackpool and a collection of local dialect words.
- A retirement home in Southampton encourages its older residents to write their memories on a word processor. This novel approach not only gives them the experience of writing, but also offers an introduction to Information Technology. At one day care centre, as a result of this approach, older people now regularly use the Internet to communicate with new friends across the globe.
- Small informal groups are set up and events in the newspapers are discussed. This encourages a sense of contemporary awareness. The technique is also applied to individuals.
- Trips are arranged to visit places significant to people, such as local parks, the seaside, the countryside, place of birth, home-town, etc. One group also used a state-of-the-art digital still camera to take photographs. These pictures were then replayed back at the retirement home as a kind of slide show but on television, thus effectively continuing the experience, informally, over several days.
- Visits are arranged from outside groups such as story-tellers, children, musicians and actors. Cookery demonstrations are also popular.
- Projects are developed where individuals are encouraged to record and write their own life histories. Oral history recordings, music and other sounds can be used.
- People are encouraged to write and read poetry, and to produce drawings and sketches based on memories.
- The use of smells. Smell is a powerful stimulant. Special packs of evocative smells in bottles for use in reminiscence work have been produced by a Blackpool-based company. Others are easily created, such as the smells of cooking or the smell of household items like bleach or a coal fire. Some smells are, of course, seasonal, such as pine, Christmas hyacinths and roses. Not all smells need to be pleasant; it is in any case relative. Some people will find some smells repulsive, others not at all. A farmer's reaction to the smell of horse manure is likely to be different from that of a city dweller. The popularity of aromatherapy has introduced many smells which are readily available and can be used as part of an overall reminiscence work package.

Age Exchange in London has pioneered a great deal of reminiscence work including the idea of themed reminiscence boxes which contain objects and other information.[12] Many museums also provide objects for use in reminiscence work along with photocopies of historical documents. Over time it is possible to build up a useful collection of artefacts and objects for use in reminiscence. Many items can also be picked up cheaply from car boot sales, auctions, market stalls and from social services departments with responsibilities for house clearance following the demise of clients. Items can range from textiles, such as corduroy and velvet, and clothes, through to weavers' shuttles and workaday tools.

The recreation of former experiences can be very rewarding. The preparation of wartime food or making up clothes on a treadle sewing machine are such examples. Some people burst forth with a completely uncharacteristic enthusiasm. In my own experience with a group the discussion moved round to discussing footwear. Inevitably, as we were in the north of England, clogs were mentioned. Suddenly a little quite man blossomed. He had started work as a clogger in a cooperative society and eventually ran his own business repairing clogs, boots and shoes. The group were transfixed by him and for a few minutes all relived the common everyday experience of a clogger mending clogs. Nor did he stop there. He went into a mime sequence, watched avidly by the group, as he demonstrated how to sew a leather clog upper using my shoe as the example. (I still have a hole in my shoe sole to prove it!)

Many reminiscence themes are identical to the subject areas covered by oral historians exploring life histories – childhood, school-days, homelife, work, recreation, wartime experiences, etc. The techniques used in oral history recording and reminiscence work are not dissimilar, and ideas and techniques can clearly be shared by both groups of workers.

Reminiscence work has largely been targeted towards the needs of the elderly, particularly those suffering from some form of dementia. Age, however, is not the sole criterion for reminiscence work. It is effective with all ages. It works well with people who might be classified as lonely, aloof or depressed. I have used the oral history reminiscence approach to great effect with teenagers in foster care, prison inmates, terminally ill patients, and those coping with bereavement. Sometimes the reason for the initial contact with such individuals was straightforwardly to record an oral history interview. However, the oral history approach is not always applicable, desirable or appropriate and it is sometimes better to abandon the tape-recorder and simply, in an act of friendship, support the person by using a blend of oral history and reminiscence techniques.

The approach adopted by Rosie Mere of the Arts in Hospitals Trust at the University Hospital of Wales in her 'Travelling On' Project some years ago is worth repeating in this context. Rosie used a life story approach to encourage reminiscence, rather than the thematic approach adopted by other reminiscence groups. There are times when a thematic approach can be very painful to those taking part and by adopting an approach which highlighted the positive aspects of a person's life, she was able to increase enthusiasm and assist in a positive way. Questions were asked in a non-threatening way and constructed to encourage talk, such as:

How have I learnt when to change direction in my life?

What have been the surprises on my journey so far and how have I dealt with them?

How do I know when I have arrived somewhere I wanted to be?[13]

The questions are interesting and illustrate a very different approach to memory capture from that adopted by most oral historians.

THE EFFECTS OF WAR ON COMMUNITY

It has already been established that oral history is extremely useful in recording the unwritten history of Britain during the Second World War. This perspective is undoubtedly important because of the secret nature of operations, projects and industrial wartime production on the home front and also because of the censorship regulations. However, this is very much a British viewpoint and it is worth for a moment exploring other viewpoints from across the world, for example the experiences of soldiers in the Vietnam War.

A project, established by the University of Massachusetts, rather than by a specific community group, studied the experiences of soldiers in modern battle. The emphasis was placed on the role of 'ethnic' servicemen and their experiences in Vietnam. The work showed that Asian American soldiers had 'died in greater numbers proportionately' and 'were more likely to be shot if captured', and 'were often shot by their own side in error'. Chinese American nurses were mistaken for Vietnamese prostitutes and many had been shocked at the dehumanization of Asian people they could relate to, introduced in training as the enemy.

Another related project called Full Circle returned some servicemen to Vietnam in order to help them to come to terms with their experiences and to replace the emotions of war with those of peace. Perhaps this is not too dissimilar to the many visits by UK servicemen to the battlefields of France and Belgium? One controversial element raised by the project was the suggestion that the rise of black youth violence was in some way related to their parents' Vietnam experiences.[14]

Although the project was an academic study it clearly had a social role to play in the understanding of warfare and its effects on communities. Such a project, coming from an ethnic community, examining not just personal experience of conflict but its effects on the community the soldiers returned to, offers an interesting avenue for exploration by oral historians studying conflict and society.

ORAL HISTORY AS A PEACE-MAKER

Could oral history be used as part of a peace-making, healing or rehabilitation process in a former war zone? As far as is known it has never been tried in that context. Oppressed communities have used oral history to record their unwritten feelings, as is vividly portrayed in the account by Robert Perks of the National Sound Archive (UK) concerning his visits to the former Soviet Union. The outpourings of the people are recorded and preserved for future use. It raises all kinds of questions about oral history in this context, such as its future use. Notwithstanding such difficulties there is potential for using oral history to bring people together in an atmosphere of common understanding.

In 1997 I was asked to produce a confidential report to explore ways in which oral history might be used to create links between Great Britain and Ireland. It soon became clear that oral history could be used as a vehicle for common understanding between communities. It needed a willingness for people from all sides of the conflict to get together for the common purpose of peace-making and friendship. The spiritual leaders of some communities often led the way, although in others it was enlightened individuals or organizations such as schools. The methodology was for mixed teams to record experiences and see the situation from the other's point of view. This cannot, obviously, produce a magic solution to end the hatred and conflict, but, by sowing the seeds in the right places, it can help in the healing process in the longer term. The real experiences of ordinary folk would be recorded to be used by generations yet to come.

There were many other suggestions in the report, and clearly the security of those taking part was taken very seriously. The hijacking of information for propaganda purposes was also considered, although assuming that museums, libraries, archives, universities, colleges and schools were involved, the original material could easily be preserved essentially intact. A further suggestion was the spread of common experience gathered by oral history work on the Internet.

Religious Leaders and Community

Oral history, especially in an active church, is also the kind of work that can, with some training, be undertaken by the members of the church as a 'community' project. Some excellent work has been undertaken on graveyard tombstone surveys using a tape recorder to record the details, and in another instance members of a church recorded memories of their past preachers and the changes they had witnessed over the years. One inner-city church group ambitiously recorded the work of the church with local prostitutes giving middle-class parishioners an insight into a way of life they knew little about.

This kind of community oral history is a very useful way of binding people together, especially if there is an appropriate focus such as a centenary exhibition in the offing. It is, if initiated by the right people in the right way, a method of bringing together people in strife – such as in Northern Ireland. The application of the techniques for friendship-building and bridge-building between communities is not easy; nevertheless such work could easily develop from a heritage, community or church-based project. The potential is there.

The vicar of a small industrial community in the Pennine area of Lancashire was concerned because, as he put it, 'his parish and community had been divided by the motorway'. A long-established community, the village is more or less linear with a north–south road. Former industries included farming, the textile industry, chemicals and coal-mining. The M65 cuts through the heart of the old village in a cutting at right angles to the old road. In parallel to the M65 are older transport routes, the canal and the railway. These, by their very nature and scale, did not match the disruptive physical effect of the motorway. It was the motorway which, ironically, allowed easy access to nearby towns and encouraged commuter settlement on the southern edge of the village. The vicar, anxious to identify important aspects in village life, and also to actively involve the local church in the community, created an oral history project in 1996. Training took place and volunteers recorded in all parts of the community, the motorway no longer being viewed as an obstacle to communications. Although a church-based project, it was not seen as evangelical but as a way of uniting the linear community. The objectives of the first stage of the project have been met, and exhibitions and publications are being planned for the summer of 1998.

It is evident that there are many different kinds of approaches to community oral history. Chapters Six and Seven deal in detail with some of these other approaches and describe how to conduct an interview. Nevertheless, it is worth at this stage summarizing some of the points to be considered in setting up any community-based project.

Primary objectives. These need to be clearly defined and the definition should include the statement 'to record people for posterity and to preserve the original recordings and transcripts in an appropriate archive and to record material for use in the secondary objective of the project'. Secondary or end objectives may include local archives, reminiscence work, encouragement of writing or storytelling, drama, interpretation of buildings, archives, photographs, etc., adult education programmes, broadcasting, and recording material for publication, exhibition, video or tape-slide work, etc.

Recruitment and administration. Who will do the work? How many people are needed? What size of group is suitable? Who will be in charge? How will decisions be made on the direction of the project? How will interviewees be selected? By whom? How many? Which sex, age? etc. How will interviewers be selected and trained? By whom? Do they have the right kind of out-going personality necessary for oral history work? How many? What sex, age or colour? Is language important?

Subject matter. What subjects are to be covered? Is it proposed to record life histories? Are the interviewees members of the group? Is the question sheet to be compiled collectively or as the occasion demands – that is, devised separately for each informant. Who will prepare it?

Time-scale. Projects snowball as interest grows. Is the project open-ended or finite? Is a time-table necessary? How long will it take to do the research? Who will do it? The use of archival, three-dimensional and other material should be looked into.

Publicity. The type and nature of publicity varies. Television reaches a wider audience but local newspapers and local radio offer more controlled responses.

Equipment. How much equipment is needed? What is most appropriate, audio or video? Video is expensive and more complex. (See Chapter Nine) What precautions can be taken to prevent equipment and tapes being stolen? What training is needed? Who will provide it?

Finance. Where is the money coming from for the project? Who will administer it?

Transcription. Who will undertake the work? What arrangements can be made for the long-term preservation of recordings and notes?

Clearance. Where will the clearance notes be housed?

ORAL HISTORY – SPECIALIZED INTEREST GROUPS

There are a number of specialized interest groups using oral history. Some of these are community-based in the broadest sense and all have explored important new issues.

Women's history is an area that has seen a huge growth in interest in recent years. Oral history has been a liberating force for women. The opportunity to record unwritten feelings and experiences has undoubtedly helped to change the role and perception of women in western society. If you were asked to name outstanding women in history – who would they be? Boudicca, Emmeline Pankhurst, Amy Johnson, Diana, Princess of Wales, the Queen, Margaret Thatcher, Florence Nightingale, Mother Theresa and Madame Curie spring to mind but these names are the stuff of official history books and do little to represent women in the real world.

In the United States there have been many oral history projects looking at the experiences of women. The Tully-Cremshaw Feminist Oral History Project has been exploring the National Organization of Women from its foundation in 1956. The Schlesinger Library of Radcliffe College, Cambridge, Massachusetts, houses the collected material and is also the home of the Black Women Oral History Project established in 1976. However, in the UK the Soroptimists (and for that matter their male counterparts the Rotarians) and the Women's Institute have yet to embrace the idea of oral history, either as a way of recording their respective histories, interacting with the communities they serve or even as a straightforward public relations exercise to increase membership.

Sport is another area of interest for oral historians. Defining sport is not easy. For this purpose it is defined as meaning 'a recreation, game or activity usually with a competitive element, having a defined winner or achiever'.

Mainstream sport is well covered by the media. It is usually the noteworthy elements of a game or performance that are most enthusiastically reported. Well-funded or sponsored sports also tend to get the best peak-time coverage, yet there are many sports which are an integral part of the social fabric of modern society but are not reported because of lack of space or time or because they are considered by the media to be of minority interest.

A recent edition (Spring 1997) of *Oral History* magazine was dedicated to 'Sporting Lives', and contained articles on football, golf, rounders and handicap running. Such recognition of sport as a valid subject is useful and timely.

Things are, however, changing. There are proposals to record athletes and others in the 2002 Commonwealth Games in Manchester. This particular project has from the outset intended to record them using not just oral history but also photographs in order to construct as accurate a record as possible. Individual athletes will be recorded at various times up to, during and possibly beyond the games. It is recognized that it is important to record feelings, expectations, desires and, it is hoped, successes as they take part in the games.

Most reported sport history is about winners. In order to get as broad a picture as possible it is necessary to record the runners-up, support staff, trainers, parents, family members, officials, sponsors and others. This wider-based approach has only just begun. It can go far beyond social cross-sectioning and may even have direct training applications.

Sport is not just the big names or winners. This local football team are standing with such pride, they must have a story to tell! (Author)

The recording and examination of training difficulties, and how they were overcome, and assessments of poor performances are all invaluable to future athletes or competitors.

In the museological sense sport can be a difficult subject. Football, golf and tennis all have their component artefacts – footballs, golf clubs, tennis racquets, trophies, clothing, banners – but they also have specific buildings such as arenas and stadiums. There is, of course, a tremendous familiarity with such facilities. Everybody knows what they are for and what they do, but as time passes they may change. As an example, horse-racing is popular across the world, but courses may close down for many reasons – the sale of land for building development, quarrying, flooding and drainage problems, etc. – and the physical remains therefore need to be identified, photographed and interpreted using archival and oral history testimony. Interviews not just with the jockeys but also with the people responsible for maintaining the courses and organizing races should be arranged. This somewhat holistic approach to recording is deservedly gaining in popularity. Recent work by members of staff at the Manchester United Football Club Museum has included, quite deliberately, early memories from ground staff, gate-keepers and, of course, fans.

In addition to the physical structures directly concerned with the performance of sport there is the area of supporting industries and services, such as cricket ball makers, tennis racquet makers, badge, kit and strip manufacturers, racing motorcycle manufacturers, snooker table makers, turf accountants, etc. Some suggestions for future recording include such diverse subjects as ballroom dancing, quoits, children's games, mountain biking, TT racing in the Isle of Man, cricket, skiing, the Tour de France cycle race, bowling, table tennis, swimming, darts, snooker, pool and billiards, motor racing, snowboarding, fishing, orienteering, dog racing, mountain climbing, running, sailing, hockey, lacrosse, dominoes, boxing, martial arts, bingo and, of course, gambling.

The current debate in Britain regarding fox hunting is an interesting one. Assuming for a moment that fox hunting is indeed a sport within the definition given earlier, if 'blood sports' are banned by law then the case for recording all aspects using oral history methodology is not just overwhelming, it is vital and extremely urgent.

CHAPTER FIVE

ORAL HISTORY IN THE CLASSROOM

The educational potential of oral history is not confined entirely to the formal classroom situation with children. Learning is a dynamic lifelong process concerning everybody. Oral history has been the focus of attention for many adult groups, whether or not they are directly involved in further education. Church groups, fellowship societies and local history societies have all explored oral history to advantage. This informal approach to education is gaining in popularity with older people, particularly as the number of people retiring early increases.

In the more formal setting of the classroom there has been a mixed response. Some enthusiastic teachers have used oral history with startling results, while others have tended simply to use oral history recordings as a resource, and many have not used it in a structured way at all.

TWO-WAY LEARNING

Oral historians soon learn to question what is generally regarded as 'correct' or the 'truth of the matter', as they experience different perspectives, ideas and facts from their informants, and compare those with accepted published accounts. The education process is two-way. Both the oral historian and the informant learn from the interview. In a way it is simply a variation of normal informal conversation working as a mechanism for exchanging ideas, thoughts and observations. Indeed, the competent oral history interviewer usually aims to achieve an informal but sociable exchange of questions and answers.

Therefore the use of oral history in an educational sense is one of exploration and discovery for both interviewees and interviewers with the ulterior motive of direction and guidance for those under formal classroom tuition. It is also, by its interrogative nature, an enforced intellectual exercise in comprehension and understanding. One of the strengths of oral history is its ability to unearth new perspectives or question the validity of accepted fact. This can potentially lead to an opportunity for the teacher if the recorded fieldwork results differ fundamentally from set texts, books or curriculum guidelines as pupils are encouraged to appreciate differing interpretations.

VISUAL ORIENTATION

Before the advent of television, radio listeners were forced to use their imaginations and create images in their mind's eye. The growth of television and, latterly, the use of computers has tended to make people more visually orientated. This preoccupation with the visual has probably been achieved at the expense of some listening skills. It is true that people still listen seriously to sound – for music or in language acquisition – but the inability to comprehend more than brief 'sound-bites' is very evident in some groups.

This bias toward visual orientation is not confined to children and students. Museum people report that whereas a decade ago people would stop and listen to a five-minute piece of oral history in a gallery, this is no longer the case and most people will now only listen for around a minute and a half.

This bias is also present in education to some degree. The resources that are available are often visually orientated without any separate audio component. Where there is a separate audio component, it remains unused if an appropriate video is on hand.

Audio, specifically oral history material, requires an effort to listen and understand. Yet the advantages to both tutor and student are considerable and often far-reaching. These advantages frequently transcend the rigidity of a formal curriculum, offering access to life skill development.

ORAL HISTORY AND THE NATIONAL CURRICULUM

Perhaps the best and definitive account of using oral history in the classroom is the recent publication by Allan Redfern entitled *Talking in Class – Oral History and the National Curriculum* published by the Oral History Society in 1996. In this important landmark publication attention is paid to the way oral history techniques and sources can be applied to parts of the (England and Wales) national curriculum (1995).

Redfern's approach is thorough, and has sections dealing with the value of testimony, sound archives and similar sources, oral tradition, music and story-telling. It also includes practical guidance on using the tape recorder in the classroom and recording of interviews, the principles of which are covered extensively elsewhere in this publication. He acknowledges that the principal utilization of oral history is likely to be in the History section of the current version of the national curriculum, but suggests that there are also applications in English, Information Technology, Geography, Religious Education and, to a lesser extent, Maths and Science. Particularly useful to teachers are his detailed suggestions on how oral history might be used. Under Key Elements and Attainment Targets he lists practical suggestions under the principal headings of chronology; range and depth of historical knowledge and understanding; Interpretations of history; historical enquiry; and organization and communication.

For example, under Unit 3a, Victorian Britain key stage 2, he suggests using sound archives resources. Sound archives are an important source of oral history material, and many of them now produce packs for school use as well. Under the heading Oral Tradition he suggests 'grandparents' memories are sometimes passed down in interviews'. It is always worth asking, even straightforwardly as a class exercise, what parents' or grandparents' earliest memories are. What did their grandparents or great-grandparents tell them? He also includes Music as a heading and lists folk songs, street songs, and Victorian music hall songs as ways of further shedding light on the Victorian period.

Finally, under the heading Printed Sources, he makes the important point that many printed sources such as factory inspector reports were originally derived from oral testimony.

There is a limit to the use and analysis of material in schools because of the constraints of time, money and relevant staff experience. The approach adopted, however, by the national curriculum allows pupils to understand the processes and evaluation of history in a way that was not really practical say twenty years ago.

THE POTENTIAL OF ORAL TESTIMONY – AN EXAMPLE

As Allan Redfern pointed out, many documentary sources started out as oral testimony. It is worth spending a moment examining a piece from the Children's Employment Commission Report of 1842 which fits well into the section Unit 3a, Victorian Britain key stage 2.

The original report collected oral testimonies and investigated the employment of women and children in industry and coal-mines. It contains the well-known interview of Betty Wardle, a housewife, from Outwood near Lever.

Have you ever worked in a coal pit?
    Ay. I have worked in a coal pit since I was six years old.
Have you any children?
    Yes, I have four children, two of them born while I worked in the pits.
Did you work in the pits while you were in the family way?
    Ay, to be sure. I had a child born in the pits and I brought it up the pit shaft in my skirt.
Are you quite sure you are telling the truth?
    Ay, that I am, it was born the day after I was married, that makes me to know.[1]

The piece is capable of considerable analysis and evaluation as evidence. The following possibilities of work come to mind.

Why was the evidence collected at all? By whom? What was their objective? Did this objective colour their collecting? Why did Betty Wardle give evidence at all? Why should she? Was she paid? Who was she? Where did she live? What was the outcome of the collected evidence? What changes were brought about? Where can information about Betty Wardle be found? What other evidence is there to support her story? How would she get to work? What was she likely to have worn? Why did she not go to hospital to have her children? The language of the report is formal for publication. How would she have really spoken?

Even this basic analysis covers many areas other than the pure history element. For example, it touches on coal-mining; English (spoken and written); geography; government legislation and Reports; health care; map reading and interpretation; numeracy (map scales, sections, etc.); women's history and work and its changes.

Resources that might be used to form an analysis include:

Maps and plans. First edition Ordnance Survey maps, Estate plans, Enclosure records, Tithe maps and assessments can help locate former coal-mines and associated features. Different maps can show the changes at Outwood and provide material for a time-line diagram. Geological maps can show coal-seams and therefore depth of mine, etc.
Coal-mine records.
Diaries and other contemporary unpublished accounts.
Published sources – newspapers, reports, etc.
Wills.
Oral evidence.

Direct supporting evidence of oral testimony is often difficult, if not impossible, to come by. There is, however, often indirect evidence. Well aware of the Betty Wardle piece in the Children's Employment Commission Report during my own research into coal-mining in the area, I deliberately included questions to determine whether there were any family memories of women working in the mines. The results were quite surprising.

> I remember an old lady telling my grandma about the fact that she'd worked down the pit and pulled a small skip fastened to her. . . . Most of the time her job was to help her father by sitting there with a candle. (Wigan, *c.* 1850)

> I remember an old lady who worked down the pit. They used to have to carry the coal on their backs. Her job was waiting of her father filling the sack and she used to have to come up these ladders with it on her back. (Wigan, *c.* 1850)

> My grandmother's grandmother used to work down the mine and was drawing the boxes [full of coal] with a belt round her. . . . They used to take the baby to the pithead at snaptime [mealtime] while she [breast] fed it. (Wigan, *c.* 1845)[2]

Under the heading Interpretations of History, Redfern suggests 'Many teachers find this element problematic, but at every level oral history can make a significant contribution to the ways in which historical interpretation is approached.' The versatility of oral material is evident.[3]

Redfern also identifies English key stages 1–4 as having potential oral history elements. These include speaking and listening, writing and an awareness of the richness of language, including dialect and other non-standard English. There is a common theme about the advantages of talking to older people and the oral history interview is one way of breaking down barriers between ages.

Although Redfern correctly assesses that, by its very nature, oral history is about the past, paradoxically it is also about the present and contemporary situations, feelings and events. An example of this contemporary approach took place in Preston when a number of schools (primary and secondary) cooperated to record memories of the Preston Guild

Celebrations which occur every twenty years. The children interviewed their parents and grandparents about the last Guild using photographs as a basis, as well as recording their own experiences and recollections of the current celebrations. This approach to recording contemporary views also helps to break down barriers between children and older people.

THE OVERTON EXPERIMENT

Several years ago an experimental project was set up in the village primary school at Overton near Morecambe to explore how oral history might be applied in teaching. The experiment was run jointly with the headmistress and staff of the North West Sound Archive. Overton is an interesting part of the north-west. It is very close to the River Lune and Morecambe Bay, a vast tidal flat. Some of the pupils came from the community of Sunderland Point about 2 miles away, an area cut off at high tide. The people of the area had a long tradition of farming and fishing, including salmon fishing. New industries included the nuclear power station at Heysham which has attracted fresh people into the area.

The project's objectives were simple enough:

- To see what the children could do for themselves. What were they capable of?
- To develop new approaches to interviewing in the classroom situation and beyond.
- To encourage community-wide involvement, the school being seen as 'the heart of the village'.

The initial topic chosen was 'school-days' on the grounds that most of the people in the village had been to school locally and so children could relate directly to that experience. The first experiment involved bringing in and introducing to a class an older member of the local community.

One of the difficulties soon encountered was that older people were somewhat taken aback when asked to chat to a large group of children. Several were unintentionally patronizing. Although the sessions were structured it still needed the teacher (in one case myself) to act as the question-master or leader. There were obvious knowledge gaps, too, on both sides. Children mentioned things on television and it was clear the informant did not know what was meant. Equally, when discussing school life in the 1920s, terms were used such as the School Board, which meant nothing to modern children. The initial experiment worked well enough, but there was room for improvement. The sessions needed structuring and an awareness of certain key differences in the age gap.

One of the most useful management tools is the mind map or logic spider. This is used to write down in a clear rational way any ideas about a particular subject and show its relationship with other subjects. A sample logic spider is given in Chapter seven.

The subject, school-days, was written clearly in the centre of the board. The whole class then participated, adding different legs to the spider such as truancy, teachers, punishment, drill, lessons and so on. When the logic spider was completed (it took one lesson) the class was divided up into groups, each concentrating on a different subject area from the logic spider. It was found that some children generally regarded as low achievers actually scored

Children from Overton School practise interviewing elderly residents from the village. (Lancashire Evening Post)

better on this kind of logic work than children who seemed to be more literate. Each team then worked on developing questions within their subject under the usual regime of Why, What, Who, Which, When, Where, How.

Children do not share the same perceptions of the world as adults, a fact that is reflected in the way they talk and the type of question they ask. 'Children will ask people how much they earn, something no adult would dare do. . . . One pupil asked a pensioner if they had a clock in their classroom. Well, no was the simple answer, but this led on to the fact that few homes possessed clocks, that there was a knocker-upper and you could see the church clock to check the time.'[4]

Working in smaller groups produced better results. The next time the old man came in he worked with a particular group who asked him questions about his past. The group tape-recorded his answers using a PZM microphone in the centre of the table attached to a cassette recorder. Tie-clip mikes were also used, particularly when noise levels were high.

The sessions allowed the staff to create the following structured approach.

1) Brief the informant to some extent about what to expect before entering the classroom.
2) The first session is little more than an informal chat. Selected members of the class may ask half a dozen general questions about school-days – no more.

3) At the first session there needs to be a facilitator such as a teacher.

4) A second session is arranged with the informant.

5) A logic spider is completed for the subject.

6) Each team works on a separate part of the logic spider. Any other research – books, old photographs, etc. – can be used as a basis for question preparation.

7) At the next session there are two options:

a) The informant meets one group per session away from other members of the class, i.e. in a separate room. The questions are asked and recorded in the usual way.

b) If the class is relatively small then each group can ask questions in open class, the informant sitting with each group in turn. This has the benefit of all the class hearing the answers at the same time, but destroys the more intimate and spontaneous atmosphere that can be achieved using the first approach.

8) Technically it is better to work in small groups with a closer microphone technique. This improves the overall intelligibility of the replies, especially when using standard cassette tape-recorders. However, whichever approach is taken it is important for the teacher to monitor the interview and spur the interview along when children, with relatively little experience, dry up.

Children also learned to be polite and to ask their questions in a non-threatening way. Frequently other subject areas emerged for discussion. The development of lateral thought was unexpected but occurred several times. Not far from Overton is the city of Lancaster where in the 1930s a particularly scandalous murder was carried out by a man called Buck Ruxton. Not only has this murder entered into the local folklore, but the children after a while actually became quite knowledgeable on the subject and were able to enlighten the interviewees!

The next stage was to involve the community in a more formal way. A meeting of all parents and villagers was held at the village hall. Some of the tapes were played and this generated considerable enthusiasm for the work and local involvement. Children then interviewed, mainly at the school, a number of local people about the village itself, asking how the village had changed, and finding out about the fishing industry on the River Lune, flooding and a host of other subjects. The headmistress and her staff collected copies of photographs and documents and started a village resource centre. Other items were donated including objects.

The village project spurred on other work including the recording (audio and video) of the last surviving haaf-net salmon fishers on the river. Other children walked around the village exploring and learning how it had changed. The information was then checked against maps and plans, parish registers, old photographs and other sources. If time and resources had permitted the project could have been taken further, booklets produced, and an exhibition held.

Other Approaches

Other schools across the country have developed their own approaches to using oral history in the classroom. For example, in Skegness, Seathorne County Primary School recorded the memories of local people recounting the 1953 East Coast floods.[5]

At Stocksbridge Secondary School near Sheffield a project with teenagers showed just how effective oral history can be as a catalyst in English work. Part way through an English lesson one of the students came in very excited with stories about a local ghost. Security men working on a local by-pass had been frightened by a ghost. The police had been called in and they too had experienced something unusual and frightening. Seizing the opportunity the teacher encouraged children to research into the history of the area and ask friends and relatives questions about tales of ghosts and the supernatural in the vicinity. They also interviewed local people about their memories. The students came back with various stories which might account for the ghost.

In terms of learning and experiencing English, Irene Orchard, who was responsible for the experiment, recounts 'Classwork included discussing the interviews, transcribing the tapes, illustrating some of the ghostly incidences, and putting together the class magazine. . . . For the next few weeks, the class . . . studied the book *The Ghost Downstairs* by Leon Garfield.'[6]

SITE WORK WITH CHILDREN

Taking children of all ages out of the classroom is not only exciting but also challenging for the teacher. The amount of information that can be gathered during fieldwork exercises is considerable but direction from the teacher is essential.

Example: visit to a canal breach.[7] The local canal burst its banks in 1936 leaving a huge gaping hole and a coal boat hanging over the drop. The rest of the canal never recovered and was eventually closed down in the 1950s because of the breach. The teacher devised a route from the nearby canal locks and buildings to the breach, bearing in mind the obvious safety requirements. Photographs preserved in the local library showing the locks and the canal breach were enlarged on a photocopier and laminated to make them waterproof. The site was examined not just as part of history but as part of geography, and numeracy.

On Site Work

Several local people who had worked on the canal and remembered the coal boats and horses before the breach occurred were invited to talk to the children on site and show them around. Informal interviewing on site by children is far more difficult than a structured session in the classroom. The same methodical approach to question preparation is, however, essential. Time line preparation is also useful so that children can relate quickly to what is being said by the informant.

Again the teacher has to take a monitoring role in the discussion. Older people sometimes have a tendency to talk down to children and that is where the teacher intervenes by asking the next question. There will also be gaps in the informant's memory. History is taught as a logical progression, with facts established over the years. It will have been a long time since some of the informants received formal education – if indeed sometimes any – so there is a possibility that the teacher knows more about the time-line of historical events

Canal breach, 1936. Old photographs can be compared with the site today (opposite), and the history investigated using oral history techniques. (Lancashire & Yorkshire Railway)

than the informant. The strengths of the interviewee – personal experiences and specific knowledge – should therefore be exploited to the full.

It is not always possible to prepare everything in advance. Walking along the canalside, one of the children discovers an iron ring set into the stone sill or banking. It is unlikely the child could have prepared for this accidental discovery. The answer from the boatman might well explain how boats were fastened to the rings by ropes as they were awaiting their turn to go down the locks. That leads on to locks and how they were worked, how horses were used and so on. Over a period of time the teacher will build into the teaching notes spontaneously derived questions about iron rings, grooves in walls cut by tow lines, sluices and so on, as part of the prepared questions that can be asked.

The informant will not be there for ever. Eventually there comes a time when

The site of the canal breach today. (Author)

information must be taken from a secondary source such as a countryside warden or local historian. The recording of the original people now takes on a new significance, and the preservation of those early interviews becomes extremely important as a resource.

Classroom Work

The possibilities for subsequent classroom analysis are considerable. The coal boats were measured and found to be exactly 70 feet in length. The children having been taught in metres were thus introduced to imperial measure and the exercise involved converting metric to imperial as part of the lesson. Measurements of the lock dimensions were also converted and simple calculations done on how much water each lock might hold.

Follow-up work in the classroom could also include the working-up of sketches into pictures. Sketch plans of the interior of buildings or features such as lock masonry can also be drawn up. Buildings of different periods have different styles of architecture, and simple sketches of the main styles related to the time-line drawing are useful in understanding the evolution of a site.

The use of maps was essential to the understanding of the area. Children measured distances on the map and related those distances to their own experience. Simple sections across the river valley were drawn in order to show the gradients – all involving simple numeracy, scales and graphs. Using a large-scale plan as a base, the map was then annotated with features not included by the original map-makers. A photocopy of the original map could be used on site and annotated by the group, the information being transferred to the master plan on return to the classroom. Features such as new buildings, trees, wall plaques, signposts, abandoned cars, etc., can be added for completeness.

The geography of the site included a river valley with steep sides, the canal being constructed on one side throughout its length. How was the river gorge formed? What was the likely effect of a sudden canal breach into the gorge? Why was the local paper-mill sited in the gorge? Why were there no roads? How was the river crossed? What caused the various pock-mark depressions to be seen near the river? (Coal-pits.) What was the effect of the pollution in the area? Where did the waste tips come from? (There was no obvious source but oral investigation, listening to tapes and map work revealed the chemical works was responsible.)

A site selection for fieldwork allows a systematic study to be done over several years from Key stage 1 to 3.

Key stage 1 is concerned with investigating change and includes fieldwork. Key stage 2 looks at land use and changes that have taken or are taking place. A major part is environmental-based and studies how people have changed the surroundings. Key stage 3 is an advancement on the other stages, and involves the development of annotated maps and other 'original' research. Redfern suggests using interviews to understand settlement and economic activity, perhaps looking at a major industry in some detail.

Tips on using a tape recorder in the open air:

- Allocate one person to be in charge of the tape-recorder.
- Always use a separate stick-type microphone out of doors.
- Cover the end of the microphone with a foam windshield. These can be easily obtained from electronic suppliers, such as Tandy, and fastened on with an elastic band.
- If it is very windy make sure the person operating the tape-recorder and microphone stands with his or her back to the wind or finds a sheltered place to record. Others can stand behind in a windy location and act as a shield.
- Except when it is very windy, hold the microphone close to the informant's mouth – a couple of feet, for example. If another person speaks then move the microphone across to him or her.
- If the weather is wet then place the tape-machine in a self-seal plastic and keep it under a coat away from the elements.
- Keep a spare tape and batteries in an accessible place, such as a coat pocket.

TRANSCRIPTION AS PART OF ENGLISH

People write in different ways, and they also listen in different ways. The transcription of an oral history interview challenges the transcriber's ability to understand not what is actually being said but what is really meant. Children working on transcripts as a group will inevitably perceive things in different ways, and often their inexperience with words and their true contextual meanings will show through.

One completed transcript read 'When I were a lad I were allus sparking my plugs'. It should have read 'sparking mi clogs'. Clogs had iron soles and young lads would strike sparks on the flagstones and pavements.

The danger with using non-standard words and sentence construction is that it can become regarded by children as standard. The use of the word 'were' instead of 'was' in the preceding paragraph is a case in point. It is not incorrect English – it is a variation of English. Teachers need to be aware of this and ensure children understand the nature of language and how it changes.

If changed to 'When I was young I liked to spark my clog irons on the pavement' the sentence is not the same as the informal speech. The meaning and social context have been changed.

Children will not be familiar with older words and their meanings and it may well be necessary to create a simple dictionary or glossary of such words to aid them in their work. This is particularly true of dialect words and place-names which have local pronunciations. When I was a child the local farm was always known as *ku'nin'gri*. Today it is much more fashionable to call it by its Ordnance Survey name – Coney Green, the old name being unknown to the occupants of nearby housing estates whose origins are outside the area.

RELIGIOUS EDUCATION

The National Curriculum suggests that religious education should have a historical perspective. Some aspects of religious life have been well recorded, particularly, for example, the Jewish faith. The National Sound Archive produces a special pack on the Holocaust for teachers and others, and other religions have also recorded their experiences and faith. Some work has been undertaken, mainly at local level, by the Methodist Church, and the experiences of Muslim people have been well recorded in Bradford, Leicester, and Kirklees. Abroad the Mormons have recorded surviving memories of the great treks across America, as well as famous visitors to their headquarters at Salt Lake City.

Oral history can be used to explore faith and belief, perhaps with the support of religious officials, such as priests or rabbis. They are likely, of course, to offer the orthodox line, whereas talking to ordinary church-goers, practictioners or believers allows areas of doubt to be considered. Atheism and agnosticism should not be ignored. Interviewees need to be selected with great care. The straightforwardness of children asking logical questions can create offence.

Whether oral history techniques should be used to directly reinforce belief or association with one particular sect is debatable. That oral history should be used to explore faith in more than one religion is more than reasonable as it can help to dispel prejudices and create understanding and tolerance while reinforcing individual conviction. In PSE (Personal and Social Education) the exploration of other people's viewpoints is encouraged and oral history offers a way of opening doors, crossing barriers and talking to a range of people.

MUSIC

The recording and preservation of traditional folk songs and their relevance to historical periods and social change are relevant to music studies. Beyond this the possibility of interviewing individual pianists, singers, composers, even instrument-makers, allows a deeper understanding of music and its interpretation. The memories of those who enjoy music are also important, and an examination of its uses, both performance and commercial, is not out of place.

CITIZENSHIP

Oral history offers a real perspective on the way people live. Memories recorded on tape allow access to social change and differing points of view. The interview technique should be used to explore the modern world. Oral history is not just about what happened yesterday or yesteryear. The potential is considerable; for example, interviews can be arranged with local leaders such as the mayor, outstanding individuals, church leaders, local councillors, doctors, youth leaders, nurses, charity workers and service groups such as Round Table or Rotary. Oral history offers an open door to people who are otherwise largely inaccessible to children.

SPECIAL EDUCATIONAL NEEDS

A great deal depends on the nature of a child's disability as to how he or she might benefit or respond to sound. Children with serious mental health problems sometimes react to simple sounds such as a musical instrument or a lion roaring.

Motivation is often a problem with children who need special educational assistance. Sound is one way of accomplishing motivation, but its application is, of course, limited by the nature of the disability.

Adults with visual impairment often make fine interviewers because of their skill in listening to the replies informants make. Sight-impaired children too, with help, can undertake interviews with success. There is no real reason why they cannot interview the same people suggested for sighted children as part of the National Curriculum.

Experiments with visually impaired children recording oral history suggest that the approach is essentially the same but needs modification of the tape-recorders, such as marking keys, to allow easier operation. Questions can be written in Braille or, for partially sighted people, in large contrasting lettering or a form they can read.

One additional area is the recording of the experiences of other visually impaired children and adults and sharing those experiences for common benefit. Assistance in the production of a talking newspaper will also give access to technology such as tape-recorders and cassette duplicators as part of National Curriculum Information Technology.

ROLE-PLAYING AND DRAMA IN THE CLASSROOM

Primary school teachers will already be aware of the potential of role-playing in the classroom. The recording of personal memories offers the opportunity to use the transcript as a basis for simple role-playing or more advanced dramatic interpretation. For example, an interview has been recorded with a former coal-miner. He recalls:

> Working on't coal-face were never easy. There were allus dirt and dust in yer face. Your face, round your eyes, no matter how much you washed you allus finished up with coal – it were like women 'ave – what do they call it – mascara.
>
> Aye, coal dust it got everywhere, in your mouth – you used be spitting out for days after – some of the men would chew tobacco you know to keep their mouth moist – 'cos you weren't allowed to smoke underground.

In another section of the interview he recalls:

> When your were working a flat seam of coal that were easy. You lay on yer side like this and swung yer pick. You had a little cracket or wooden [wedge-shaped] support under your shoulder while you were doing it.

And finally:

> When you were working you could hear the roof moaning – we called it rock weight. What it were – first there were little bits of coal trickling down then you'd hear the timbers moan and crack. Then the floor would start to come up to swell and it were time to get out. I've seen it come so quick you had to scurry and leave all your tools behind. On another occasion it come up and it were just the height of a wooden clog sole and this fellow he yelled for his mother. He were trapped by clog sole between the roof and the floor. We had a job on getting him out, I'll tell yer.
>
> On another occasion, roof come down. Whummf! Mi light went out. I shouted and Bill Smith come wi a new light. But it were too late; allus I could see were a hand sticking out from under the roof-fall. It were too late, he were dead. Only a young lad, young Tommy, aye he were only young. It weren't his day were it?

This original transcript can be converted into a simple single-scene interpretation as follows.

SCENE:
Underground in a coal-mine. The date is 1888. The seam is very low, approximately 2–3 feet maximum height. Suggest using several desks placed alongside one another to give length, the role playing taking place underneath.

The room should be darkened, the only light coming from tiny hand torches, the type that can be kept in a pocket or handbag. The light should be weak as though the battery is fading. New batteries would be too bright. These torches simulate the pit lamps which would have been hung on hooks or placed on the ground. Blu-tack is useful for temporary fastening of lights to table legs or other pieces of furniture. In many pits naked flames were used and while this is the desired level of illumination, the use of candles or naked flames in the classroom is clearly dangerous and impractical.

The idea is to create a claustrophobic atmosphere, one of confinement and hopelessness and darkness.

CHARACTERS:

Young boy – first day down the mine

Collier – an older man with a very bad cough. (Spits and coughs a lot. He is obviously in ill-health.)

Second collier – Man who brings the lamp

SOUND EFFECTS:

Taped or class making squeaking noises to simulate the rock-weight. Sound effect of an explosion to simulate a roof fall.

PROPS:

Pit lamp. If it is not possible to get a real pit lamp draw two to scale and use those instead. Stick them to the torches with Blu-tack or adhesive tape. Cover the table legs with thick vertical strips of paper to simulate pit props.

Use a large cushion for the cracket.

Use a 'pretend' pick or, if space permits, use a yard brush with a shortened handle about 3 feet in length.

MAKE-UP:

The two older men have blackened faces and hands with mascara round the eyes.

The old man has a moustache.

Use red lipstick on the boy's legs to show blood after the roof-fall.

Large jacket or thick dark blanket to throw over the boy to simulate a roof fall.

COSTUME:

The young boy is dressed in long trousers (jeans will do) with only a loose shirt with sleeves on the upper part of the body. On his feet he wears ideally clogs but suggest a boot – anything with a thick sole.

Collier: Similar dress but no shirt.

Second collier: As above.

Scene commences. The lights are out. No light is visible from the set except the light pushed forward in front of the older collier. The boy does not have a lamp. The two characters enter from stage right on their hands and knees, shuffling along under the assembled tables, the older man leading. He is clearly having difficulty and constantly coughing and spitting out. The two arrive, the young boy passing him to sit stage left. They both sit facing the audience. Nothing is said. The old man coughs and wheezes, taking deep breaths for at least 30 seconds.

Narrator

Old Tom is a coal-miner or collier. He has worked down the pit all his life. His job is to hew or cut the coal from the coal seam using his pick. The young boy is called Bill. It's his first day down the mine. He is very frightened. They are both tired even before they start work. They have walked and crawled underground for at least half a mile. Bill's job is to shovel up the coal into a sledge which will be pulled along the passageway to a point where it can be taken to the surface.

Old Tom now leans on his side supporting his shoulder on a cracket, a kind of wooden stool, so that he can swing the pick at the coal.
(This will need some experimentation to get it right – which is fine, as this is what it's all about. Old Tom's back should be towards the audience, the coal-seam is at the rear. Working in a confined space is not easy and if a yard brush with a shortened handle is used to represent the pick, care must be taken to ensure the boy does not end up as a real casualty.)

Old Tom continues to cough and spit while swinging the pick. After a few minutes he stops and turns towards the boy.

Narrator

Old Tom is already dry from the coal dust. It is in his eyes and in his throat. He reaches for his watercan, he searches round but can't find it. He feels in his pocket and pulls out a piece of chewing tobacco. All the miners chew tobacco. Like smoking it's dangerous and unhealthy, but everybody does it. It helps to keep his mouth moist. He gives a piece to young Bill.

Young Bill bites a piece off with some force. He turns towards the audience and with the light shining on his face from the lamp pulls the most awful face and shouts as loud as possible: 'Aaaargh' it's 'orrible, mi mouth's on fire.'

Narrator

Many coal-miners even until just a few years ago used to chew tobacco underground. They were not allowed to smoke because of the risk of explosion. Men who chewed tobacco also had a horrible habit once they had finished with it.

The young boy, who is still holding his throat and gasping for air, suddenly takes a deep breath and rounds his lips and spits the pretend tobacco towards the audience in the most vile way imaginable. The old man laughs.

His face changes and he puts his hand up to quieten the boy. He puts his hand to his own ear as though listening to the roof.

Narrator

The mine is beginning to creak. All mines creak. The timber props are making a noise. Little trickles of rock are starting to come down from the roof. Every old miner knows this could lead to a roof fall. What will happen next?

Old Tom signals to the boy to follow him back along the tunnel, stage right. The boy begins to follow but suddenly the lights go out. There is a loud dull thud as the roof falls. During the time the light is out the boy lies on his stomach centre stage looking right towards the audience. His lower body is covered with lots of coats or crumpled paper – whatever – to simulate the roof fall. He is moaning loudly.

A light appears stage right. The old man starts to uncover Bill. He pulls a face when he sees the boy's legs. He shouts 'Help, help, I need some help down here'. While the narration continues a second collier arrives with a lamp to assist. Together they slowly begin to drag the boy stage right. At the end of the narration the lights are extinguished.

Narrator
The worst has happened. The roof has collapsed. Bill's legs are buried and crushed. Old Tom will do all he can to uncover him but it is not easy. The other miners will come. They will have to drag him along the passageways to where the coal is hauled up the shaft. He will have to wait there for an hour in agony. The coal-mine owner will not stop winding coal just for an injured boy. Eventually he will be taken by horse ambulance to the infirmary six miles away. He will be crippled and unable to walk for the rest of his life.

The difficulties of acting out the roles in such a confined space illustrate the problems faced by real miners. In some parts of the country where coal seams were steep, up to 1 in 2, it would be like trying to work lying on the average staircase at home.

The dialogue in the scene has been kept to a minimum, partly for dramatic effect. The narrator is the key to understanding what is going on. Older children may feel confident in using dialogue either scripted or ad libbed.

Role-playing and Drama on Location
The use of oral history testimony to form a basic role-playing exercise or simple script is not, of course, confined solely to the classroom. Increasingly, historic houses and museums provide access to areas where role-playing can be carried out in authentic settings or with authentic artefacts. A country house might offer access to the kitchen area where children could act a scene of a banquet or meal being prepared, or use the ballroom or dining-room to understand how people lived. Some organizations have full-time education officers who can help by providing teachers' notes well in advance of the event. Others provide actors who involve children in role-playing. At Wigan Pier, The Way We Were Museum, in a reconstructed classroom an actor playing the part of a teacher takes children through a lesson with all the formal strictures of Victorian England.

Not all role-playing needs be indoors. Scenes can be recreated in actual locations where recorded events took place. It may be a place recalled in childhood as a picnic spot allowing a Victorian picnic to be recreated or perhaps an old Second World War pillbox, with children playing members of the Home Guard.

FREEZE-FRAME HISTORY

This is a slightly different and less structured approach than direct role-playing or dramatic interpretation. The key to the success of the freeze-frame approach is for the teacher to be instrumental in how the scene is contrived, directing the children as required and improvising as the scene develops. Taking, as an example, the coal-mining tape used earlier the teacher may wish to make the point that local coal seams were extremely steep and that working on the level as portrayed was not a common local method of working. Some seams were as steep as 1 in 2. The teacher can create the incline using a chair and a long piece of plank or board. (Mathematics, angles and ratios.) With appropriate safety very much in mind each child can then lean on the board as though hewing coal. The local working experience is then much more meaningful for children. How did local miners work in the dark hewing coal at an angle steeper than the stairs at home?

The National Curriculum offers a superb opportunity for teachers to use oral history. Redfern identifies a number of very specific areas where oral history can be used in association with other material. There are, however, many other subjects not directly mentioned in the National Curriculum, such as local politics or the development of skill training. These non-mainstream subjects can be extremely important in cultures and educational systems outside the UK. (For further information see the section on 'Oral History in the classroom in developing nations'.)

So, in summary, what are some the advantages and disadvantages of using oral history in the classroom?

Advantages	*Disadvantages*
Expands the imagination	Requires a structure to
Increases observation power	be devised by the teacher
Extends vocabulary	to take best advantage of
Increases listening skills	the situation
Cross-curricular (IT, English, interview skills numeracy, history, etc.)	
Logic development	Takes time to develop
Inter-personal skill development	
Personal confidence development	
Links into the local community	
Offers a way of measuring change over time	
Offers a way of acquiring knowledge of the past	
Offers way of exploring life in the local community, especially with older people	
Encourages literacy and self-expression (Communication of knowledge)	
Allows exploration and analysis of other viewpoints	
Creates an awareness of other evidence and its value	
Introduces and familiarizes students with the concept of using libraries, museums and archives as sources of information	

Training and Awareness Among Teachers

Although many teachers have used oral history indirectly in their work a more systematic employment of the technique requires training for teachers. At the present time there is very little high-quality professional training available on oral history and this needs to be remedied.

My own experience of introducing teachers to oral history has been that once the subject is understood then there is enthusiasm. However, to sustain interest in oral history among all the other things teachers are expected to do is difficult and it needs an active leader to develop an oral history programme inter-woven with the requirements of the national curriculum. A training programme for UK teachers at all levels must include:

- Awareness of the potential of oral history in relation to the national curriculum
- Practical interview skills development training
- Classroom project development

Many schools have active parent-teacher organizations. One way forward might be to encourage a minimum of, say, two adult members of the PTA or governors to undertake an oral history programme. The adults would need training in the techniques but could reinforce the role of oral history in the classroom, as well as forming a link between adults and children, another requirement of the national curriculum.

This also gets round the problem, to some extent, of knowing exactly who the adults are and their trustworthiness around children. This indirect management could then be spread further in close liaison with staff, to include careful selection of older people to talk to children in class or be interviewed.

VIDEO AND ORAL HISTORY IN THE CLASSROOM

Little has been said about the use of video either in the classroom or out in the field. It would be unreasonable to impose on children all the standards suggested in Chapter nine, Oral History on Video. A decision has to be made as to why video is being used at all. Is the primary reason for using video to give children experience with equipment as part of Information Technology or is it truly to record accurately oral history? The bias has to be one way or the other. If it is for oral history, the recording of local people and so on, then longer scenes and more questions, plus preservation of the original camera tape is the order of the day. If familiarity with equipment is the priority then story-boards need to be drawn up, scenes set out, and short concise interviews undertaken.

It is, of course, possible to do both by recording in oral history style long interviews with local people and then to use the material copied from the original camera tape into a conventional production at the editing stage. The following suggestions may be helpful.

- Research the subject thoroughly and prepare, using a logic spider, a simple question sheet. Keep the total number of questions short but to the point if IT is the objective, much longer and searching if oral history is the objective.

- Ideally use video after an oral history interview using audio. Much latent information will have come to the surface during the audio session and can be used as a basis for compiling questions.
- Make sure the person using the camera knows how to operate it before an interview is attempted.
- Always use a separate microphone such as a tie-clip type pinned to the informant. Practise before the informant arrives.
- Choose a quiet location with good light.
- When recording, switch on the camera and wait for about a minute before asking questions. This allows the camera to build up to speed.
- Indoors, always use a tripod.
- Indoors, zoom in on the interviewee and manually focus. Then come out to a slightly wider angle. Then leave it alone! Zooming in and out, or 'hose-piping' as it is known, is poor practice.
- Concentrate on the person, not the interviewer. Don't worry about mistakes, they can be edited out later. If a mistake is made leave a gap of a few seconds to allow space for copy-editing and then continue.
- At the end of the interview always thank the person on tape.
- Keep the original camera tape safe or in an archive. Use the edited version or a copy of the original for teaching purposes.

ORAL HISTORY RESOURCES

In addition to any recording produced in the classroom there are other organizations that hold collections of oral history material. Not all offer a loan service, but many publish educational packs of material, recordings, photographs and teachers' notes. A selection of these organizations is included in Appendix one.

RECORDING EDUCATION HISTORY

This is an area where pupils of all ages can make a significant contribution to the public record. There are still people around who have played a considerable part in the development of education and they should be interviewed as soon as possible. One example of this is a recording made during the 1960s with Edward O'Niel, a former primary school headmaster with revolutionary ideas. His early experiences of teaching sixty children in an inner-city school classroom changed his views about teaching for ever. He was later to pioneer, at a small village school, a practical, hands-on, almost unstructured approach to education which attracted the attention of academics from around the world. He opened the school after hours – unheard of in the Britain of the 1920s and 1930s – for everyone in the village to come and learn.

The richness of his memory and the way his character comes across in the interview is noteworthy. How many more fascinating educational pioneers have been missed?[8]

ORAL HISTORY IN THE CLASSROOM IN DEVELOPING NATIONS

Much of what has been written earlier applies to developed nations with or without a national curriculum. Many schools and education programmes in some developing nations have few, if any, resources. Textbooks are sparse and often old and chalk-board plus word-of-mouth teaching remains important.

The idea of a formal classroom is unknown in some parts of the world. Education is built, partly at least, on perception, oral tradition, and instruction from older people. Oral historians in Britain understand the wealth of information available from older people, but it rarely has a purely practical role to play. The shoe-maker, the rope-maker and the farmer pass down memories of interest to the social historian, but only rarely relate methodology at a detailed technical level that can be attempted by others. Museums have taken the lead here, preserving tools and equipment, with crafts surviving as visitor attractions rather than as practical workshops to aid human survival.

The educational requirements in developing nations differ from those in the UK. Although politically literacy is often seen as the number one priority, almost as high on any list of priorities is the need for people to have a basic ability to earn a living, feed a family, support others or simply survive as individuals. The concept of recording older people simply because 'they are there' or 'as an academically interesting thing to do' is very much a western perspective. Recording older people because they can help you learn how to survive and develop potential is a very different view of the role of education.

Adult education, the use of oral history with older people in the form of reminiscence work, as undertaken in the west, is not developed.

An opportunity surely exists to bring together adults and children as a way of passing on useful knowledge and essential skills. The young benefit and the older people receive respect and dignity. A value is placed on their knowledge, wisdom and existence. The same feeling of well-being and of being wanted, a sought-after benefit of reminiscence work in the west, is a significant bonus.

The pairing-up of children with a mentor, a process described in detail in Chapter Three as a tool in training ethics, could be applied in developing nations. The process does not involve an apprenticeship nor necessarily a formal teaching of skills, but a shadowing in the workplace or similar environment on a regular basis.

Although the advantages of using oral history in the classroom have been outlined earlier, because the outcome in some developing nations is fundamental to survival it is worth examining some possibilities again.

Language Skills

Fluency in a mother tongue is essential. In countries such as India it is often important to be able to speak or at least understand other indigenous languages and dialects. The migration of people across India for work means that many different languages are spoken. Some basic knowledge of English is becoming important as westernization begins to take effect. The Internet, radio and satellite television are often transmitted in British or American English and any use of information technology means some capability in using and understanding English.

The development of interpersonal skills has been discussed elsewhere. In reality there are restrictions on how this may be applied within the conventions of particular cultures. For example, women may not be allowed to contribute on equal terms with men in a discussion group because traditionally women are not seen as decision-makers. To what extent education has the right to change such practice is a matter for serious consideration; it is not simply a matter of women's rights, and there may be other considerations such as the introduction of imbalances which could adversely affect both men and women.

Health Education
Oral history techniques are used to discover and explain how isolated communities in poorer countries deal with diseases such as malaria, leprosy, Aids, bilharzia, etc. The oral history approach can reveal taboos and perhaps even local approaches to treatment. The oral history process, having created trust, allows the teacher or health worker to reinforce the health education message in the context of local culture and practices.

Problem Solving and Logic Development
The preparation of question sheets using mind maps or logic spiders as basic templates creates an awareness of the potential of using the technique for other purposes, including learning from books and problem analysis.

Practical Skill Training
This approach has been adopted by a number of agencies. I know of two such projects in India; doubtless there are many others across the world. One is at Guwahati in Assam where a local orphanage educates boys and girls for life outside. They are taught carpentry, cookery and basic literacy. A larger project, also in India, is the work of the Boys' Town Movement where orphans (nowadays boys and girls) are trained to support themselves and others.

Businesses
Oral history can also be used to look at business and the way it operates. It can open doors to the right people and give an insight into the management and organization particularly of small businesses. It can also identify weaknesses in traditional industries.

ADULT EDUCATION

Although there have been some exceptions formal state adult education has largely ignored the potential of oral history. Learning and involvement in oral history has tended to be beyond the classroom with organizations such as libraries rather than education authorities taking the initiative. There are numerous projects which have involved local people directly in oral history or reminiscence work without resort to the classroom. The Workers Educational Association was one of the early pioneers in using oral history with adults, holding seminars and courses and even sponsoring two radio series based on oral history in the 1970s.[9] Reminiscence work is, of course, adult education in its broadest sense, the initiative having been taken by social workers, carers and others.

The use of workshops to involve and utilize existing oral history material within the community is capable of considerable expansion. For example, in Australia 'Most of the collecting institutions and state branches of the Oral History Association of Australia organise workshops and services for community and interest groups.'[10]

It is clear that oral history has an important role to play in education at all levels and with all ages. In the UK its value is increasingly being recognized and used within the formal state system. Beyond the classroom, its use, particularly among older citizen groups, is becoming commonplace.

Its potential in the developing world has yet to be fully realized and exploited as a cost-effective educational tool and resource. The use of oral history as an investigative tool, and as way of preserving oral cultures, is still in its infancy.

The evolution of oral history and education will continue. In the future, it could well be accepted in the classroom as a fundamental methodology for teachers, not just in the UK but throughout the world.

CHAPTER SIX

RECORDING ORAL HISTORY: PLANNING

Successful recording needs careful planning and the right equipment. The tape recorder has changed the way that oral material is collected and preserved. It has many functions: it is a notebook, an interrogator, an acquirer of dialect and language, a permanent record keeper, etc. Oral history has taken off partly because of advances in recording technology, and those advances are still continuing.

EQUIPMENT

Equipment is now so advanced that there is no excuse whatsoever for making a technically inferior recording. Broadcast quality is attainable even from budget-priced systems, but the days of cheap cassette recorders are numbered.

During the past ten years or so, major technical advances have been made in sound recording technology. Gone are the days of struggling under the weight of a mains reel-to-reel tape machine. Modern equipment is portable, lightweight and often battery-powered.

REEL-TO-REEL TAPE MACHINES

Nevertheless, in these days of digital recording, it is worth including in this review the portable reel-to-reel machine. The workhorse of the oral historian has for many years been the reel-to-reel battery-powered portable Uher Report 4000 series. The Uher, in both mono and stereo versions, is still a very good machine and is often available second-hand for a reasonable sum of money.

Technically, at 7.5 inches per second tape speed the Uher meets broadcast standard, and even when working at the lower tape speed of 3.75 inches per second it still gives quality speech recording suitable for oral history work, providing a modern high-quality electret-type microphone is used. However reel-to-reel tape is becoming harder to obtain and is expensive compared with cassette tape. The Uher is portable and operates on rechargeable batteries or mains. However, it is heavy, and running at the broadcast quality speed of 7.5 inches per second, a 5 inch diameter reel of tape lasts only 16 minutes per side on standard play tape. Recording and replay times are doubled when using the machine at 3.75 inches per second on standard play tape. Long play tape at 3.75 inches per second allows around 45 minutes per side. (A recommended tape supplier is listed in Appendix One.)

One serious disadvantage with the earlier Uhers were the multi-pin DIN microphone plugs which are a nightmare to wire and require a special locking collar on the plug to

Reel-to-reel portable tape recorder. (Author)

ensure a good audio earth. Modern microphones are often on ¼ inch jack plugs or XLR–type plugs and a special adaptor has to be made to use them on the Uher.

Cassette-Recorders

The introduction of the cassette-recorder in the 1960s provided an attractive alternative to the Uher. The early cassette machines were quite adequate for speech, as long as a separate microphone was used rather than an in-built microphone. The introduction of the Sony professional series and the cheaper Marantz series proved that almost broadcast quality was possible from cassette. The Marantz series is now one of the most popular of all the cassette systems used by oral historians.

Recordings intended for posterity should be made to the highest quality that can be afforded. Avoid the cheap cassette-recorders at the bottom end of the range, especially the kind used in schools for group and field work.

Another approach adopted by some oral historians is to use a mains-powered stereo cassette deck. Cassette decks cost less than, say, a battery-powered Marantz and usually offer two microphone inputs, although increasingly these inputs are not included as standard and it is essential to check with the supplier that live microphone recordings can be made. (It is relatively cheap to have a battery-powered unit made to use microphones at line level input on the rear of the machine.)

The cassette deck is intended to be part of a larger system which has an amplifier and loudspeakers, so the deck itself is not fitted with an internal speaker for listening to play-back. However, almost all decks have a headphone socket and, when budgeting for a machine, you should include about £15–20 for a pair of headphones which then allows the tape to be heard on site or back in the office. Cassette decks are widely available from high-street stores.

DAT (Digital Audio Tape)

This is a comparatively new development in sound recording. The system differs significantly from both reel-to-reel and cassette systems by recording the information digitally. Digital recording is perhaps best exemplified by the compact disc which is renowned for its superb sound quality. Many CDs are in fact originated from DAT, which gives some idea of the quality DAT is capable of producing.

Battery-powered DAT portable machines can be purchased for around £500 and are small and lightweight – ideal for interviewing. Tapes can only be recorded on one side but are available in lengths of up to several hours, giving more than enough running time for oral history interviewing.

All systems have their advantages and disadvantages, and the DAT is no exception. The machine works like a tiny video-recorder, storing its digital codes on a special DAT tape.

DAT (digital audio tape) recorder with tape. (Author)

Sound archivists, concerned about long-term storage problems, have suggested that the DATs might become unstable in time. The author's experience of using DAT for some years is that they are very reliable; I have only experienced one failure from an early tape batch when the cassette mechanism jammed. Even then the recording was playable after a simple repair. The DAT is, in my view, the best technical way to record oral history interviews; however, for long-term storage and safety, a second copy should be made on another medium such as cassette, Mini-disc or even reel-to-reel archival tape – with extra copies for everyday use.

DCC (Digital Compact Cassette)
The digital compact cassette is intended to replace the ordinary compact cassette and in some ways is very similar to DAT, but is intended for the domestic market. Its overall technical quality is, however, not as good as DAT, but should be more than adequate for the home user. Equipment will allow the replay of both standard cassettes and DCC, but, at the time of writing, the system is competing with Mini-discs and there is great debate as to which system will prevail.

Mini-disc
DCC's rival, the Mini-disc, is a small disc which can be recorded by the home user and is intended eventually to replace the tape-cassette. Mini-disc is beginning to make its mark. The BBC use the Mini-disc system for news-gathering in the field, in many cases replacing the old workhorse, the Uher reel-to-reel machine. Mini-disc is now being targeted at the domestic market and is available from high-street outlets at around £300 per machine.

Mini-disc recorder. (Author)

Recording is possible from microphones and the discs are re-usable. The recording quality is not quite as good as DAT but the difference for oral history work is so marginal it can be ignored.

Recommendation. In order of recording quality I recommend DAT, Mini-disc, professional cassette-recorders and, on a convenience basis, last of all reel-to-reel portable. Mini-disc at the present time is becoming increasingly popular in oral history work and is likely to become the standard field recording machine in the future.

Microphones

A golden rule in oral history recording is always to use a separate plug-in microphone (or microphones). Never rely on in-built microphones. Invariably they give a fair recording of the tape-recorder's motor and in an interview situation they are too far away from the interviewee to be useful.

Tie-clip Microphones   The most widely used microphones for oral history work are tie-clip mikes. Usually two microphones are used: one is pinned to the lapel of the interviewer and the other to the lapel of the interviewee. This is by far the best way of ensuring good sound quality during an interview and the microphones are so small and lightweight that even elderly people completely forget they are wearing them within a couple of minutes.

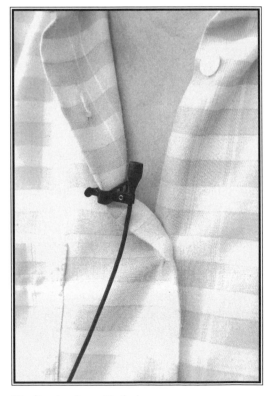

Costs vary greatly. At the professional end of the range, microphones from companies such as Sony, Sennheiser and AKG can cost several hundred pounds each. While they are superb and well worth buying if the money is available, these microphones are designed mainly for professional studio work or in orchestral situations (such as on a violin). At the other end of the range are small condenser electret-microphones selling at around £20 each from electronic component suppliers. These microphones are cheap enough to carry as spares and offer excellent quality for oral history recording. Incidentally electret-microphones have a small battery in their base which must be removed when not in use.

Stick Microphones   Stick, or hand-held, microphones also have their place in oral history work, and while costs can be high

Tie-clip microphone. (Author)

for the quality studio models, battery-powered electret types give excellent quality for oral history recording.

Stick microphones are also useful as back-up mikes should the tie-clips fail for any reason, and are essential when interviewing in the workplace or out of doors. Although professional stick-type microphones can cost hundreds of pounds, an electret type from Tandy or Maplin's Electronics will cost £25–50.

PZM Types PZM (pressure zone) microphones are a comparatively new kind of mike which have a specific application in oral history work. Most microphones receive information through the air directly via sound waves, that information being transformed into an electrical signal which goes into the tape-recorder. The PZM mikes have a flat plate and work on a slightly different principle. The microphone is placed on a flat surface such as a wall or a table, which forms a boundary for the sound wave. The sound wave is received in a special capsule in the microphone. The sound is largely free from reverberation from the boundary on which it is mounted or attached, and picks up in an omni-directional pattern effectively. In an interview situation where the only practical option is to have people seated around a table, and where more than one interviewee is to be recorded, the system works well if the microphone is placed in the middle of the table, and obviates the need for extra equipment such as an audio mixer. Some audio engineers claim the microphones possess a clarity of sound not found in other microphones. A budget-priced PZM microphone suitable for oral history work is available from Tandy stores.

Other Equipment

Lightweight aluminium flight-cases are a useful way to carry around recording equipment and accessories. There are, however, some disadvantages to using flight-cases: opportunist thieves well know that such cases are likely to contain items of value. Some professional photographers now use well-padded sports bags for their everyday work, thus disguising the fact that they are carrying valuables.

There are two schools of thought about using equipment cases in the interview situation. One says it puts people off seeing expensive-looking cases and the other that it looks professional and encourages rapport.

At a practical level the aluminium flight-cases offer good protection and usually retain their micro-climate for very long periods, certainly overnight if bubble pack is used internally to cover the kit. DAT machines are, on very rare occasions, prone to condensation on the tape heads which can take several hours to clear. The flight-cases, suitably insulated, will help to keep the machine 'warm' until it is needed.

Other indispensable items include headphones, a set of jeweller's screwdrivers, standard electrical screwdriver, 3 and 5 amp fuses, gaffer tape, notebook, pen, spare tape and batteries. An extension lead with a circuit breaker is essential if battery power is not an option.

The Interview Situation

People react in different ways to being interviewed and the skill and experience of a good interviewer will often help to allay a person's fears. Being interviewed can be a somewhat daunting experience, particularly for the elderly who often see it as an important social occasion, a special moment in their lives, which could involve the interviewer in the ritual of tea-drinking and the consumption of many home-made cakes.

Occasionally people have been put off the whole idea of being interviewed because of a bad experience with a news reporter 'who got everything wrong' or, worse still, a local radio reporter straight off the 'how to interview people for radio course' who thrusts a microphone two inches from a person's mouth and then wonders why people fail to respond in a meaningful way. The relationship between the interviewee and interviewer must work from the beginning and, while there are tricks of the trade which will help to establish that confidence quickly, the interviewee's personality plays a significant part in the proceedings.

Good, professional interviewing is not easy. There are many things for the interviewer to be aware of. It is easy, for example, to become preoccupied with the technicalities of sound recording and lose sight of the original objective of the interview. The introduction of cassette-recorders, DAT and now Mini-disc has made high-quality sound recording easier. It has not, however, made interviewing easier. That still relies on the human qualities of preparation, trust, empathy, experience, skill and personality.

The clear objective of most interviews is to acquire information and this requires communicating successfully with the interviewee. The technology should be, desirably, a high-quality audio recorder, but the technology is ultimately secondary to the acquisition of knowledge – the pencil and notebook certainly have their place.

The audio recorder functions as a modern substitute for the notebook, but more so, recording accurately things the pen cannot, such as dialect and accent, the timbre of a voice, intonations, song, music and sounds. In addition, of course, the technology is there to offer a permanent sequential record of events, as well as being a practical tool for the oral historian and researcher.

Initial Research

Let us assume that it has been decided to make a recording about farming methods in order to complement and interpret a museum's existing collection of tools and equipment.

First of all it is necessary to do the research. A good starting point is often the office filing cabinet, other members of staff, and then family and Museum Friends. There is also the local auction mart, agricultural college and similar organizations. The library will have news-cutting files. Look for names and background information. Check in telephone directories, trade magazines, trade directories, lists of electors, pension funds, trade unions, retirement homes and so on. Gradually suitable candidates for interview will become apparent.

Even an announcement on the Internet might bring results, while a phone call to the local paper suggesting perhaps a feature article with an appeal for names always works well. If the paper is not able to offer a feature then write a letter to the editor for publication, again appealing for potential interviewees. Local radio is another way of contacting the right people, particularly the BBC local radio stations which generally have an older target audience.

Television is extremely effective but it requires a shift in thought to use it and control it to your advantage. Television people think in terms of images, particularly, of course, moving images. They are only likely to be interested if the subject is tele-visual, and within practical travelling distance of the studio. Personal contact is the best way to ensure attention – press notices often go straight in the bin.

Television will bring more results than any other publicity medium. Be prepared to deal with it: you may receive literally hundreds of replies. Do you really want hundreds? On the other hand I have recorded some interviews which would otherwise never have been made simply because I would not have found the interviewees through normal channels.

Approaching and Selecting People for Interview

Names and addresses of potential informants need to be sifted through and a primary selection made. Decisions need to be taken about the type of interview to be recorded, each person being considered on his or her merit.

Close wording of the original appeal is an important ally at this point. Ask for 'help and assistance' in the Oral History Project, but never actually suggest that an interview is an inevitable consequence of their responding to the appeal. This allows latitude in the selection of individuals, a way of thanking people for their 'kindness in replying' and 'their help with information for the project' without being loaded with the obligation of interviewing someone who clearly has little to offer.

The Interviewer

The question also arises as to who should actually undertake the interview. On one project, in which an estate worker was recording an oral history of his place of work, problems soon arose when he wanted to interview his employer. Not only was there a marked class barrier but, of course, the employer was also the interviewer's manager. The problem was resolved by using a second oral historian to record the employer, along with a suitable confidentiality closure on the interview barring the employee's access to it for a given period of time.

Will a better interview result from someone with a sympathetic ear to the informant, from an aggressive argumentative stance, or by presenting the role of a passive observer? Sometimes the circumstances dictate the stance an oral historian has to take. Which stance should be taken when interviewing a terrorist, or a person with extreme religious conviction or facing perceived persecution? There are no hard and fast rules, except to record the fact that a particular stance has been taken for a specific reason or reasons.

Should women interview men or men interview women? Should white interview black or black interview white about race? In the United States during the monumental oral history project undertaken by Bob Blauner's team on American race relations it was found – particularly in the early days of recording in a racially charged atmosphere – that most of the interviews had to be undertaken by same race interviewers.[1] This raises the question of what differences in opinions and attitudes might have been recorded if interviewers of different races had, somehow, gained the confidence of the groups at that time and if, somehow, it were possible to compare both forms of interview.

Make use of the telephone. Talk to people about their experiences, but not in detail at this stage. Thank them for their interest and ask, if they are clearly likely to be suitable informants, 'if they would be willing to be interviewed at a later date'. My own approach is to say something like 'What I would like to do is to come over and see you and talk about it a bit further and bring with me a small tape-recorder, if it's OK by you.'

Using the telephone to acquire information and aid selection also establishes an important link between interviewer and interviewee which will help considerably at the interview session when rapport is needed quickly. The telephone is, of course, a transducer of sound, a microphone in their living room. Listen carefully to potential informants. Do they stutter? Have they a foreign accent? Do they have a strong dialect accent? Are they deaf? Do they really know anything about the subject? These are all important clues in deciding whom to approach for interview and how to interview them.

Another approach used to locate potential informants, gain publicity and learn about the subject under study is to use BBC local radio. Short telephone phone-ins on dialect, traditions and customs, local history or whatever will usually provoke an immediate reaction. A straightforward appeal for informants also tends to work well on local radio stations.

Occasionally, because of distance or cost, it is worth considering recording an interview directly over the telephone. A good example of this is a tape preserved at Wessex Film & Sound Archive of an interview recorded by telephone with a former nurse living in the United States about her memories of the US Army Nursing Corps in England during the Second World War.

Not everyone has a telephone. Some responses to the appeal may come by letter, or from a well-meaning friend or relative. Assessing potential interviewees from such sources is far more difficult. Admittedly a letter may offer important clues to a person's overall knowledge of a subject but offers no clue at all as to his or her ability to communicate orally on the subject.

Well-meaning relatives are a mixed blessing. 'Oh you must talk to Uncle Joe, he's been in farming all his life', is a typical remark, but do they really mean 'Talk to Uncle Joe, *because* he's my Uncle Joe'? And if you do Uncle Joe he may well decide 'not to be bothered', or indeed have little to tell. Some people are simply not good communicators and it is easy for well-meaning relatives to inadvertently embarrass their 'uncle joe'.

Most interviews are likely to be conducted in a person's home. There are many advantages to this approach, in particular the fact that the interviewee is in a familiar environment and is likely to be more relaxed and forthcoming than in a formal studio setting. There are times, of course, when recording at home is not a serious option; for example, where there is noise or interruption from other family members, or if the interviewee is living in a retirement home. Mobility can be a real problem for the elderly and so the oral historian must be prepared to travel and spend time recording in widely different acoustic environments.

Intelligibility is all when recording oral history. A certain amount of background noise is acceptable – after all the recordings are not being made for BBC radio but for posterity. Imagine for a moment that an oral history recording existed from, say, eighteenth–century

London and that in the background were the sounds of a London street. How fascinating that would be to historians today. So in oral history interviewing, it is not taboo to include reasonable background sounds provided that the recording remains sufficiently intelligible for future generations to understand. A brief line on the Clearance Note identifying the background sounds would be useful.

There are, however, occasions when oral history interviews are recorded in studios, or similar places, sometimes at the specific request of the informants. They may not wish their family to know they are making a recording, or they may wish to tell the world they are being interviewed for posterity! I have recorded interviews in board rooms, prison remand wings, retirement homes, hospices for the terminally ill, schools, on ships, down mines and even over the telephone. The oral historian is there to interact socially with the informant and to record memories – even if it means working on a Sunday afternoon in a retirement home miles away to get that once-in-a-lifetime interview.

Each location, when viewed from the sound recording perspective, is a challenge. An ideal 'studio' would be quiet with a dry-sounding acoustic, with very little reverberation or echo, similar to that in a room with heavy drapes, thick carpets and perhaps books around the walls. In reality this ideal is rarely achieved and reverberation, or 'room coloration', is always present. Try to avoid recording in rooms with high ceilings, little furniture and solid floors. Avoid rooms near busy roads or loud sources of sound. If the only room available is near a sound source then encourage the interviewee to sit at the end of the room farthest away from the sound source.

Tie-clip microphones in these situations keep the distance between a person's voice and the mike to an absolute minimum. As a general rule, the nearer a microphone is to a person's mouth the more background sound will be eliminated. In practice, a tie-clip microphone should be no closer than about 6 inches (15 cm) to a person's mouth in an ordinary interviewing situation. Closer than that the sound of his or her breathing becomes obvious and distorts the sound.

There are, of course, exceptions to every rule. Close-miking, as it is called, at distances much closer than 6 inches (15 cm) is sometimes the only way to record in a particularly noisy environment, such as a factory. The interviewee accepts the obvious limitations imposed by high-noise levels and expects the interviewer to stand very close, breaking the rules of personal space. The interviewer needs to hold a stick microphone very close to the lips of the informant, possibly as close as 1 inch (2.5 cm) and then swing it back to him- or herself for the question. In order to reduce the effects of plosives in the voice, a foam windshield is vital in these situations. A weaving shed in a cotton mill or a generating plant are examples of locations where close-miking would be essential.

Traditionally, in oral history recording, the approach is on a one-to-one basis and is usually approached as a biographical or life history interview. While this is likely to remain the most popular interviewing method there are others worth exploring.

Types of Interview

1 *Group Interviewing* A successful approach, pioneered by the North West Sound Archive in England, is the group interview approach. Often groups such as the Women's Institute,

Soroptimists and Civic Societies ask for a speaker for their winter meetings. Rather than offering a straightforward talk to their members, consideration is given as to how the needs of the oral historian might be met at such sessions. On the night the group is divided into three or four separate 'teams' depending on how many people are present. A member of staff or a volunteer is then assigned to each group. This person will act as the interviewer. A microphone is set up on a stand and the group is seated in a semi-circle around the microphone, the interviewer facing them. A popular subject, such as school-days, traditions and customs, dialect or marriage, is chosen and the session then starts. There are several permutations to this procedure; in some cases, each group tackles a different subject area, changing over part way through the evening to a different subject or interviewer. Another approach is to ask people to bring a meaningful object or photograph from their childhood as a basis for discussion. Many important objects and documents, including rare photographs, have come to light using this approach.

The maximum number in each team should be no more than five people; three is ideal. This technique applies not just to clubs and societies wanting speakers but can apply equally to retirement homes for the elderly and with school children in the classroom.

The principle advantage is that a great deal of new information is acquired quickly, albeit in a superficial way, sometimes from people who would not willingly be interviewed on a one-to-one basis. A disadvantage is that a particularly loquacious member of the group may dominate the session, and it is the responsibility of the oral historian to ensure that questions and replies are spread evenly across the group. It is also very important to identify on tape who the people are and where they are from, otherwise the exercise loses some validity.

At the end of the session perhaps some four hours of material will have been recorded. It will quickly become apparent which people are worth interviewing on a one-to-one basis. Suppose that the oral historian is researching farming methods; although the general discussion will follow a particular subject line it will be easy, in most cases, to ask a few supplementary questions to each group about farming and see what happens.

This approach is very similar to the approach adopted by the oral history team of the Moscow State Institute of History and Archives in their work recording in Samarkand in 1990. 'It is a collective approach to Oral History. . . . It enables each [interview team] group member to interview alone or in a pair or in a group, depending on ability and confidence, and encourages an on-going analysis of interviews as they happen. Information and problems are shared as they happen. It was an approach which also catered for different ways in which people retold their experiences.'[2]

This approach is certainly an interesting one. However, there are clear dangers in relying solely on group oral history. The Moscow team analysed their results and did not rely completely on group response and common memory.

In group-based oral history it is essential to examine to what extent there is dramatic embellishment and inaccuracy. Could there be agreement by common consent or peer levelling within a group to save face, hide facts or promote a particular theme or thought? Many of these things do occur, not maliciously, but as part of normal conversation and discussion. (See Chapter Four)[3]

Oral history is always throwing up surprises. During an interview about running an off-licence in an inner city, the old lady recalled that as a child she remembered 'Red Indians' coming into the shop for 'fire-water'. The photograph she produced confirmed this improbable story, the 'Red Indian' was a member of Buffalo Bill's Wild West Show in the early part of the twentieth century. (Author)

2 *Life History/Biographical* The one subject all people know about is themselves, and it is the one subject that in many ways is easiest for a beginner to undertake.[4]

A questionnaire is an essential *aide-mémoire* to the interviewer covering childhood, school-days, homelife, parents, adolescence, marriage, work, etc. This type of interview can take several sessions to complete. One colleague summed it up nicely: 'It's like peeling an onion, you take off the first layer and there is another fresher layer beneath.' It is the kind of interview most often used to record the memories and reminiscences of the elderly. It chronicles social attitudes preserved in their thinking, as well as providing information.

Ask questions in a logical, structured, chronological sequence. Relate dates of events to their age. I always ask early on in the interview for their date and place of birth and when they married. This means it is possible to work out the year if they say they were twenty-five at the time of some local event.

The dialectologist needs to know a little more than the date and place of birth of the informant, particularly where the informant's parents came from, their work and something of their migration and geographical movements.

Ask what their earliest memories are. The results sometimes are quite surprising – one very old lady clearly remembered General Booth, founder of the Salvation Army, running his fingers through her hair! Next ask if their grandparents or great-grandparents ever told them stories about the past. The question is well-worth asking, and the results can again be surprising. One old man talked about the Rainhill locomotive trials of 1829 and Stephenson's *Rocket*, and another about the clan wars in Scotland.

Many people have a skeleton in their cupboard. There might well be areas that the informant does not wish to discuss and this must be respected. Such is the rapport that can build up between interviewer and interviewee that often things are said that in normal circumstances would be left un-said. One elderly lady told me in some detail about her honeymoon and her innocence in matters of sex! I asked her if she really wanted me to record this and she replied that it was important for other people to know what it was really like living in 'prim and proper' Victorian England.

Clearly much of this applies mainly in the UK. The recording of life-stories is seen as extremely important in other countries, especially in the developing world. It is a way of preserving the truth of past events as seen by the people, a truth that is often not represented in official literature and records. It is a way for people in formerly oppressed nations to preserve their language, culture and traditions. As yet it is an under-used methodology, but with enormous potential for heritage professionals, aid workers and teachers the world over.

Another approach to recording biographical interviews is that adopted by the National Life Story Collection housed at the National Sound Archive at the British Library in London. It starts from the pretext 'Every man and woman in this country has a story to tell of his, or her, own life. These life stories are the raw material of our history and our understanding of change today. They are as much part of our heritage as buildings and landscapes.'

The collection concentrates on in-depth interviews covering family background, childhood, education, work, leisure and later family life. In addition there is a collection of manuscript autobiographies, usually unpublished accounts of the lives of interviewees. Many different specialist collections have been created as a result of the project, including Leading Citizens; 'The Living Memory of the Jewish Community'; City lives – bankers, legal professionals, and others working in the City of London; Lives in Steel – steelworkers; Artists' Lives, Medical Lives, Missionary Lives, etc.

The oral history of British photography is a project supported by the Arts Council, the Victoria & Albert Museum, the National Museum of Photography, Film & Television and the National Sound Archive. A series of interviews is being recorded chronicling the lives and memories of British photographers. Those already interviewed include Ken Baird (landscape), Jane Brown (portraiture), Maurice Yates (submarine photography) and Raymond Kleboe (*Picture Post*).

3   *Survey and Cultural Interviewing*   Development and relief agencies have now started to use oral history. As long ago as 1991 a conference was held on oral history and Third World development at the National Sound Archive in London. It became clear that techniques were already being developed and oral history was being used as an investigative tool and a means of self-expression. The Save the Children Fund has, for example, used oral history to uncover the reasons for the reluctance of Somali women to participate in a national immunization programme.

Concern has been growing at the apparent ineffectiveness of aid over the years and the recognition that workers lacked sufficient local cultural knowledge to maximize the impact of aid. There were many issues to consider, such as different cultural and social priorities.

Oral history needed to be a useful, practical tool rather than, as one worker put it, 'the mining of information for pet projects'. Workers themselves now recognize that they have to learn far more about the people they are attempting to help by understanding their cultural and social position. Oral history, if used honestly in this context, gets away from the sometimes patronizing approach adopted by some agencies. It opens doors, builds confidence and encourages healthy debate and argument.

Oral history is not the panacea for all problems. Some people will assent to suggestions given by the interviewer so as not to lose face, or to preserve rites, while others give misleading answers simply because the knowledge was so entrenched into their everyday lives that they were unable to put the meaning into the right words. Acceptance, absorption into the community, and discrete observation are also important complementary skills for the oral historian or development worker. Traditional and local stories and village gossip are also part of testimony and may reveal facts that seem to contradict earlier statements. Some field workers have observed that quantifiable information is often sparse in interviews, but overall perceptions emerge that are vital in the understanding of cultural priorities, value systems and moral frameworks.

The Sahel Project is in many ways a landmark and represents an important stage in the story of oral history. The project set out to 'explore the culture, history and environment of the Sahel through the memories and recollections of its people' and 'to explore how the application of oral history techniques can assist the development process'.[5] The Sahel is a region of north Africa including Mauritania, Senegal, Mali, Burkino Faso, Niger, Chad, Sudan and Ethiopia and is essentially a marginalized area to the south of the Sahara suffering from effects of desert expansion.

In 1988 the voluntary agency SOS Sahel reviewed its policy towards the elderly. One of the motives for the project was to include the memories of older people rather than marginalizing them. The project was funded by a number of different agencies, including NORAD, the European Union, HelpAge International and others and targeted older people who remembered what the land was like before the drought.

The increased desertification interrupted traditional ways of living and the continuity of cultures. Young people across the Sahel are, ironically, better educated now than in the past and there has been a general attitude that such methods were old-fashioned and have little to do with the present. The project did not 'set out to accumulate facts, but rather to find the stories, improve the techniques for their collection and, most important of all, demonstrate their value and utility'.[6]

Over 500 interviews were completed at nineteen sites in seventeen languages in nine countries. Four main categories were selected for interview: refugees, pastoralists, farmers, and fishermen. Women proved particularly difficult to interview, largely for cultural reasons, although their inclusion was considered essential to the survey. There was also a reluctance to talk about land practice, irrigation techniques and animal care to 'educated westerners' on the grounds that they might be considered ignorant and out-dated.

Nevertheless the interviews were able to reveal methods of improving soil fertility, the control of animal breeding and pasturage. Healing methods and herbal remedies were also collected. Overall, the project collected evidence of change, both cultural and agricultural. There were distinct pointers to some of the reasons for desertification, such as unreliable rainfall, pressure on land from rising populations and the clearance of bush for cultivation.

Important lessons were also learned by the development agencies. A number of pre-conceived ideas were shown to be inaccurate and misleading. The very practice of oral history recording in villages and communities, where little contact had previously been made, led to closer ties and understanding. In Senegal the Fédération des Paysans Organisés used the interviews they recorded as part of the project for their literacy training programme.

In the Sahel Project oral history was used to accumulate a wealth of information. Although not a primary aim of the project, local languages and dialects have also been recorded for posterity. The end results of the project will benefit both the communities of the Sahel and the development programme. Closer links and a deeper understanding now exist between indigenous people and the development agencies. The agencies, because of this deeper understanding and awareness, can also plan and manage their own resources more effectively.

In some ways survey interviewing does not fit readily into any specific category. The very fact that interviews are recorded with different people about a particular subject or life history is, by its very nature, a survey. Academics in the main have used oral history techniques to examine facts or situations on a comparative or statistical basis. Dr Elizabeth Roberts at the Centre for North West Regional Studies at the University of Lancaster has, for example, compared social and housing conditions for working-class women in Preston, Lancaster and Barrow-in-Furness. Simplistically, it would seem that comparisons between locations and the individuals living in those locations are straightforward. In practice, however, this is far from the truth. As in all interviews, there comes a latent level of understanding about social and moral issues, a conceptualization in the mind of the researcher into why and how things occurred. Purely statistical approaches have been tried with varying degrees of success. The problem with using oral history in this way is often that it is not possible to obtain a complete cross-section of people to be questioned or interviewed.

A carefully contrived series of standard questions offer researchers a basic way of comparing like with like. However, if the cross-section sample is incomplete, this can lead to significant cumulative errors occurring. An example might be looking at how a cotton mill functioned. A standard question might well be about wages and income at a particular date. The information would come from weavers, spinners, tacklers and others employed in the mill. To complete the picture of income, the mill manager, or owner/s, would also be need to be interviewed. The chances are that these people are no longer alive while there are still plenty of weavers and spinners left. The record is therefore incomplete. The other danger in a purely statistical approach is misunderstanding of context. Why did wages vary? There may well have been local reasons for this, such as the loss of a major customer or straightforward meanness of the mill owners. One perception will be gained from the workers and another, assuming survival of mill owners and management personnel, from them.

4   *Local History and Community Histories*   Although this listing of interview types suggests that the styles and approaches are quite different, in practice there are often overlaps between them. Local history is really a subject rather than a form of interviewing, although the nature of the questions asked can be different; they are likely to be parochial in outlook, offering details of interest to a community or amateur historian. For example,

details about local tramcar operation, shop-keepers, events, local placenames, buildings, characters and former industries. Local history interviewing involves biographical, subject, survey, photographic interpretation and other approaches.

Interviews rarely stand on their own as a sole source of information, and in the local history field this is particularly true. The interview must be seen as being complementary to other sources of information and subject areas, such as buildings, objects, archives, pictures and photographs.

Community history and immigrant oral history is seen by some as being separate from local history, which has traditionally been archive, book, object and photograph based. However, local history research has over the past few years begun to address the huge changes taking place in society. It may, for example, involve recording more modern or contemporary experience within a specific population group. Blackburn Museum and Art Gallery has recorded the memories of Asian immigrants and the history of their community both in Blackburn and in India and Pakistan. Important work in community and ethnic oral history was undertaken by Rob Perks in Bradford, along with important complementary photographic survey work.

5 *Dialect and Language*   A great deal of language and dialect recording in the English language has been recorded by specialist dialectologists and linguists but this does not mean that it should be avoided by others. On the contrary, the more recording takes place, the more chance there is of a recording surviving. The approach, however, is more specialized than for other forms of interviewing and great pains are taken to ensure that the informants are true native speakers, born in the area under study and without too many outside influences. Having found a suitable person, the questions are phrased in such a way as not to supply the actual word or phrase the dialectologist is seeking. A typical question about a key might be: What name do you give to the object you place in a lock in order to undo a door? Another way is to show a picture of a door and point to the various parts, asking what word would be used. There are also ways of recording accents and inflections by asking people to pronounce a set series of test words or recite the alphabet or numbers to 100.

Dialect and language is an area often overlooked in the museum world, but there are some notable exceptions, such as the recording of the Welsh language at St Fagans by the National Museum of Wales and the preservation of Manx speech at the Manx Museum on the Isle of Man.

The University of Leeds School of English pioneered to a large extent in the field recording of the English dialects. The result of their extensive fieldwork 'The Survey of English Dialects', is not only an important piece of work for dialectologists but also contains extensive oral history recollections about English country life, including some handed-down family memories reaching back into the eighteenth century.

To some extent an interviewer with a different accent to the interviewee can influence the way that the interviewee responds. The respondent will 'put it on' and or even 'talk posh' for the sake of the recording. This is a constant problem with dialect and language recording and is part of what is known as the 'levelling out effect' of language to a point where people's accents change to become acceptable to both sides. Usually a good warming up informal session reduces this effect, and certainly towards the end of formal interviews informants are often less inhibited about using language and accent.

Some dialectologists insist that the only true way to record uninterrupted language and dialect is to record without the persons actually knowing they are being recorded. While the logic of this approach is reasonable, it is not usual to record people without their knowledge for whatever purpose. Another approach using radio microphones could be a solution. The persons wear the radio microphone in an everyday work situation and eventually, after some time has passed, they will begin to use language in a natural uninhibited way. The actual recording is made some distance away by a dialectologist using a suitable receiver and recorder.

If the recording contains embarrassing material then, by negotiation, it is within the right of the informant to have a closure placed on the recording in the museum or archive, either until his or her death or an agreed date for release. It goes without saying that anonymity should also be part of this closure agreement. Some dialectologists destroy or erase recordings made without the informant's knowledge after extracting linguistic information.

The recording of local people reciting their own dialect writings has only a very limited value to the dialectologist. Modern writers largely attempt to write and recite in an old style which, while it has an entertainment value, usually produces inaccurate writing and pronunciation. On a slightly different tack, interviews could be recorded about why people write dialect and how the subjects they write about were chosen.

6   *Interpretative – Locations*   The tape-recorder is a most useful tool for interpreting locations of various kinds whether in the countryside or in town, or even within a building. Walking round a country village with an elderly resident, recording as you walk, is a good way to obtain detailed local information. The small visual items so easily missed, such as an iron hook in a wall, can suddenly trigger a long-forgotten memory. In my own experience a former German artillery officer suddenly and dramatically switched back to his wartime experiences in a chilling way as he visited as a tourist a former German gun-emplacement in the Channel Islands. He totally relived the experience, pointing out where various mechanisms and equipment had been housed and the rigid procedure they had to follow.

Returning people to a long-forgotten location can have dramatic effects, producing outpourings of knowledge triggered by the environment. Walking round a country village or walking round an old mine site can be very evocative and revealing. Photography and video come into their own on these occasions, although they have in some respects different roles to play. Photographing various features mentioned on a village walkabout, such as iron rings in the wall, is essential in the understanding of the tape in future years. Maps and plans must also be annotated with the locations and direction arrows showing where photographs were taken. It is then a short step to creating from the original sound tape a tape-slide or computer presentation, or a village trail for children or tourists.

The newer formats of Hi-8, Super VHS and digital DV video-cameras are light enough to carry around and work in very low light levels and can complement the oral historian's interrogative approach. (See Chapter nine)

7   *Interpretative – Photographs and Documents*   The merits of this approach have already been discussed in Chapter two. Many public libraries, archives and museums have large collections of photographs, yet often surprisingly little is known about them. Most photographs are likely to have been taken within living memory as photography only became commonplace and popular from the turn of the twentieth century onwards. The idea of basing interviews on photographs and documents does not seem to have been pursued by oral historians to any great extent. The field is wide open, with enormous amounts of work most urgently needed.

Documents are not exempt from oral history methodology, as was shown in detail in Chapter two. Diaries can be understood better if background information exists from other family members or friends. Business archives and technical drawings can all be explained by interviews with former workers and management. Ephemera, posters, tickets and so on can easily form a talking-point in any oral history interview, practical aids to effective recall. There are many more categories of modern archives that could benefit from oral history, such as computerized records, local government records, family history, trade union records, wartime documents, etc. In one instance oral history techniques were used to find out about the provenance, background, history and social context of medieval documents discovered in a wooden chest.

As a further example, Bedfordshire County Record Office in 1994 ran a reminiscence evening for Fire Brigade personnel which was attended by over fifty people. The Archive holds important records of firefighting in the county. Photographs from the archive were displayed and 'names put to unknown faces'. Another by-product of the session was the deposit of other material brought in by some of those attending the evening as guests.[7]

8   *Interpretative – Objects*   Almost all museums and art galleries possess objects without sufficient provenance or detail. Oral history techniques do have their limitations, relying on the time span covered by human memory, but oral history presents the opportunity to learn and understand more about objects in care.

Each interview is based around the object under scrutiny, whether it be a tool or perhaps some domestic item. The object is the starting point for a number of enquiries. For example: How was the tool used? Who used it? When? Why? Who made it? How was it acquired? What did it cost? How common was it? and so on. This approach not only provides the curator with information about the tool but also on the social, and perhaps even religious, circumstances surrounding its use. Too many objects in museums have, in the past, been displayed without adequate understanding and interpretation.

Some museums have long since recognized the usefulness of recording interviews and background information concerning their collections for many years. For example, St Fagans (National Museum of Wales), the Imperial War Museum in London, the Manchester Jewish Museum and Kirklees Museum in Yorkshire have all used this approach.

The North West Sound Archive in England has always regarded recordings as artefacts in their own right, particularly now that recording technology is changing and magnetic tape may well soon be a thing of the past.

In a pioneering venture Croydon Museum used oral history methods to collect objects and involve the public in developing a new museum in a very real way. A London suburb with a population of over 300,000, in the 1980s Croydon suffered something of an identity crisis and was described as being a place 'where nothing much happens'. One person remarked 'There's no history in Croydon, it's a modern shopping centre'. With attitudes like that to cope with, the museum curator was faced with tremendous difficulties. First, a series of roadshows were held in local libraries to attract local people and get them to bring in photographs and objects. The results were mixed, but people were surprised to discover that anyone was actually interested in them as part of Croydon's history. After a period of experimentation it was decided to contact individuals who had offered to lend items during the roadshows. Over a span of several visits they were interviewed about their lives, and any relevant objects, such as toys from childhood, were photographed. Family photographs were copied and interviews completed of their life or family histories.

The curator then organized an exhibition called the 'Living Memories Show' which aimed to attract visitors from all groups in Croydon, but in particular those people who do not normally attend museums. The show was chronological (representing each decade from the 1930s to the 1970s) rather than theme-based, and featured, where possible, objects identified during the interviewing and research stage as significant to those people. The designer worked in part from cassettes and photographs and used existing objects to reconstruct a 1930s kitchen or back parlour. In the other areas oral history was used to illustrate the lives of three women during the 1950s, '60s and '70s. Objects including an evening dress featured in the display. Almost 9,000 people came to the Living Memories Show during the three weeks it was open. The museum has now developed a collecting strategy for the future and a policy involving local people of all ages, sexes, denomination and colour.

Gaps in the existing collections were identified. A special religious questionnaire was sent out to places of worship and scripture bookshops and a 'death questionnaire' to funeral directors, florists and monumental masons in an appeal for objects.

Very few people came forward initially from Croydon's ethnic minority groups but this was resolved by hiring historical researchers to encourage groups to become involved in the work of the museum. Contacts were made with local Irish people, South Asian people, Afro-Caribbeans, and gay and lesbian groups. All the researchers felt that there were distinct advantages to be gained from being from the same background as the people they interviewed. This approach also demolished a number of widely held stereotypes. The Irish interviewees lent the museum several exhibits including boxing boots and a policeman's whistle.

Every exhibit in the museum has both a conventional label and a touchscreen featuring the voices and photographs of the donors. The exhibition takes on an air of being 'that of a well-designed junk shop', yet reveals stories that are sad, funny or interesting. Some are 'even dull – just like real life'. Hence the title of the eventual museum-based exhibition – Lifetimes.

This important approach using oral history in relation to objects is an important advance in community awareness, understanding and museum thinking.[8]

The British Empire and Commonwealth Museum based at the former Temple Meads station in Bristol tells the story of the Commonwealth from John Cabot's voyage to Newfoundland in 1497 to the handover of Hong Kong to China in 1997. Oral history plays a major part in the museum's activity, recording the participants of Empire and Commonwealth before it is too late. There are twenty volunteer interviewers around the country recording mainly life histories of people from Africa and Asia. The Museum produces an impressive catalogue covering a wide range of subjects from the Mau Mau to Mahatma Gandhi and from typhoid to Tsetse flies. Four full-time transcribers are employed to deal with the influx of recordings.

In both these examples, oral history has been used not just as a way of reaching people but also as a way of gathering objects, papers and photographs for permanent preservation, thus enriching collections. The interview process involves active interpretation or understanding of the objects and their significance to the people being interviewed.

9   *Craft and Industrial Processes*   The recording of craft and industrial processes is again something museums should be doing quite widely, and indeed some already are. Industry is changing rapidly and museums cannot preserve everything, nor is it desirable to preserve some aspects of industry. Nuclear or chemical industry plant, some ships, craft processes such as charcoal-making, or salmon fishing are natural candidates for photography and/or video alongside oral history recording and the preservation of smaller objects representing the industry or craft.

10   *Actuality*   Radio, television and the newspapers all cover everyday events. So why bother recording contemporary material at all? Radio and television are, as we have already seen, very selective. By the time news reaches the home it has been refined, changed and edited, sometimes in a most alarming way. For most purposes this condensation of news is fine, but for posterity more is needed.

To what extent the heritage professional should become a detached reporter or incident observer is open to debate. There are historical precedents for such independent observers, so why not the oral historian?

Contemporary recording can have value as time passes. I myself recorded a number of interviews with prisoners and prison officers at Strangeways Prison in Manchester, England, a few years before the riots took place. Not only was it possible to record attitudes, feelings and tensions, but also detailed life stories, crimes and other offences. Prisoners arriving at the prison went first to the Reception Area. I included a very detailed description of this room – colour, smell, feeling, furnishings, notices and other impressions – in as detached a manner as possible. I also recorded the general ambience of the room and something of the reception procedure as prisoners arrived from court. Language here was not always the politest but was an essential ingredient in understanding how men survived in prison in the 1980s.[9]

On another occasion, following a street riot, I found myself in a position of being hounded by local people who insisted on telling their side of the story. The role of neutral observer can indeed be a useful one.

It is, of course, not just national news that is worth recording. There are local stories about break-ins, fires, road accidents, retirements: the local papers are full of good stories, often with inadequate detail. These stories are often the basis for good oral history. The opportunity to follow them up and record them offers the incidental advantage of establishing good permanent contacts with journalists and others.

11   *Political Interviewing*   This is included here for completeness and might be considered perhaps as part of contemporary or actuality interviewing. The technique employed in most oral history recording is subtle and friendly, but political interviews can be a very different matter. At a local level most politicians respond well to the usual oral history approach but politicians practised at dealing with radio and television journalists can be evasive or aggressive. A directness is required in order to break through this barrier. Most politicians are naturally defensive about their careers and do not like to be reminded of their weaknesses and failures; even a promise of closure with 'no access to the recording in their lifetime' may not be enough. Remember the Watergate tapes?

One way of recording politicians is using the biographical approach, not asking in the first instance about their political life. Start with childhood or schooldays. The political stuff comes later, when trust has been established.

In media interviewing a balanced interview is theoretically the aim. In oral history work this is not essential, as long as details of why a particular bias was introduced is kept with the recording documentation. Which approach would have revealed more information about someone like Adolf Hitler: one with a detached viewpoint or one which deliberately empathized or even sympathized with his viewpoint?

12   *Technical Interviewing*   A great deal of research is required to record technical interviews successfully. As a practical example, in order to record interviews on the secret development of jet engines during the Second World War several levels of interview were necessary. These ranged from eliciting comments from the man who physically beat metal to shape over a tree stump for the panels used on the prototypes to acquiring answers to some very different detailed technical questions raised with the operation manager, who was concerned with engineering metallurgy.

Another example is an interview with Sir Harry Platt, the pioneer orthopaedic surgeon. It was necessary to seek the help and expertise of a medical colleague who was able to assist in the construction of the question sheet and ask technical questions at the interview session. The oral historian acted more as a sound engineer, monitoring the whole interview most carefully and then asking those additional questions about everyday things, such as 'And what did your wife think about that?'

13   *Children's Playsongs*   When Iona and Peter Opie published their book *The Lore and Language of School Children* it revealed a new world in which language, words and phrases

were being transmitted from child to child and from generation to generation in parallel with but often quite independent of the language used at home or in the classroom.

Apart from the fact that children's street and playsongs are delightful to record, they do have a darker side. The songs are often, in adult perspective, racist, obscene and very cruel. Oral historians are, however, also in the business of recording reality and actuality, and should not be offering judgement on the material being collected. It is up to others to interpret and understand. All recordings must be seen in this light. Recording children these days is not without its difficulties. It is a sad fact that in western society so many children have been molested or abducted in the street that approaching children at play may be seen as a suspicious act.

Classroom projects in primary school are often a starting point, although there are some limitations. Children are not likely to reveal their more risqué presentations in front of the teacher. When I record children I always work with another person who is known and trusted by the children, but who also understands my requirements. When working in the street I usually make the microphone visible and obvious so that people are under no illusion about what I am doing. In addition I carry identification and the name of a responsible individual who can vouch for my activities.

Children's skipping songs and street games are also ideal material for video-recording, but care must be taken to ensure that the image does not take priority over the clarity of speech or song. A separate off-camera microphone is essential and, for archival purposes, the takes should be continuous so as to ensure that the 'performance' is captured entire.

14   *Folk Songs and Folk Memory*   Much information is passed from generation to generation by word of mouth. The suggestion that questions should be asked at the beginning of an interview about memories passed down from great-grandparents or grandparents is a good one and should be pursued. It is not just family memories that can be collected in this way. Snatches of long-lost folk songs and rhymes are often there in the memory, but remain hidden until someone asks a pertinent question. Long-lost traditions and customs can also be rediscovered in this way. In the UK many Morris Dance traditions are passed on verbally and/or by practical example, and should be recorded using both oral history and possibly video.

Story-telling has not featured strongly in a traditional way in England for many years, television and radio having arguably taken on that role. Yet in other cultures, story-telling and poetry are meaningful and a vital part of everyday life, the importance of the bard in Welsh culture and Scandinavian sagas being two such examples.

Ordinary folk, too, have their stories passed down from generation to generation. Ask: it is surprising what still survives just below the surface.

15   *Traditions and Customs*   In the previous section the importance of recording the memories of folk songs was emphasized. There are many rural traditions and customs still surviving and, although strictly speaking these are not oral history but oral tradition, they should be recorded as completely as possible and then interviews conducted about what such traditions and customs used to be like and changes that have taken place.

There is a need to record as many traditions and customs as possible before they change or disappear for ever. Sound recording is certainly an effective way, complemented by photographs or colour slides. The video again comes into its own here, following the rules laid down earlier about continuous takes and the need for a separate microphone. Putting the date at the beginning of the video is also useful. (See Chapter Nine)

16   *Family History Interviewing*   This approach is still very much in its infancy. However, interviews with members of the family about their lives can add important and significant information to support other documentary research. Interviewing one's own immediate relatives is not easy. Sometimes there is a reluctance to talk about childhood days in detail. There can be embarrassment about revealing details of past relationships or the irrationality of youth. There is a strong case for allowing someone from outside the family to record immediate relatives. The imposition of an outside interviewer changes the rules. Family secrets can be unlocked in ways not always possible in the established intimacy and familiarity of family. Some elderly relatives, as soon as they see a microphone, clam up, simply because of that familiarity and social bonding in the family. 'I don't want the rest of the family knowing that' is a not uncommon retort. However, a great deal depends on individual character and relationships within families. Both approaches are probably worth trying.

Family interviewing is worth doing for another reason. The recordings survive as a permanent memorial and private record of loved ones.

17   *Miscellaneous*   Further types of interview have been suggested by Slim, Thompson and others in 'Ways of Listening', an article in the book by R. Perks, and A. Thomson, *The Oral History Reader* (Routledge, 1998). These include single issue interviews such as information about a specific event, and regular diary recordings.[10]

CHAPTER SEVEN

RECORDING ORAL HISTORY: THE INTERVIEW

ASKING THE QUESTIONS

There are various schools of thought on how questions should be compiled and asked, and indeed whether question sheets should be compiled at all. There has been much debate, particularly in Australia, about the relationship between listener and interviewer. To what extent should the interviewer dominate the interviewee, 'control contents and set the agenda'? There has been accusation of 'European cultural arrogance' in the recording of Aboriginal and Islander history. The argument suggests that 'Aboriginal histories are presented in different forms and different emphases. Interviewers need to listen and hear aboriginal voices and their particular ways of telling the past.'[1]

Risking the possibility of further perpetuating European cultural arrogance, to what extent does this approach obviate the question and answer process? The dangers of consensus group interviewing have been discussed elsewhere. It is recognized that some societies only talk in groups, or individually, in turn, and, because of the unfamiliarity of western interview approaches, they may not react or respond in the expected way.

The need to understand and be sensitive to different cultures and their ways of thinking and behaving must be a primary consideration for oral historians. Who makes the better interviewer – a native speaker or an outsider, a man or a woman? The difference in this context between recording established oral tradition and oral history can sometimes become blurred.

I would argue that oral history is primarily about asking questions and seeking answers. Without that, recordings are devalued, whatever the end objectives may be. It would not be unreasonable to suggest that the recording of oral tradition and oral history are almost separate issues. Oral history is interrogative by nature and only rarely authoritarian. Oral tradition can be investigated using oral history methodology just like any other subject.

It is important to allow and even encourage hitherto unheard groups to talk, but it is the oral historian's job to ask questions and record the replies for posterity. This also raises the question, what is the purpose of recording at all? For whom is it intended? If the purpose is to create an archive or resource for a disparate group of people, then outsiders asking detailed questions might be inappropriate. Yet the outsider is detached and objective, and can often see the greater picture. The risk of allowing uncontrolled ramblings is a great one. Interviews do need a sense of direction and purpose.

The author interviews a former wartime air-raid warden in Stockport's complex of tunnelled shelters.
(Stockport Express)

The Question Sheet

So what are the advantages and disadvantages of using structured question sheets? Jan Walmsley, in her work with people with learning disabilities, has shown that it is quite possible to interview using Life Maps – a series of symbols – which can be logically followed or evolved as interviews progress. This approach is capable of considerable application in oral history, not just for those with learning disabilities but also with children, individuals whose first language is not English, the elderly, and the hearing impaired, and perhaps as an aid alongside conventional question sheets.[2]

One of the most useful adjuncts to constructing a question sheet is the technique described earlier for use in the classroom – the logic spider. Taking English village life as an example, each leg of the spider represents a subject related to village life: police, funerals, christenings, childbirth, heavy snowfalls, shops, haymaking, schools, bus services, etc. Many of these legs can be further divided so that, for example, haymaking might include headings such as tools, time of year, storing the hay, workers, etc. Each of the spider's main legs then forms a heading with sub-questions beneath.

LOGIC SPIDER

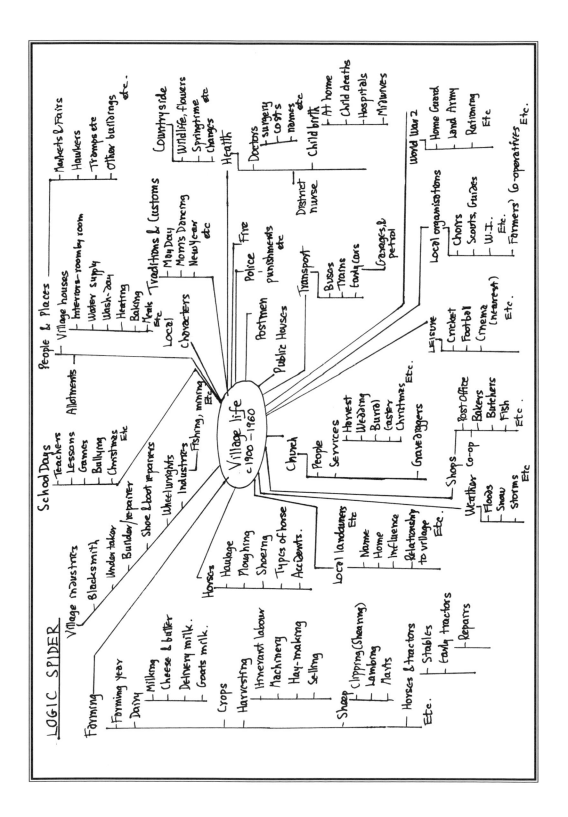

Village life c.1900 - 1960

People & Places
- Markets & Fairs
  - Hawkers
  - Tramps etc
  - Other buildings etc.
- Village houses
  - Interiors-room by room
  - Water supply
  - Wash-day
  - Heating
  - Baking
  - Meals etc
- Countryside
  - Wildlife, flowers
  - Springtime
  - changes etc
- Health
  - Doctors
    - surgery
    - costs
    - names etc
  - Child birth
    - At home
    - Child deaths
    - Hospitals
    - Midwives
  - District nurse
- World War 2
  - Home Guard
  - Land Army
  - Rationing Etc

Traditions & Customs
- May Day
- Morris Dancing
- New Year etc
- Local Characters
- Postmen
- Public Houses
- Police
- Fire
- punishments etc
- Transport
  - Buses
  - Trains
  - Early cars
- Garages & petrol
- Local organisations
  - Choirs
  - Scouts, Guides
  - W.I.
  - Etc.
  - Farmers' Co-operatives Etc.

School Days
- Teachers
- Lessons
- Games
- Bullying
- Christmas Etc
- Allotments

Village industries
- Blacksmith
  - Under taker
  - Builder/repairer
  - Shoe & boot repairers
- Wheelwrights
- Industries
- Fishing, mining Etc

Farming
- Farming year
- Dairy
  - Milking
  - Cheese & butter
  - Delivery milk.
  - Goats milk.
- Crops
- Harvesting
  - Itinerant labour
  - Machinery
  - Hay-making
  - Selling
- Sheep
  - Clipping (Shearing)
  - Lambing
  - Marts
- Horses & tractors
  - Stables
  - early tractors
  - Repairs
  - Etc.

Horses
- Haulage
- Ploughing
- Shoeing
- Types of horse
- Accidents.

Local landowners Etc
- Name
- Home
- Influence
- Relationship to village Etc.

Church
- People
- Services
  - Harvest
  - Wedding
  - Burial
  - Easter
  - Christmas Etc.
- Gravediggers

Leisure
- Cricket
- Football
- Cinema (nearest) Etc.

Shops
- Post Office
- Co-op
- Bakers
- Butchers
- Fish Etc.

Weather
- Floods
- Snow
- Storms Etc.

Question sheets – advantages and disadvantages:

Advantages	Disadvantages
Acts as a useful memory aid	Creates an agenda set by the interviewee
Offers comparative study between interviewees	Does not easily allow the informant the opportunity to express him- or herself in ways different to that of the interviewer.
Allows careful construction of difficult questions	The questioner might miss unresearched areas subsequently revealed by the informant
Useful as a learning aid to would-be oral historians on how to ask questions	It creates a more formal setting than true friendly conversation
The question sheets remain alongside the tape as a permanent record	

In practice, most oral historians use a question sheet (or sheets) with headings and key words. The important questions are first of all the place and date of birth of the informant and then any family background he or she is prepared to give (on or off tape); the occupations of his or her parents; migration – where he or she or the family moved to and from; the size of the family, brothers, sisters, etc.; school/s attended; type of work; when he or she was married/divorced, etc.; and religious and political interests.

It may not be appropriate or relevant to ask all of these questions; a great deal depends on the nature of the interview. Nevertheless the interview should include the informant's place and date of birth.

Research into an individual or subject can only go so far and I have found that the minimum needed is a list of subject headings worth exploring with the informant. In practice, such a list of subject headings needs to be broken down further into questions that can be easily understood by the informant. Be careful not to supply the answer within the question, as in the following example:

Q: Was it because of your life-long interest in folk music that you play the guitar so well?

Several issues are raised in the above question. First of all, there are the assumptions that it has been a life-long interest, and secondly, that the life-long interest has been confined to folk-music. Thirdly, flattery has its place – but not here.

It may be necessary to break the question into several sub-questions in order to avoid unduly influencing the informant.

Q: When did you first become interested in folk music?
Q: Why?
Q: How/when did you learn to play the guitar?

The essential questions are always: Why? Which? When? Who? Where? What? How?[3]

In some cultures it is common for people to answer 'yes' and agree with the questioner so as not to lose face or offend the interviewer. Most people tailor their replies somewhat to the expectation of the interviewer; this must be guarded against by asking follow-up questions that will ensure that the meaning is clear.

Some interviewers include accuracy check questions on their question sheets. They will deliberately supply information that they know is wrong, such as a date or a name, to see if they are corrected by the informant.

Keep the questions largely open-ended, avoiding the type of question which solicits a direct 'yes' or 'no' answer, unless of course that is required to confirm facts, dates, and so on. 'Yes' and 'No' answers and brief summaries are also useful ways of changing the direction or subject area of an interview by rounding up one section and leading into the next. For example:

Q: . . . and so by the end of 1945, you changed your job.
A: Yes. I went into farming for a couple of years.

The need to avoid supplying answers to questions is apparent.

The level at which the questions are asked is also important. Who is the research aimed at – children or scientists, artists or technologists? A scientist is likely to be interested in the technical minutiae, while a child is only concerned with the most general sense.

If it is for gallery or exhibition replay then the interview needs a narrative approach; if it is for research, say for an exhibition, a more detailed level of questioning might well be appropriate.

Recording the Interview

Most oral history interviews are recorded in the home of the informant. Preparation for the actual recording session should begin in advance. The equipment needs to be checked over and batteries recharged overnight if necessary. Organize a check list of equipment to take with you.

The timing of the interview may well influence the way it goes. Elderly people in retirement homes tend to be governed by the clock for meals and bodily functions. Very elderly people tend to snooze after lunch and a morning session may well be more appropriate. However, most of the interviews I record are made in the afternoon or early evening. I always leave the choice to the informants and fit in with their arrangements as far as possible.

Arrive early in the area where the person lives. Spend a few minutes nearby, but out of sight, going through the question sheet, rehearsing names – people are easily put off if you get their name wrong – and check the batteries in the microphones before going into his or her home.

On arrival, always offer some identification, even though he or she may be expecting you. It is polite and immediately puts a person at ease. In Britain shaking hands is largely acceptable when meeting for the first time. There are some exceptions, however; some elderly ladies were not brought up to shake hands with men and it is quite alien to them. Always attempt to shake hands when first meeting, or at least to touch them on the shoulder in order to make a physical contact. That first physical contact is extremely important: an immediate affinity occurs that is hard to break.

Look around the room where the interview is to take place. Listen for acoustic problems and extraneous noises. Cover up the budgerigar or parrot: it will soon think it's night and stop cackling. Turn off the television or radio (with the informant's co-operation, of course) and any other equipment making intrusive sounds. Look around the room for visual clues about the person to be interviewed. Are there any musical instruments? Are there photographs of him or her? Are there shields and trophies in a cabinet? Is the garden full of roses? All these are clues to the person, and can be used to talk about anything at this early stage except the subject of the interview. In Britain the weather is always a good standby, closely followed by the state of the traffic. This 'warming-up' period allows you to get to know the interviewee better and form a common bond early on. (Some people are so uninhibited that such a warm-up session is unnecessary: they start talking as soon as you enter the room and keep on talking until the recorder battery is flat!) I often simply introduce myself at this first stage and mutter something about the weather. Then I say something to the effect that 'I'll just nip out to the car and get the tape-recorder', leaving no illusions as to why I am there.

Ask where the informant usually sits. Try to accommodate him or her as far as possible, because he or she is likely to be more relaxed in the usual chair. Avoid a situation in which the sun shines directly into an informant's eyes.

Still chatting generally, as a first step wire up the tie-clip mikes. Run the mike cable under the person's arm and around the back of the chair to prevent him or her from fingering or playing with the cable. In the case of an elderly person I usually lift the arm very gently in order to position the cable, thus reinforcing that all-important tactile bond mentioned earlier.

Sit at a slight angle to the informant so that he or she cannot actually see the tape-recorder, but in such a way that you are able to preserve eye contact. Do not sit too close – 5–6 feet is reasonable, although this varies from culture to culture. While still talking plug the microphones into the tape machine and switch on. Check the recording levels carefully and without telling the informant, start recording.

Start the interview by saying something like 'Now where did you say you were born?', and the session is underway, the interviewee being led gently into the recording process. Never, as some people do, say something like 'This is a recorded interview with Mrs Smith about her life as a vagrant, recorded on 24 April by Joe Bloggs'. It is guaranteed to switch people off.

Photographs are used routinely in interviewing by the British Empire and Commonwealth Museum in Bristol. This photograph shows workers at a coconut plantation in the 1930s. Both the Indian and British workers have been interviewed by the Museum. (British Empire and Commonwealth Museum)

Objects, photographs, even newspaper cuttings can act as a catalyst to get people talking. The British Empire and Commonwealth Museum, for example, often use photographs as a discussion point, encouraging in the process the exhumation of long-lost pictures and family albums. Other interviewers have constructed time-lines for the interviewee to relate to.[4]

Interviews involving descriptions of localities or structures can use maps and plans to plot information. This approach is particularly useful to local historians, natural history conservationists, town and country planners, archaeologists and industrial archaeologists. As the interview progresses, not only does the base plan act as a stimulus for recall but becomes an annotated complementary document to the tape. Another similar approach is the use of detailed technical drawings of machines, buildings and structures.

A good interviewer will try to empathize with the story being told by the informant. This human consideration, while important in order to get the best from the person being interviewed, should not over-ride totally the need for objectivity, but it should and does provide a stimulus for additional questions as those experiences are shared.

Where do you draw the line? Ross Livshin, a Manchester-based oral historian, has been recording survivors from the Jewish Holocaust. A high degree of sensitivity and understanding was essential from the outset. Interviewees were often extremely apprehensive before the interviews took place, some not having spoken about their experiences since the war. Presented, possibly for the first time, with the opportunity to tell their stories, some of the informants simply could not continue and broke down in tears, along with the interviewer. The interviews could involve many separate sessions – one involved fourteen separate sessions – all treated with care and understanding. Reliving such horrific experiences on tape brought other attendant problems that the oral historian needs to be aware of. Some could manage just one session before being forced to abandon the project, unable to continue because of painful memories. Others would make the recordings and then not be able to sleep at night for many months. Others even needed professional help following the sudden release of such long-suppressed emotions. The need for high professional standards in such oral history recording is plain to see; it also illustrates how personal oral history interviewing can be. Many friends are gained by sharing the memories of private, and sometimes painful, experiences. Oral history recording is as much to do with people as with the acquisition of information.

It is the hallmark of the amateur to constantly interrupt with interjections like 'er', 'I see', 'Oh really. How nice', 'Sorry', and 'Yes, I know him well' – but everybody at times forgets the golden rule about keeping quiet and listening to what is being related. Even now, after thirty years of oral history recording, I occasionally forget and manage to add the odd 'yes', but it becomes objectionable to the listener when it occurs constantly throughout an interview and actively interferes with the intelligibility of the reply.

Body language and empathy, if you will excuse the phrase, go hand in hand. The skills of body language understanding are extremely important in oral history interviewing. Nodding the head and an encouraging smile work wonders. Shaking the head, or looking very puzzled, often solicits an enquiry of 'You don't understand that do you?' or something similar, followed by an explanation. You might feel like an idiot, but it works.

Some oral historians even use mirroring techniques as effective tie signs in an attempt to bond themselves more closely to the informant.[5] In other words, they mimic the body language of the person they are interviewing. This is a particularly effective technique in reminiscence work and it certainly has its place in oral history recording providing it is not obvious and therefore patronizing. The head height alignment to an informant can also be crucial and is related very closely to eye contact and personal space requirements. Older people and children especially respond better if your eye line is roughly at the same height or slightly lower than their own. Nobody likes to be looked down upon.

People respond better if their attention is held and eye contact is maintained, but this is quite difficult to keep up for long periods. Too long a gaze and the informant wonders why the interviewer is staring. This is especially true if the person is of the opposite sex and appealing. Yet eye contact is vitally important in understanding and reacting to the person being interviewed. If prolonged eye contact needs to be maintained, try to look at the forehead just above the nose, rather than directly into the eyes of the interviewee. This allows the gaze to be continued for longer than normal. For both the interviewee's and interviewer's comfort there are ways of breaking a gaze during a long interview. Check on how the tape-machine is working – just the briefest of glances is needed – or look down at the question sheet; this is sufficient to avoid uncomfortable, unnerving eye contact.

Oral history interviewing is generally relaxed and informal. Two volunteers practise interviewing using Mini-disc as part of the National Canal Oral History Project based at the Boat Museum, Ellesmere Port. (Author)

Eye contact becomes difficult when either party wears spectacles. Light reflecting on the lenses from, say, a nearby window, will interrupt eye contact. If the situation is such that changing position or closing the curtains is not practical, it immediately places the interviewer at a disadvantage. Returning the gaze to the forehead position is all that can be done. Some informants with failing eyesight or hearing would also benefit from the interviewer sitting in a well-lit position so that body language can be observed and lips read clearly.

There are times when the opposite is true, and maintaining eye contact is counter-productive. Looking down at question sheets during a long silence is a useful way of inducing a reply from the interviewee. Silence, 'the pregnant pause', is certainly a useful ploy in interviewing and almost always forces a reply from an informant. It can become a near battle of nerves to see who answers first, but eventually the informant will respond, breaking the silence.[6]

Interviewing people who have little or no sight means that the interviewer must rely far more on listening and communication skills. The timbre and character of the voice becomes important. How the question is asked and how it is conveyed carries information of significance to the informant. Listening to the reply, and to the inflections in the reply, is crucial to understanding in such situations. It is one the reasons why sight-impaired people make such good interviewers – they listen to responses in a way a sighted person has difficulty doing without training.

One of the hardest parts of oral history interviewing is listening to what the interviewee is actually saying and interpreting that response. What does it really mean? All the time, while listening to the replies to your questions, you should be preparing the next. At first this multiplexing idea is not easy, but it comes with practice, and there is always the question sheet to fall back on.

The interview has then a 'warming-up' period; a little further on and the interviewee has forgotten the tie-clip mikes and often switches into a mental state which, in some ways, can make the interviewer seem quite superfluous. The out-pouring of memory is such that the presence of the tape-recorder and interviewer are somehow less important to the informant than the memories being recalled. This state of out-pouring can vary considerably from individual to individual and may last from a couple of minutes to half an hour or more.

There are always interruptions during interviews: it is part of life. These interruptions vary from someone at the door, a dog barking, the telephone ringing, the district nurse wanting to give injections, to low-flying aircraft. Work around the interruptions as far as you can. Some tips to minimize the effects of such interruptions include answering the telephone yourself and saying 'Mrs Smith is in the middle of being recorded at the moment, can I get her to ring you back?', while callers at the door, particularly friends, will often remain quiet throughout the interview session, fascinated by the whole event. It may even be necessary to postpone the interview as a last resort.

Gauging the way the interview is proceeding is also important. Is the interviewee answering the questions you want answered? Are you allowing him or her to ramble into subject areas not relevant to your enquiries? Occasionally during an interview the informant may say something for which the interviewer is quite unprepared. During an interview on aircraft noise, recorded deliberately close to the main runway at a major international airport, the informant, a lady, was asked if she had ever been in an aircraft. Her reply changed the course of the interview in an instant as she explained she would never go in an aircraft after seeing a passenger jet crash in the fields at the rear of her home. The jet then bounced into a row of houses and blew up, killing all the passengers and a number of others. Quite unprepared for this response, it was necessary for the interviewer to go back to basics and use the Why, When, Who, Where, What, Which and How questioning system.

It would have been unlikely in normal circumstances that she would have agreed to such an interview, but in the context of an interview on aircraft noise she was willing to relate her experiences. It also illustrates how confidence and rapport can be established very quickly with an informant.

A point will be reached towards the end of an interview when it will be obvious to both parties that the interview is drawing to a close. At the end of the interview always thank the informant on tape. 'That was great, thank you very much for your time' or something similar works well.

Inevitably the reminiscence process continues after the tape-machine has been switched off and packed away. There will be further memories to record on paper and preserve with the tape. On many occasions people will also produce old photographs, documents and objects. One technique I use, if I suspect that the interviewee might do this, is to cheat slightly. I pretend the interview has finished but I leave the machine on standby. The tie-clip mike is removed and this encourages the interviewee to rummage through drawers or photo albums. The tie-clip mike can be very carefully held in the hand as the photographs or objects are described and discussed. It is, of course, courtesy to ensure the informant realizes, knows and accepts your furtive procedure. Make the microphone obvious the moment you wish to record further and say something like 'I am just going to get this on tape'. Use gentle but assertive language rather than a request.

The end of the interview is a good time to consider object, document and photographic retrieval. It is always worth asking if they have any old photographs. If they have many, it may well mean another visit and another interview to interpret them.

It is essential in such cases to produce a written receipt there and then for the informant, saying what is being taken away and for what purpose. There is, unfortunately, other paperwork to complete too, especially the clearance and deposit note. Copyright in a recording exists in most countries. It is there to protect the interests of the copyright owner, particularly in the music recording industry. However, in UK copyright, any sound recording which is 'published' has protection for fifty years from the date of release. The copyright of an oral history interview, that is the actual recording itself, has a copyright independent of that of the informant. As a general rule, the copyright lies with the person, persons, or organization that paid for, or commissioned, the recording to be made. An individual giving out information has a literary copyright in the words and is entitled to enjoy that copyright until seventy years following the year of their death (EEC directive 93/98).

In order to simplify this complex area most sound archives and oral historians either ask to own the literary copyright or ignore the copyright element completely and seek the permission of the informant to use 'their contribution' in certain specific ways, which offers protection to the interviewee on how the recorded material might be exploited.

Clearly this approach works in most countries, providing the permission is given in writing. A standard form is reproduced in Appendix 4, which oral historians are free to copy and amend.

Occasionally, a situation arises when it is impossible either to complete a clearance note or to seek copyright clearance in the normal way – for instance, vox pop street interviews or with the very elderly. In these circumstances, the street statements are assumed to be 'cleared' by the fact that assent for the vox pop was given, providing the names of the informants are not known. With the very elderly it is often wise to seek permission from their nearest relative or simply to ask if they, the informants, have any objections as to how it might be used.

A frequent question asked at training sessions is how long an interview should actually last. It varies, but on average is about 45 minutes to an hour. Occasionally it is longer, but it is important to monitor elderly informants carefully, as fatigue soon sets in.

Within a very short period of time, usually by the following day, a thank-you letter should be sent to the informant. Such letters are greatly appreciated; sometimes, many years after an interview has taken place, relatives contact the oral historian to relate the death of the informant, having traced the name from much-prized letters.

Some oral historians insist on taking a photograph of the informant and keeping it with the recording and subsequent transcript. This is, of course, a splendid idea. The best time to take the picture is after the interview has finished and a relationship has been established. This means taking the photograph on the day of the interview and indeed this may be the only practical way if visiting again is a problem because of distance. In my experience it is better to go back and concentrate on photographs rather than sound. As a matter of courtesy I usually offer a copy of the photograph and a copy cassette to the informant should he or she desire them. (See Appendix three)

VIDEO AND FILM – ITS PLACE IN ORAL HISTORY RECORDING

The whole process of using video for oral history is dealt with in Chapter nine. A brief summary though, particularly of the relationship between oral history and video, is not out of place.

The moment a video camera is used in an interview situation (and it takes a minimum of at least two people to record successfully), 'the rules of engagement' are changed. Some people do not like their 'photo' being taken and may object to the presence of a camera; indeed a video-camera could easily destroy the confidence and confidentiality that has been built up between the interviewer and interviewee. Professional television producers might well question this, but the oral historian is in a far more privileged position, being able to ask questions and receive confidential replies in the certainty that they are not to be transmitted on a public broadcast system without their permission. Again the oral historian can place a closure on a recording for fifty years, ensuring strict confidentiality and, if necessary, anonymity.

The approach and objectives of the oral historian are different from those of broadcasters. Oral historians are concerned with extracting as much accurate information as possible, while the broadcaster needs to condense that information and, in the case of television, make it visually interesting as well. In order to condense information into a given time slot much is lost on the editing room floor. Questions are often discussed in advance and responses sometimes rehearsed. Watch any public broadcast television and listen to the questions and answers.

When television interviews are recorded on location the entire interview with an informant is shot as a first stage. The camera position is then reversed and the interviewer is then recorded asking the questions. The whole sequence is then edited back at the studio, giving the illusion of a continuous interview.

Quite often questions are loaded, or contain inaccurate assumptions. The quality of this style of interviewing is deteriorating and the oral historian must be aware that the standard demanded by posterity in oral history interviewing must remain high at all times.

The editing process interrupts the original uninhibited flow of the interview. Bias creeps in and the final programme is far from being an 'original document' in the way the oral history tape must be. That is not to say that television programmes cannot provide vital useful information; they can. Television has resources to be envied by the oral historian and often undertakes research well beyond the resources of the heritage professional.

Even basic video-recording usually needs an experienced camera operator and an interviewer. Indoor shots may well need extra lighting and the personal, intimate relationship between interviewer and interviewee is certainly tested to the limit. In order to comply with the requirements of true oral history interviewing the camera must be kept running and only switched off when a change of location or natural break takes place. The camera is in effect acting as an illustrating tool for the notebook, NOT the other way round. The visual image, while extremely important, is, in oral history terms, complementing the information or message from the informant, often with important body language.

The direct application of television as an oral history medium has been tried successfully by the Brazilian Film and TV Museum in São Paulo. Television was seen as a practical way of recording artistes recalling their own, and Brazil's, musical heritage. Impromptu performances by some of the interviewees show how effective and important the visual element can be, particularly with practised performers stimulated by the environment of a television studio. Traditional sound interviews would have gone into more detail and could have been recorded in a complementary way to the video. Unanswered questions raised during the shooting of the video could be asked again, without the pressure of time that always seems to accompany video-recording. Whether true or an illusion, it does impose constraints on the interview situation. Equally it would probably also work the other way, recording sound first, and video second.

CHAPTER EIGHT

STORAGE, CATALOGUING AND RETRIEVAL

Although Mini-disc is beginning to challenge the situation, most recordings are likely to be made on recording tape in one form or another: cassette, DAT, reel-to-reel or video-tape. Modern magnetic tape is designed and manufactured to be robust; nevertheless, it deteriorates in time and care needs to be taken to ensure proper care and handling, as well as correct storage to ensure its longevity. Mini-disc also needs to be handled with care.

THE STORAGE ENVIRONMENT

The place used to store recorded materials needs to be secure and should ideally have some form of environmental control. There should be at least simple monitoring equipment such as a hygrometer and a thermometer to check relative humidity and temperature. The room should not have large fluctuations in its environment and should vary only 5 per cent or so in temperature and humidity in a twelve-hour cycle.

All plastics should be stored away from light, tape, Mini-disc and CDs included. The windows should be blacked out to avoid daylight and occasional rays of sunlight. Blocking out the windows helps prevent a number of flying insects attracted to the light emerging in the spring from wooden structures.

The air in the room should be clean, ideally with filtration to remove particulate dust and pollutant gases, with human access strictly limited and controlled.

There is a certain amount of argument as to whether magnetic materials should be stored on steel or wooden shelving. Steel shelving on two occasions in my own experience proved to be magnetized when tested. Wooden shelving on the other hand can emit harmful substances and needs to be chosen with care.

The recordings themselves should be stored in acid-free archive board boxes or containers. This gives added protection and buffers the recording against sudden unexpected changes in temperature and humidity.

Temperature and Humidity

The storage of magnetic materials has been a subject of some controversy in the last few years, particularly following the catastrophic and expensive failure of a well-known studio professional tape. One of the commonest tape failures is the binding agent holding the ferric oxide to the polyester base of modern tapes. This failure is a direct result of hydrolysis of the binder over a long period of time (in other words, a gradual chemical decomposition of the binder brought about by the interaction of water in the form of moisture from the atmosphere). In early acetate-base tapes the effect is so marked that the recording layer can actually peel away from its backing, leaving clear plastic. That, combined with the inevitable stretch which occurs with polyester bases every time they are played, means great care is needed in their preservation. At least one tape of American manufacture, if stretched accidentally, instantly loses all its oxide leaving just clear tape and dust.

My own recommendations for tape storage (given in the Society of Archivists Information Leaflet no. 4), of 45–55 per cent RH (within 5 per cent) and 50–60°F (10–16°C), are, in the light of recent experience, in need of downward revision: 10–12°C at 40 or 45 per cent RH. These revised figures do not prevent long-term deterioration of magnetic tape but do slow down the hydrolysis. In too dry an atmosphere, the problem then arises of loss of inherent moisture in the binder which can also cause a loss of oxide powder.

Magnetism

Tape is affected by magnetism and care must be taken to ensure that recordings are kept well away from magnetic sources. Some of these sources can be quite surprising – magnetic door catches, microphones, loudspeakers and television sets. Keep important tape collections (including computer floppy disks) at least 3–4 feet, or further, from known magnetic hazards. The earth's magnetic field is not thought to affect magnetic recordings.

Direct Heat

Direct heat such as sunlight can not only warp reels and cassette cases, but will also partially erase the tape.

Labelling Tapes and Boxes

When labelling boxes, cassettes, reel-to-reel tape, etc., use permanent archival quality fine black marker pens.

Play-back Deterioration

Every time a tape is played it inevitably suffers some damage. This is particularly true of tapes played back on old, badly maintained tape machines. Microscopic pieces of dirt scratch the tape along its length and magnetism can build up in tape-heads and on guide rollers if the machines have never been demagnetized.

Cleaning tape-heads and guides is not difficult. Buy cotton buds from the local chemist, along with some denatured alcohol or ionized methylated spirit. (If in doubt refer to the manufacturer's handbook.) Dip the cotton bud into the liquid and squeeze off the excess. Rub the tape-heads and guides gently until clean. Polish very gently with a clean dry bud. Never use anything metallic near the tape-heads – it could do permanent damage to heads and tape. Clean the rubber composition pinch roller in the same way. Do not apply excessive pressure. The tape-heads and guides in average use should be demagnetized at least once a year by a qualified engineer. NB: This cleaning procedure applies only to reel-to-reel and cassette machines. DO NOT attempt to clean DAT or video machines or CDs or CD players in this way. Seek the advice of a qualified audio or television engineer.

'Sanctity of the Original Object'

Treat the original recording as an important original object and the copy as you would an important document. The original recording should therefore be played as little as possible. Copy them to cassette format or Mini-disc for study purposes and public use, and keep them in separate buildings so that, in the case of theft or fire, one set survives.

Fire Protection

Magnetic recordings are prone to significant damage by fire and heat. Water from fire hoses, burst water pipes and sprinkler systems cause major damage to card and paper accompanying recordings. Experiments have shown that water in the short term can damage tape bases resulting in a loss of quality on play-back. Recordings surviving fires may need urgent specialist treatment and an appropriate disaster plan should be prepared for such an eventuality. Advice on disaster planning can be obtained from most Record Offices or Area Museum Councils in the UK.

The best immediate extinguisher for tape is the CO_2 gas type which leaves the tapes, boxes and accompanying paper substantially intact. However, always seek the advice of a professional fire officer for appropriate fire protection and escape. Remember burning plastics release toxic vapours.

Cataloguing and Transcription of Interviews

Once the recording is complete and the clearance note and deposit agreement signed, the recording should be copied as soon as possible for security and work purposes. Other documentation will now follow, usually some form of basic accessioning process.

The cassette copy at this stage will require listening to in detail. There are advantages if the original interviewer can be persuaded to jot down a rough summary as soon as possible after the interview, while it is still fresh in his or her mind. The basic summary of an interview is an extremely useful guide to content but not a definitive one: only a full transcription can provide that. For example:

> Joe Lansdale – Canal memories b. 1890 Recalls falling into the canal aged four – men working the ice boats – how he rescued a drowning child – horses falling into the canal – the great canal breach of 1936 – steering boats by night – strike breaking in 1911 – people living on the boats – cargoes. Etc.

Transcriptions are time-consuming and difficult to do. It takes a trained worker roughly 7–10 hours to transcribe one hour of real-time interview. It also assumes that the transcriber has a good general knowledge of the subject and has a good ear for regional and other accents. Lay-outs for transcripts are really a matter of personal choice. Nowadays many people use word processors with a wide choice of printing colours and typefaces.

Sample Transcript

Interview with Mrs J. Collins, of Hillhead, Chadderton, Oldham. Recorded 16 July 1986. Mrs Collins worked for AV Roe & Company covering the wings of aircraft during the First World War.

Q. How did you pin the fabric to the aircraft frame?

A. Well, we had to . . . it was like putting a pillow case on. Like this you know, say that was the tip of the plane, it was bonded either side. I made this just before you came. We used to have to get it like that, one girl at that side and one at that and gradually work it [the fabric] on.

Q. Sort of like putting your socks on, isn't it!

A. Yes. Then we'd carry on until we got it fitted, right round the tip of the wing.

Q. As tight as you could or . . . ?

A. Yes, well and then we'd . . . one girl would be at that side and one at the other and then we'd come right down gradually, until we'd got to the end.

Q. Working it along?

A. Yes and then when we'd got it like to that end, we'd go right back to the tip and then the seam would have to be level down that side of the wing and rounded. . . . and then there hadn't to be a crease or anything, and then when we got it to that end, we'd turn it in like that.

Q. What happened to the end pieces?

A. Yes, and then we had to sew it right across, turn it in and sew it across.

Q. By hand?

A. Yes – needle and cotton.

Q. And how long would it take you to cover a wing like that?

A. Er, well all I can tell you is that it usually come about as we was sewing it across after we'd been working perhaps for about two hours. Then when it got after 12 o'clock you couldn't . . . you know it was hard work to keep your eyes open just at that time and after it got about half past twelve you'd be wide awake again and carry on with another wing.

Annotations are often necessary. Errors in dates can be corrected, placenames inserted, references given, but the transcript should be capable of being read intact without alteration. Transcripts are always second best to the recording; gone are the inflexions and nuances of language and communication. The interviewee might say that something was OK or fine, but by saying it in a certain way, she could mean the exact opposite. Besides actually hearing the voice itself gives the exercise a remarkable quality and makes history live in a meaningful way.

Other useful guides to the information contained in transcripts include indexing, line and page numbering, sectioning and headings. Headings are extremely useful where it is not possible or reasonable to produce an index. An interview of four A4 sheets is perhaps better summarized at the beginning then given meaningful headings in the transcript where necessary.

Our sample transcript of a lady employed to cover the wings of aircraft during the First World War is a case in point. She went later to work in other factories and also recalled vivid memories of her childhood. Other transcript headings from that interview transcript include: Drilling hand-grenades; Johnson's wire works; Making Midland cologne perfume (1926); and May queens.

Long interviews or folios of transcripts are more useful to a researcher if they are line numbered and indexed. Indexing is a highly skilled operation although increasingly word processors offer some form of automatic indexing facility. These index generators produce only the most rudimentary indexes and are, frankly, no real substitute for the skills of a professional indexer.

Sample index to transcripts. (The numbering 6/22 refers to interview number 6, page 22)

Air-ships *4/20, 7/8*
Air Travel – *Transatlantic competition to the "Queens" 1/9*
Alan Cobham's Flying Circus (1929) *2/25*
Alcoholism *17/7, 20/1*
Aldred, Albert *11/4*
Alston, J. *9/11*
Amalgamated Cotton Mills Trust *14/7, 18/10*
   see also textile industry
Ammon Wrigley Fellowship see Wrigley, Ammon
Anaesthesia – Accrington Victoria Hospital (*c.* 1960) *4/2*
Andrew Knowles and Sons Ltd (colliery owners) *2/5*
Anglo-Afghan War (1919) *7/20*
Animal-cruelty
   Horses *17/9, 2/28*
Apprenticeships
   Aircraft engineering *2/25*
   Engineering (*c.* 1927) *1/6–7, 2/25*
   Locomotive engineering (*c.* 1940s) *16/7*
   Reed-making (*c.* 1936) *1/4*
   Weaving (*c.* 1920) *8/9*

Sectioning is simply dividing up the page of a transcript into two equal sections. The top half of an A4 sheet is simply called 'a' and the lower section 'b'. Each page is numbered consecutively from the first page and offers a reference point for the cataloguer and indexer, for example:

> Aircraft manufacture 2/25a
> Engineering (*c.* 1927) 1/6–7b, 2/25a

The easiest way to catalogue recordings is to give each tape or interview a straightforward running number starting with the year of accession. ie: 1994.1, 1994.2, 1994.3, etc. This number is marked on the tape and box containing the reel or cassette and is a unique marker. The simplest sort of catalogue can be kept on card or loose leaf in a ring-binder. Computers do have their place, for example in searching for obscure terms, but for small collections a card and/or loose leaf catalogue is just as good.

The details of each recording are put on to a 5 × 8 inch catalogue card or typed on to an A4 sheet. For example:

> 1982.1019 Family memory of the Peterloo Massacre (1819), with the accession number, title, a summary of the contents, the duration, a note of copyright ownership and any technical or provenance notes.
>
> Interview outlines a family memory of an incident immediately after the Peterloo Massacre in which soldiers are reputed 'to have cut people down' in the Ancoats district of Manchester. (2 mins 6 secs) Living conditions in the area during the informant's childhood in the same area are then described.
>
> 8 minutes 15 seconds
>
> Copyright Smith Enterprises 1982 Speed of recording 7.5 inches per second Other information: Recorded on a Uher 4000L Report by John Jones 16 May 1982 at the home of Mrs M. Donaldson, 24, Anyroad, Sale, Cheshire. Photo of Mrs D. available.
>
> Restrictions: YES/NO (If yes, refer to separate file containing Clearance notes and/or correspondence)

These cards or sheets are filed in accession number order in a card drawer or loose leaf file. The next job is the key-wording of a different size, 5 × 3 inch, index card. At its simplest, the only items that need to go on to these cards are the interviewee's name, the main subjects mentioned and, of course, the accession number, in order to locate the main 5 × 8 inch entry card. For example:

DONALDSON, M. (Mrs) 1982.1019 Family memory of Peterloo Massacre.

PETERLOO MASSACRE (1819) 1982.1019 Family memory of Peterloo Massacre, by Mrs May Donaldson b. 1901. Recorded 16 May 1982

Other keywords might include *Manchester, Peterloo Massacre* (1819); *Manchester, Ancoats; Childhood; Textile Industry; Civil Unrest,* etc. Sometimes headings need to refer to other more formal or accepted headings. This needs the introduction of so-called SEE reference cards:

Locomotives, steam engines SEE *Railway steam locomotives*

SEE ALSO references point the user towards related and similar subjects which might not be obviously related, for example: *Birds* SEE ALSO *Dinosaurs*

These cards are then filed in alphabetical order and form an immediate index to the main cards which are filed in accession number order.

Another option is to construct another short index in chronological order of events, so that our example would represent the year 1819. For example:

1819 Peterloo Massacre 1982.1019
1829 Rainhill Locomotive Trials 1991.003
1830 Liverpool & Manchester Railway 1993.1234
1900 January 5th. Air-crash on playing fields near Southampton 1993.9987
1900 March 17th. Strike of steel workers at Markland Foundry and Broad's shipyard 1995.8777

The best place to get advice on key-wording is the local history librarian or existing catalogues in the museum, archives or library. Useful books include the *Sears List of Subject Headings, Social History and Industrial Classification* (SHIC) and the index to the Dewey Decimal Classification.

Dialect and Technical Words

Inevitably as recordings are transcribed there will be words not present in the standard dictionaries. It is well worth recording these words separately on a card index and filing the results in alphabetical order. The basic information required is:

Headword. The accepted main form of the word.
Pronunciation. Use a simple dictionary phonetic form or refer to the International Phonetic Alphabet.
Definition. Carefully define the word. If this is difficult to do, then preserve the sentence and context.
Accession number of recording.
Bibliographical references, etc. Dictionaries that have been checked. Any other forms of the word. Use of the word in literature.
For example:
PUSHER pu'shə' A small cap worn by drawers at Towneley Colliery. The cap was worn with the neb to the back and the front was cushioned with grape cork. This was because the drawer (qv) pushed coal-tubs up-hill underground using his head against the rear of the tub. Sample: 'I used to wear mi pusher nearly all the time in't pit.' 1982.0031 *Wrights English Dialect Dictionary* p. 1102.

Computers and Cataloguing

Computers do speed up searches for information, but are only as good as the information supplied to them. In a card catalogue a minor spelling error within a group of cards – for example, Railwasy instead of Railways – does not matter, but in a computer it does. Every letter and every entry must be consistent.

The templates suggested for the card layouts will also work for computerized systems. The principal advantages of the computer over the card index is the facility to provide more than one copy as a print-out, the speed of the search, and its flexibility in looking for more than one thing at the same time, for example, steam engines but not steam locomotives of the Great Western Railway. The computer can also search all the records, not just the main entry at the top. If there is a brief mention of, say, a person's name then that can be searched for even though it is not in the main keywords. This search capability is also particularly useful with tape transcripts held in word processor files.

A computer entry sheet might contain the following field names:

TITLE
SUMMARY
DATE OF RECORDING
DURATION
COPYRIGHT
RESTRICTIONS: Yes/No
KEYWORDS (In any order)
IDENTITY NUMBER The unique identity or catalogue number

The completed entry might look something like:

[TITL] Family memory of the Peterloo Massacre (1819) Mrs M. Donaldson.
[SUMM] Interview outlines a family memory of an incident immediately after the Peterloo Massacre in which soldiers are reputed 'to have cut people down' in the Ancoats district of Manchester. (2 mins 6 secs) Living conditions in the area during the informant's childhood in the same area are then described.
[DATE] 16 May 1982
[DUR] 8 mins 15 secs
[COPYW] Smith Enterprises 1982
[REST] N (None)
[KEYW] Donaldson, M.; Manchester; Ancoats; Peterloo Massacre; Riots; Civil Unrest; Childhood; Textile Industry; etc.
[IDEN] 1982.1019

Each section or field will be limited to a maximum number of characters, usually a maximum of 254. It is an exacting but useful discipline to condense interviews into that 254-word summary. While computers are useful tools, they do have limitations. Keep the entries very short. Card catalogues can hold far more information.

There are two principal ways of arranging subject headings or keywords into alphabetical order. There is no right or wrong way to alphabetize, it is a matter of personal preference. Other ways include telephone book alphabetization and computer software alphabetization.

Word by word	Letter by letter
Wash-day*	Wash-day
Washing – children's clothes	Washing – children's clothes
Washing Day	Washing Day
Washing textiles	Washings (Mine tailings)
Washings (Mine Tailings)	Washing textiles
Washington House	
Washington (Tyne and Wear)	
Water-wheels	
Weaving	

NB: Compound names should be treated as one word.

Computer word processor programmes tend to have their own rules for sorting, although the programme used to prepare this text sorts the main list using word by word.

The word THE is not normally alphabetized except when it is part of the title. For example, The Stock Exchange or *The Sinking of the Titanic*. Common practice does, however, seem to be tending towards missing out 'The' altogether unless it fails to make sense.

CHAPTER NINE

ORAL HISTORY ON VIDEO

The ubiquity of camcorders with their instant synchronized sound has enormous appeal to the average person – it is so easy to record family holidays or the children growing up. It is therefore tempting to assume that recording oral history on video is also relatively easy. That, however, is simply not the case. Recording oral history is in a different league and usually needs more than one person to be involved because of the technology concerned.

There have been numerous community projects where video has been used to record what has been accepted as being good oral history by the participants. Many of these projects are team-based, consisting of short sequences edited together to form a running programme. It is not intended to belittle such enterprising projects – there are some excellent productions around – but for many reasons they are failing to record true oral history – they are being too selective. Those selections are the result of editing, often on a team basis, of what looks and sounds good on the screen – not on what is important, or accurate. The most significant statement in an hour-long interview might well sound boring on television but is crucial to the oral historian.[1]

Understandably, video work is based on well-established television techniques. While this approach is not in question as a mass end product it is simply not good enough for the demands of posterity, and new approaches need to be adopted.

AUDIO v. VIDEO

Why use video at all? Superficially, the arguments for using video against audio recording are overwhelming. There on the screen is the image of the person talking. The facial expressions, the body language – it is all there. There are, however, arguments for and against. It is not unreasonable to argue that there is a case for using both methods in a complementary manner or, as some oral historians have done, using the original audio interviews as a basis for an edited conventional television production.

Audio is relatively cheap; it is discreet and can be undertaken on a personal one-to-one basis; anonymity of the informant is maintained; and does not necessarily need a team effort. The quality of modern audio is at least as good as that obtainable from compact discs and is considerably easier and cheaper to use than video.

Video records the face, body language and location, but generally needs a team effort. It is considerably more expensive and complex to set up, the equipment is larger and often requires access to a vehicle to transport to site. The anonymity of the informant is difficult to achieve and the presence of a TV camera is so daunting to some informants that it can and often does modify their responses in such situations. Some informants, particularly very elderly, frail people, regard video as too intrusive and daunting and will not allow themselves to be recorded. Institutions such as hospices for the terminally ill may allow an audio machine but would be very concerned at the potential disruption of a video-camera, however considerate the interviewer or team may be.

Video produces a more saleable product than audio and has the advantage (or disadvantage, according to the point of view) in an image-orientated society of being accepted without question. It is also a medium that satisfies potential backers as television is more familiar than audio and is deemed to have some artistic merit or entertainment value.

METHODOLOGY

There are many difficulties to overcome in devising a working method for videoing oral history. The rudeness and generally cavalier attitude of people working in television is one of those difficulties. Oral history interviewing is personal, often intimate and for some informants, a major social occasion. The video-camera intrudes and should be seen as a technologically advanced notebook – simply, a tool.

The objective is to record as accurately as possible the memories and reminiscences of an informant – not just something that would make 'good television', or a 'great talking head', or 'Ask about the blitz – we have pictures of that'. The primary objective, as in audio oral history, must be the complete informal conversation.

Interviewing is, admittedly, an artificial extension of 'the informal conversation' but the target should be just that: as far as possible an informal conversation. It follows, therefore, that video (and indeed audio too) should be as unobtrusive as possible.

EQUIPMENT

Any camcorder that is either Hi-8, Super-VHS or one of the new digital DV cameras will do. The camcorder must have a facility allowing a separate microphone to be attached directly to the camera. It should also be possible to set either automatically or manually the white balance of the camera to match the colour temperature of the lighting being used. It is essential that the focus can also be manually operated; autofocus, although useful for following live action subjects, has little place in an interview situation.

The old 8mm video and VHS are simply not good enough quality for serious oral history work. Access to Betacam professional or similar is preferred, but this is a very different order of cost. It may, however, be reasonable to hire such a camera (and operator) if the occasion is worthwhile.

The success of the BBC2 series *Video Nation* where people are invited to record their comments and opinions on their camcorders for transmission illustrates just how far the technology has come and what it is capable of. The set-ups are straightforward, often without any additional lighting. The latest generation of digital video camcorders will offer even better technical quality.

The introduction of sub-miniature television cameras of the type used in surveillance in programmes such as the *Cook Report* or which take the viewer on a death-defying journey in a Formula One car, may have an application in oral history recording. The cameras are so discreet they can be hidden in handbags, clocks, toys, briefcases and other unsuspected items. Usually the mechanism – the recording end – is quite separate to the lens end and is connected either by cable or radio link. The picture quality is getting better even at low light levels and should be considered seriously as a tool for the video oral historian.

A sub-miniature camera hidden in, say, a handbag or briefcase could placed on a table in front of the informant. Another approach is to place the camera optics discreetly alongside the interviewer so that the person in effect, looks directly to camera. This has the advantage of presenting a more intimate image of the informant, a situation very difficult to achieve with a camcorder sitting rather obviously on a tripod in full vision. Another advantage is that the interview can be undertaken by a single person much as in audio recording.

It is unacceptable and unethical to record without the person's knowledge and some suitable form of words needs to be used to ensure the person is aware of the camera. Lighting is also a consideration. Professional crews use powerful twin Photon Beard Red Heads/Blondes or their equivalent giving 800–2000 w per lamp even for simple interview situations. Although these lights can be hired and may be necessary for large areas, the main aim is to light informants in as sympathetic a way as possible without blinding them. Remember the rule – be as unobtrusive as possible.

There is a fundamental difference between professional television and oral history video-recording. Professionals like to use lots of light in a controlled way. They have access to large amounts of often expensive lighting kit and they use it. Oral history takes the opposite approach. Keep adding light until there is sufficient for the camcorder to record an adequate image of the informant. The background is secondary as long as it is not obtrusive.

Dependent, of course, on the time of year, use what light is already available. First of all there are domestic lights that can be switched on. Remember, though, all this electricity is going on someone's electricity bill. Some of the more powerful lighting units use almost as much power as electric fires and that order of cost is a serious consideration for some elderly people. It may be appropriate to offer a one-off payment towards their bill if several long sessions are involved.

There are often table lamps, main house lights and wall lights available. These all help light the scene. Useful and relatively inexpensive purchases might include a couple of desk lamps, and floor spotlights – the adjustable type attached to a vertical rod embedded in a floor stand. For more powerful continuous lighting investment should be made in the kind of lighting used by some still portrait photographers, provided by the Photax company. This tungsten-based lighting is not as powerful as Photon Beard Redheads but it is far cheaper to purchase and is actually recommended by the manufacturers as a continuous light source for video work.

Lighting sources can also be used in association with reflectors. There is now a wide variety of both coloured and white-surfaced reflectors available as fill-ins either from daylight or artificial light sources. The reflectors are available from professional photographic suppliers.

Overrun tungsten lights such as photoflood bulbs also give a brighter output but are considerably hotter than ordinary bulbs and care has to be taken in using them in domestic lighting fitments. They can, for example, melt or set fire to plastic fitments such as shades. Strip lights are more of a problem and can cause strobing effects and cast a greenish light and are best left off. Quartz lights that sit on the front of cameras providing an instant bright light are unsuitable for static oral history work as they blind the interviewee.[2]

On the audio side the minimum requirement is a pair of tie-clip microphones of the type used in audio oral history. If the camera does not have a separate stereo input for the microphones then they will need to be fed through a simple sound mixing unit and then fed into the mono microphone input on the camera. A mixer also offers the opportunity to listen to the sound on headphones and check that all is well before recording takes place. Sound inputs on to camera are often poor 3.5mm jack plugs or phono plugs. Care has to be taken to ensure that the microphone cables are not jerked out during recording. It is easy to do, as the author knows only too well!

Other microphone possibilities include directional microphones on gooseneck stands near the informant and well away from the noise of the camera. On-camera directional microphones are fine with quiet cameras when the camera is close to the informant. The interviewer's voice will, of course, be off-mike and lower in volume.

Tripods are essential to ensure a steady image especially over long periods. Ensure they are the type that have rubber caps on the feet. People do not appreciate holes made by tripods in their best rugs.

Additional equipment should include headphones, carrying cases, fuses, screwdrivers, extension leads, circuit-breakers, gaffer tape for fastening down cables, spare tapes, spare battery packs as appropriate, close-up attachments, stick mikes with wind-shields for outdoor use, and a vehicle to convey it all!

PREPARING THE QUESTIONS

Question preparation is exactly the same as preparing questions for an audio interview. Television journalists in particular discuss the topic thoroughly with the informant and then, because of the constraints of time, limit themselves to perhaps no more than half a dozen questions. They may even 'direct' how replies are given. For example, the reporter might say: 'When I ask if it was your own idea, I want you to tell me about the project. I'm not really interested in the rest.'

This kind of directed reporting has no place in oral history interviewing. Interviews should run for as long as it takes – possibly up to an hour or more. Answers, as in audio oral history, must never be implied – let people be themselves. The spontaneity of reply is one of the key differences between mass television approach and oral history approach.

A clipboard is a useful accessory for holding the question sheet.

PREPARATIONS FOR RECORDING

Having said it is unwise to discuss questions with the informant before the interview because of the risk of destroying the spontaneity of the reply, there is a case for interviewers to introduce themselves to the person they intend to interview. If a previous audio oral history recording has been completed then that introduction and its resultant friendship and trust should be intact. The interviewee will see the interviewer as a point of contact and a controlling influence throughout the mêlée of video-recording. That continuity is extremely important, especially with elderly people in whose home the interviewer and video team are guests.

During the pre-visit it should be explained fully what will happen. Avoid giving too much away about the questions and if asked directly say something like, 'Oh I've not quite completed my list of questions yet — but I'd like to chat about your childhood memories — school-days, things like that.' Keep it vague.

The visit will allow time to work out where the camera should be positioned in relationship to the interviewee. Look for potential lighting problems, such as archaic electricity sockets. Ask if he or she minds moving a chair slightly — if so, well that is his or her privilege and it may be necessary on the day to work round it.

Lighting the Scene

Remember to use natural light as much as possible — think windows and heated conservatories in the winter, the garden, back porch, conservatories, etc., in the summer. Try to avoid a camera position in which the subject is in front of a brilliantly sunlit window. It is far better to place the interviewee to one side and use natural daylight with a fill-in lamp from the side. Light the subject not the interviewer, who is not important in lighting terms. The golden rule is — keep it simple.

RECORDING THE INTERVIEW

As the interviewer, arrive early and talk the interviewee through what is going to happen. Reassure him or her if necessary.

Many people will want to respond by putting on their Sunday best. If that is what they want to do, fine. The priority for the oral historian is not the screen image as in conventional mainstream television; it is the conversation. The application of theatrical make-up in oral history video interviews is overkill. It is unnecessary.

Timing of the interview is important. If natural light is being used the time of day and therefore direction of light can be crucial. Just before lunch is a good time to start recording before the sun reaches its azimuth and people are beginning to feel peckish. After lunch, the sun is lower in the sky and, for at least the first hour after eating, being interviewed is probably the last thing most people want to do.

If the interview session is a long one, there will inevitably be breaks for the toilet or for a cup of tea. These are opportunities to change the camera position slightly according to the available light or to vary the focal length of the lens on the camera, making it a little more wide angled or close up as appropriate. It is also an opportunity to simply switch off the lights and let things cool down for a few minutes.

Inevitably during this down-time the informant will talk about things you know should be on camera. Say something like 'Please don't tell me now, tell me in a few minutes when we've had a cuppa.' Then prompt with something like 'You were just saying during the break about smashing windows when you were a boy. Tell me again.'

Extraneous noise is always a problem. The bottom line is whether or not the conversation is intelligible. If it is, then off-camera sounds are simply part of the contemporary environment and might well be of interest in their own right to future researchers.

Set up the camera on a tripod or other firm base. The convention in mass television is to fill the screen with an interesting image. The result is that there tends to be either a head and shoulders view or a close-up of the face. This approach is fine as long as there is a separate camera operator. There are no rules – just conventions – so it is quite acceptable for oral history work to use a wider angle and include the whole of the person and possibly even the interviewer in shot alongside the informant. A great deal depends on the location, lighting, and so on.

When the camera is set up on a static tripod without operator and is set to record the interviewee's face or head and shoulders, a problem arises immediately if the person moves forward or sideways. Pictures in telephoto have little depth of field, a phenomenon that occurs with all lenses, but is especially noticeable when used in this way. The actual plane of sharpness is quite small in telephoto; it is affected by the aperture being used in the camera. The more light there is, the smaller the effective aperture can be, resulting in greater depth of field. This is one of the reasons why television studios are so bright.

The wider the angle of view used on a zoom lens, the greater the depth of field or zone of sharpness. That is why, as was discussed above, it is acceptable to use a wide angle approach rather than a close telephoto approach. Also, when shooting live action out of doors – such as following someone around – it makes sense to stay in wide angle until circumstances dictate otherwise.

Therefore, because the primary consideration in oral history is the capture of knowledge and experience, the normal priority of bright illumination for good depth of field and saturated colour must take second place. In setting up the camera lens ask the interviewee to answer a couple of test questions. This will allow an assessment to be made of the likely position (distance from camera) the informant will assume. Zoom in on the informant and focus on the eyes. Then zoom out to an appropriate wide angle. If for any reason it is necessary during the interview to zoom in closer, the shot is likely to remain in focus.

The height of the camera in relationship to the informant, the eye-line, is also important, although mainly for aesthetic reasons. The camera height should be roughly level with the eyes of the informant.

The composition of the picture should be viewed carefully through the camera viewfinder or monitor. While a carefully composed and lit picture would be an advantage, it is not essential for oral history work where to some extent the camera is recording contemporary situations as they are – not how a television producer would like them to be. Having made that statement it is nevertheless important to avoid such things as flowers appearing to grow out of someone's ear or standard lamps projecting from the top of someone's head. The scene should also be checked for flare from lights and other reflective surfaces.

During the setting-up process the interviewer should take on the role of reassuring the informant. On a pre-arranged signal from the camera-operator, the camera (after a test recording has been made and checked) will roll. A tip given to me by a friend who used to be a foreign correspondent for the BBC is to cover up any tell-tale red lights or signals on the camera that would tell interviewees the camera is running. In other words they should be unaware that the camera is rolling, much as they would be unaware that recording has begun in audio work.

The conversation might begin with something like 'Tell me a little about your childhood. Where were you born?' And, as in audio work, the interview is under way. Eye contact must be maintained with the informant. This is far more difficult to achieve in video than in audio because of constraints such as the position of lights and camera. The position of the interviewer is therefore restricted but the interviewee should be able to see that person clearly and not be blinded by lights.

Identification of individual takes should be on audio rather than the intrusive clapper board. For example, the interviewer might say 'Right, now this is the second session, I want to explore with you your memories as a farmhand.'

End the interview as in audio, and always thank the informant on tape.

VIDEO-RECORDING ON THE MOVE

Examples of this approach include someone walking through a neighbourhood pointing out buildings and insignificant features such as iron rings in the wall that trigger memories. For example, a recording was made in a complex of vent tunnels beneath a glass cone in a glass works in St Helens. The use of colour to identify different flue products and temperatures, as well as live discussion among the experts present, allowed a technical and detailed understanding to take place.

The interiors of buildings can also be interpreted using video in this way. There are, of course, lighting problems and here the quartz camera-mounted light plays its part. Keep in wide angle shot as much as possible to retain maximum sharpness of image. Use a stick microphone with a good wind-shield to record the sound. It is possible to go to extremes and mount microphones on fish-poles placing the microphone overhead, although this is largely unnecessary for oral history work. If the subject is kept within, say, ten feet of the camera a hand-held or directional microphone plugged into the camera is usually adequate. In noisy locations simply hold the microphone closer to the informant's mouth, as in audio recording. Seeing the interviewer in shot is perfectly acceptable.

Avoid zooming in and out. In long takes, hand-holding the camera can become exhaustive and unsteady, so lean against a wall or other support.

Continuity, Reverses and Cut-aways
Continuity is important for mainstream television, but less so for oral history work. Static indoor scenes in oral history recording are likely to be long-running with few changes.

The camera-recorded video-tape is likely to be sequential, but continuity becomes more significant when working from a master tape (a copy of the camera tape) for edited productions.

Every interview should have what is known as an establishing shot, a practice older film-makers always used but which today is largely ignored. An establishing shot places the interview location in context. In the case of an interview in someone's front room, take an establishing shot of the outside of the house, including street and garden. Establishing shots should be recorded or placed at the beginning of every interview sequence whether in or out of doors.

One difficulty that can arise is when an informant refers to a photograph or small object or perhaps a distant building or place. Make notes of such cut-aways during the interview and record them separately on the end of the video-tape, identifying them using the audio track.

Reverses

Reverses are scenes shot in a single camera situation after the interview has been completed. An assistant notes the actual questions asked and the interviewer records the questions on camera. It is important to get the axis and camera and lighting angle correct for reverses, the camera being in place of the interviewee looking back towards the position of the interviewer. Purists will insist on this approach to break up what in conventional television terms may be seen as boring. However, in practical terms, it may be easier for the interviewer to record a piece to camera on the end of the completed video-tape briefly introducing him- or herself and adding any comments about context and the informant's background, including copyright ownership, for the benefit of subsequent researchers.

If a copy of the interview is sent to the informant as a keepsake it may, of course, be prudent not to include very personal observations and background notes.

There are perhaps more moral issues to address in video oral history than in audio. If a situation arises where a particularly disturbing event is recalled and the person being interviewed is clearly distressed and perhaps begins to cry – should the interview be stopped? There are many people in television who think that a crying person makes 'good television' and that it is not unreasonable to continue. The interviewee has accepted the situation of having cameras and lights and should expect difficult questions to be asked. The nature of this kind of personal intrusion is far more pronounced than it is in audio and a serious value judgement should be made on the spot. Wait for 30 seconds to a minute with the camera running and then ask if the informant wishes to continue. The informant has the option on the clearance note of not releasing that section of the recording to the public and this should be pointed out to him or her.

When the recording session has been completed it is usual to ask the informant for permission to release the tape. There is a well-established practice in oral history, but, as video has a much greater potential for subsequent use and abuse the clearance note should reflect this. An example of a combined audio/video clearance note is given in Appendix Four.

CARING FOR THE RECORDING

The recording made in the camera should be regarded as sacrosanct and the greatest care taken in its preservation and use. Copy the camera tape over (warts and all) on to a Hi-band U-matic, digital or larger format video system with a pulse track added. The latest professional studio systems allow the camera recordings to be dropped directly on to computers for manipulation and editing. This feature will soon be possible for home or community use. The latest top-of-the-range digital camcorders have an output known as a Firewire intended for direct transfer to computer for in-computer editing and compilation. Whichever system is used, analogue or digital, it effectively releases the original camera copy for preservation in an archive. Once the raw state camera copy has been transferred to computer it should be copied across on to another storage medium, thus giving a second security copy.

The original camera-recording should be stored in a separate location to the analogue or digitally generated camera copy tape so that in the event of fire, theft or plain accident one copy will survive. There is also a very good case for preserving any edited master tapes in the same manner.

Tape is a relatively unstable long-term storage medium. New technologies are arriving which will eventually do away with tape; for example, Mini-disc video systems are currently under trial for domestic camcorders. This rapid change in technology will create difficulties for video archivists in the future as re-writable optical storage systems take over. There will be a very good case for not just preserving the original camera-recording but also play-back equipment (including computers?) of the same vintage.

SUMMARY

- Record a conventional oral history interview first, with a video camera present. Consider whether audio would be better than video or vice versa.
- Check the room before recording (electricity supply, natural lighting, camera position, etc.).
- Build up trust between the interviewer and interviewee. Keep in contact with the informant; tell him or her what is happening.
- Do not give too many details of the questions in advance.
- Use natural lighting where possible.
- Minimize the inconvenience.
- Use low-power tungsten lighting. Do not shine lights directly into the informant's eyes. It is important to retain eye contact throughout the interview, just as in audio interviewing.
- The informant should look at the interviewer not the camera.
- Take your time – do not be dictated to by the technology. It is there as a tool and for no other reason. There should be no commercial pressures or time constraints.
- Unlike conventional television, the interviewer is the person in charge, not a remote producer or the team as a democratic whole. On the day it is the interviewer's responsibility not only to get it right, but also to orchestrate events.

- Always include an establishing shot before any interview, indoors or outdoors. It gives the interview location a context.
- Always thank the interviewee on tape.
- Try to supply a copy of the camera-recording as a thank-you keepsake.
- Clearance of recording. Spend time, if necessary on a completely separate occasion, going over the clearance note. Point out how the material might be used, especially if there is a commercial potential in the pictures. If necessary, work with the interviewee to produce a joint document that satisfies both parties. Respect his or her right to say no. If a commercial use does arise it might well be appropriate at that point to enter a formal contract.
- Take great care with the original camera-recordings. Preserve them in an archive along with question sheets and other notes. Store master tapes and originals in separate buildings to ensure something survives in the event of disaster.

Finally, it must by now be apparent that video oral history done properly is technically far more difficult and demanding than audio-recording. It is also far more time-consuming and expensive and should be seen as complementing audio oral history rather than supplanting it.

VIDEO DIARIES

Various television programmes, particularly BBC2's *Video Nation* series, have featured the edited highlights of so-called video diaries. Video record is perhaps a more accurate term – for keeping a record on a daily basis, as the term diary would imply, is not necessarily a feature of such recordings. There are several forms of presentation made to camera in video diary work and it raises the question as to what extent such accounts are truly oral history.

The following examples will illustrate the point.

Example one. A women sits in a lonely croft in the north of Scotland. She talks about her opinions of the world and strongly about the government's newly introduced policy on immigration control.

Is this oral history? She is talking about contemporary issues and expressing deeply personal opinions not necessarily based on her own life experience. It is dangerous to accept such isolated opinion as oral history evidence without details or social markers and background information on the person. It is perhaps marginal oral history, but good television.

Example two. A man travels on his own across the ice to the South Pole. He takes with him a camcorder and religiously every day records a report into the camcorder about his progress, his feelings and experiences.

Is this oral history? It is a man recalling his life experience and memory (albeit very recent). Yes, it is therefore oral history – but perhaps boring television.

Example three. A man walks with a camcorder around a now-derelict cottage, once his childhood home. He talks about his home life, his parents; he identifies where the bedroom used to be, where furniture was situated; and points out features in the garden such as the well where they drew the water.

Is this oral history? Yes, he is recalling childhood memory, not with the use of a question sheet but by the building acting as a catalyst for recollection. In audio terms the oral history interview would need to include photographs taken to allow identification of the features being described.

Example four. An elderly woman recalls her life in a series of separate reports to camera recorded over a long period of time in her own home. She writes out a rough script and reads it to camera.

Is this oral history? Yes, she is recalling her own life history and experience, albeit from a prompt script.

So what are the pros and cons of the Video Diary approach?

Advantages	Disadvantages
Instant visual recording of contemporary events	Image selection by the producer
Immediacy and spontaneous response	Scenes and words can be rehearsed and appear spontaneous
Allows free expression without the intervention of an interviewer	Cannot by quizzed by an interviewer
Can be recorded on a self-op basis over a long period of time	Technical limitations – e.g., lighting, battery duration
Can be kept as a family or public record	Uncertain longevity of video tape as an archival storage medium
It can be broadcast to a wider audience.	

CHAPTER TEN

USING ORAL HISTORY

The interviews have been recorded, catalogued and preserved. What next? Although some interviews will necessarily have closures or time restrictions placed on them, most interviews are likely to be available for public use. Funding agencies, interviewees and interviewers will wish, quite naturally, to see an end product of some kind. Although the point has been made elsewhere about rarely using original master tapes but rather copies, it is, nevertheless, worth repeating again. Copying is straightforward and 'mirror' quality copies are easy using digital technology.

So how can oral history recordings be used? Many practical suggestions for using oral history have already been outlined throughout the text in this work. Here are a few more detailed suggestions and applications.

1) EXHIBITIONS

Oral History and Sound in Displays and Exhibitions

In museum display terms, sound adds an important and all-too-often missing dimension to a display or exhibition. The use of sound, including oral history, is not well understood by exhibition planners and designers, for example – video systems playing next to sound replay systems is very common. Sound is much more versatile than most people imagine. It can actually be focussed or pooled, made to rise vertically or pass horizontally.

Money is often included in a budget for a video or tape-slide sequence, yet for a fraction of the production cost it would be possible not only to have interviews recorded but also playing at several positions in the gallery in one form or another. The video and tape-slide sequence do have their place, but when budgets are tight – as they nearly always are these days – money can be saved without compromising on quality by a little lateral thought.

When planning to use sound in an exhibition or display there are several factors to consider. Usually estimates are based on three components: sound production/preparation, replay equipment and installation. The cost of sound production is open-ended. It can cost relatively little or, if you employ a well-known actor, a great deal. Straightforward oral history recordings are, however, relatively cheap to produce, depending on how much editing and preparation is required on the copy tapes being used. A master tape is prepared by the studio and then transferred on to whatever replay system has been decided upon.

Some museums have combined the replay of oral history interviews with background sounds, or linked pieces of the programme together with scripted narration. Although the master tape is primarily required for the gallery's sound replay system, with some careful

Lord Hunt, leader of the successful 1953 Everest Expedition, listening to his recording of his experiences as an Indian Army Officer in the 1930s in the oral history room of the British Empire and Commonwealth Museum. (British Empire and Commonwealth Museum)

thought during production that same master could be used to produce a cassette tape available for purchase in the museum shop.

One of the difficulties present when using orally derived material is dialect or language. Recordings made of elderly people with strong dialect accents can be very difficult to understand. Similarly, foreign accents and cant language will not be readily understood by the average visitor. Who will actually listen to the recordings? Local accents are quite acceptable when the visitor is local. Museums and heritage sites with foreign visitors may have to be more selective about which sound-bites are used to ensure they are understood. The less satisfactory alternative is labelling or short printed extracts in English or other languages.

Despite those obvious difficulties, oral history extracts work well in museums and heritage centres and give an authentic feel to the place. Oral history also works well out of doors too, although very few attempts seem to have been made to use it in this way. In Chapter five mention was made of a canal boat being left high and dry after a canal breached in the 1930s. The area is now a country park. An outdoor replay unit with an interpretative panel operated by presence detector would give instant replay of an eye-witness account.

Not very long ago there was really only one kind of replay equipment available for heavy long-term use in museums and galleries: the tape loop. There were various manufacturers, the most popular being the Reditronics Message Repeater, a reliable workhorse. These machines relied on endless tape loops in a sealed cartridge, but sadly these machines are no longer manufactured and the special thickness lubricated tape is becoming harder to find. Broadcast quality tape loop machines are, however, in regular use, not in the heritage world but in theatres for spot sound effects and in radio stations for Station Idens, commercials, jingles and links. A direct consequence of this is that tape loop machines are aimed at the broadcast end of the market and are now expensive items.

Tape is, however, not quite dead and gone. Cassette-based systems are used extensively by various companies who offer tape guides to visitors in stately homes, castles and country houses. Visitors hire the cassette-players and carry them from location to location listening to the soundtrack which can offer exciting and realistic interpretations of a site. Their principal advantage is that they can be used where it would be difficult to employ other forms of sound reproduction; they are private, require no installation (except the re-charging racks) and are particularly suited to sight-impaired users.

Technology has, however, moved on from tape giving two other alternatives, namely Solid State or EPROM-based systems, and compact disc. The chip-based systems are widely used in industry from floor messages in lifts to aircraft system messages for aircrew. In the heritage world solid state systems are becoming increasingly popular for short messages, particularly where hi-fi quality is not paramount. The basic systems offer telephone quality sound which is adequate for many straightforward messages. The more elaborate systems offer better quality sound and longer running time, but at a price. At, say, 5–10 minutes of chip sound it rapidly becomes more economic to think about compact disc as a cost-effective alternative.

The chip-based systems have no moving parts to go wrong, nor do they require tape heads and pinch rollers to be cleaned at regular intervals. They do fail occasionally and it is physically possible to accidentally wipe the recordings from the chip if you try hard enough – but then it is also possible to erase tapes and break CDs.

The CD-based system, as everyone knows, gives consistent superb quality sound reproduction. Indeed it is the only way in exhibitions to reproduce some sounds such as birdsong or the shrill screams of bats, but for oral history use its principal advantage is its long running time of approximately 72 minutes on commercially available CDs – far in excess of tape loops. Solid state chip-based systems are simply not economically viable at such durations and quality of reproduction, at the present time.

Because of the way that CDs work it is possible to produce them so that they control other equipment such as lights, or a slide projector. Some museums, for example Berwick-on-Tweed, have used them to switch sound around in a gallery from one hidden location to another. The recording of the programme and the setting up of the system relies on close co-operation between the sound engineer, audio engineer and museum curator.

Once the replay equipment is in place and the recording is ready to be played back, you need to decide on the best method. Here again there are some interesting choices available. Mention has already been made of the use of loudspeakers in museums. Speakers can be hidden safely among, for example, room settings, or installed in such a way that the sound – particularly from compact disc – can actually be focused and steered precisely to head height, thus zoning speech to key areas. Using speakers allows sound to be zoomed up or down, left or right, indeed anywhere within a confined space. At Clitheroe Castle special all-weather hi-fi speakers were used with quadraphonic sound to represent a ghost telling the story of the castle keep drifting around effortlessly within the interior space of the keep.

Some systems replay the sound from the replay machines into special infra-red transmitter units which are installed on the ceiling above a particular display or at some other convenient point. Regarded as a light bulb, the light is emitted and received by a special headphone or wand-handset used by the visitor. They are reliable systems, really only prone to interference by natural daylight infra-red, their principal disadvantage being their very high purchase cost.

Oral history recordings about canal horses can be heard on handsets at the Horses and Ponies Protection Association Museum in Burnley. (Author)

In radio transmission systems the sound signal is transmitted on a licensed frequency, or frequencies, and the signal is picked up again on special headphones or hand-held wands. They are occasionally prone to interference in city areas, but can offer several different frequencies, say for an additional language or soundtrack. Again such systems are expensive and need regular maintenance under the terms of the licence.

Induction loop systems are another way to transmit sounds. The signal is fed into a special loop of wire, hidden usually on the floor or ceiling of a gallery. While people are in the loop area listening on special headphones or wands they will hear the soundtrack. The system can be installed so that the hearing-impaired, using the T-setting of a hearing aid, can also receive the sound via their existing hearing equipment. Induction loop systems work particularly well on archaeological sites where the cables can be buried under a simple gravel cover without detriment to the excavation.

One of the most popular ways of listening to oral history recordings is by telephone handset. Traditional experiments have shown that most people do not listen to sound for more than about a minute, unless it is a declaration of war. In western society in particular, people today are visually orientated rather than sound orientated, but that does not in any way invalidate the use of sound. Sometimes a minute is all that is needed. In some museums they have taken the view that the visitor can dip into a running soundtrack, listen to as much as they wish and then replace the handset. An experiment conducted at Towneley Hall Museum and Art Gallery during a temporary exhibition showed that if the presentation of the idea of using oral history interviews is done correctly, people will sit and listen to the recording for anything up to 45 minutes, some even returning several times to hear it through.

At Hitchen Museum they have developed an interactive console in their social history gallery featuring the memories of four local people. The recordings are replayed through a commercial system known as Babelbox. The unit can be programmed to store up to four recordings of up to two minutes' duration which can be changed according to future needs. The console is being built by the museum's technician. Other similar solid state systems are available and it is possible to extend running times as finance permits.

2) ACADEMIC RESEARCH

Oral history is a rich source of information for the researcher, particularly in areas where written or manuscript evidence is sparse. Most curators record oral history because they recognize that the oral source is likely to be the main one available about a particular subject, and that is reason enough. Others record because they recognize the importance of community history and the fact that ordinary people can participate.

The great temptation is to use oral history for simply taking a few notes, then wipe the tapes. Others have painstakingly transcribed the tapes and then wiped the cassettes, thus destroying a primary source of potentially historical evidence. The validity of oral history compared with newspapers, manuscripts, documents and photographs, has been dealt with elsewhere, but there still remains a reluctance to use oral history techniques in certain quarters simply because it is oral and not indelibly written down somewhere. This attitude, prominent among some academics a decade ago, is slowly being redressed as in the light of experience traditional archives and other sources of information are re-examined in relation to the oral evidence now being accumulated.

So how can heritage professionals utilize the academic possibilities of oral history recordings in their care? Some museums have established their own specialized sound archive departments housing large collections of material. The Imperial War Museum has extensive oral history collections in the Department of Sound Records; St Fagans at the National Museum of Wales has recorded the Welsh language and culture for many years; and in more recent times the Bradford Heritage Recording and Kirklees Sound Archive at Batley Museum has actively been recording in Yorkshire. Across the Pennines the North West Sound Archive was developed at the Manchester Museum before acquiring its own premises, and there are other smaller collections of material held by museums, libraries and record offices from Shetland to the Channel Islands. Some organizations have gone further and operate loan collections or recordings to accompany school loans; others such as the Imperial War Museum have produced tape-cassettes for sale. Other than the primary research required by museums and to some extent record offices, the collections tend to be used mainly by students, researchers and writers.

Listening to interviews done by the Bradford Heritage Recording Unit. The tapes are accessible through the library service. (Tim Smith, Bradford Heritage Recording Unit)

Other less obvious semi-academic uses of recorded material include research for radio and television. Local radio in particular will use good quality copies (never lend the original) and television, too, will request oral history tapes from time to time. My own work, for example, has been used on national News, *Newsnight*, *Songs of Praise*, *Horizon*, *World in Action* and many other programmes. *Coronation Street* has 'borrowed' from time to time story-lines from oral history recordings held by the North West Sound Archive.

3) PUBLICATION

In the early days of oral history, publication was virtually impossible. Few of the mainstream publishers were interested. The work tended to be local and had little to offer the wider commercial market. The *Oral History Journal* was the only useful major outlet for quite a long time, but even here it was never practical to publish complete works.

The will to publish in book form was, however, too great to be extinguished and as oral history began to be funded, particularly by the Government Manpower Service Schemes, publications began to appear. Another group that funded local publications, in full or in part, were libraries, who had always identified local studies as a professional activity. Museums and archives also played their role, but really it was not until Paul Thompson's book on oral history *The Voice of the Past*, published by Penguin in 1978, that oral history publication started to become the norm. Groups such as the Federation of Worker Writers and Community Publishers (1976) actively represented the interests of members who ranged from working-class writers through to local history and ethnic minority groups.[1]

Many organizations soon followed. In fact there were so many it is impossible to give more than the briefest of examples. Age Exchange, based in London, was one of these, publishing work on wartime evacuees, and the recollections of older Londoners who lived and worked on the River Thames.

The use of recollection was not new to publishing, of course. There are many publications based on local reminiscence and even some commercial magazines such as *The Dalesman*, which rely heavily on memories of the past. Publishing reminiscence material is not new but it is, and was, always highly selective and editorialized.

There is an onus on heritage professionals to ensure that the material they publish is as accurate as possible. The very fact that the publication will be selective and edited will, for pure researchers, invalidate the material to some extent, and they will always require access to the original recording and/or transcript. The printed word is never a true substitute for the recording.

However, for most non-academic purposes, school use and general readership, it is reasonable to compile an oral history based on selection. Publication also has the advantage of encouraging others to come forward with their own memories and reminiscences, photographs, objects and documents. There is also the advantage that illustrations can be included to explain difficult text, such as a drawing made up by the skipper of a fishing boat showing the boat's layout and the way it operated when trawling.

Photographs of the informants can be included in the publication, as well as old photographs and complementary documentary material, along with a bibliography and index.

4) DRAMA PRODUCTION

Oral history interviews have been used to create scripts for dramatic productions with sometimes extraordinary results. Some years ago a project involving oral history was set up using unemployed youngsters from Merseyside. Many of the youngsters were fairly wild in their behaviour. Full of bravado they set out recording interviews with the local elderly people who had volunteered their services.

The tapes were transcribed and made into a play and the elderly people who had taken part in the project were invited to the performance. One of the interviews had been with a First World War veteran who had lost several friends in the trenches. As the sequence of 'going-over-the-top' was re-enacted, the old man started to cry. The atmosphere was so charged and emotional that the performance spontaneously stopped and there were tears in the eyes of those present. The effect of that production was to create a long-term relationship between the old man and the youngsters; indeed they became very protective towards him. Oral history certainly has its place.

Another example, this time from the United States, was the Warner Women's Oral History Project from New Hampshire who produced a performance entitled 'It had to be done, so I did it'. The production was based on sixty interviews with women living in rural communities recorded in the 1980s and consisted of a series of readings and sketches chronicling their experiences.[2]

Age Exchange based in Blackheath Village in London works with a Reminiscence Theatre Company who perform plays based on the memories of older people. They operate a booking service, and their plays are performed in libraries, schools, community centres, retirement homes and theatres. Their past productions have included 'What did you do in the war, Mum?', 'Routes – memories of immigrants from India', and 'When the lights go on again' – memories of the end of the Second World War. There are also special workshops in which actors, children and older people explore memories and their dramatic potential.

In the museum world, at the London Transport Museum actors are employed as actor-interpreters to work alongside an exhibition called 'Women in London Transport'. The scripts of the two characters, a 1950s ticket audit assistant and a 1960s canteen assistant, were written using oral testimony where possible. Oral history also provided background information and gave the actors an historical perspective.

5) REMINISCENCE WORK

Reminiscence work has already been covered in some detail in Chapter four. However the application of oral history techniques is worth mentioning. Professional carers can use oral history interviewing skills very effectively with the elderly, particularly the 'why, which, when, where, what, who and how' questioning technique, alongside other prompts such as the smell of perfumes and spices, creative writing about the past, drama, music, sounds, photographs, even video-tapes of local places such as shops, or visits to beauty spots and buildings. Some museums and libraries have ventured down the road of reminiscence work but, generally speaking, it is an area often best left to trained reminiscence workers and professional carers.

Having said that, there are exceptions to every rule and oral history has been used successfully with the terminally ill, not by the carers but using an oral historian to superb effect. The very fact that the memories were to be 'preserved for posterity by an official body' changed the rules of engagement as it were and it was possible to record the most intimate of information.

At the request of a hospice I recorded several interviews with a man who had led what seemed to him to be a very ordinary mundane life. In fact his life proved to be anything but ordinary as he revealed how he had travelled around in his youth as a journeyman carpenter repairing barns, gates and farm buildings. He had made a very thoughtful decision that he wanted to leave a record of his life as a kind of memorial for his family, as well as leaving a record for future generations. The psychological lift it gave him had to be seen to be believed: he felt valued and his life had a sense of purpose and direction.

The use of memory for therapeutic purposes is, of course, not the exclusive right of the oral historian. In 1995 at St Barnabas Hospice in Worthing, writer Jennie Fontana and visual artist Heather Hodgson worked with two terminally ill patients. They produced a painting entitled 'Blowing a Lapwing's Egg' which was directly based on one of the patient's recollections of her father's chemist shop.[3]

There is, of course, an additional important role for museum curators, librarians and archivists as providers. The reminiscence worker needs basic materials to work with, such as simple (and replaceable) household objects, copies of photographs and a historic framework in which to utilize these things effectively. Curators, perhaps in association with local history librarians and archivists, could arrange seminars for carers, giving a brief outline of important local events, objects, documents and other materials available for loan including oral history tapes.

6) USING ORAL HISTORY – NATIONAL CURRICULUM (HISTORY)

The National Curriculum (History) key stages one and two encouraged the use of oral history. Although the many reforms have weakened this approach, nevertheless teachers still use oral history in the classroom. Many primary schools in particular have developed school projects bringing elderly people into the classroom to talk to the children about the past.

Kirklees Sound Archive at Batley Museum, NW Sound Archive, the Imperial War Museum, National Sound Archive and others have all produced special oral history packs for school use. The Kirklees packs are exceptionally well produced, having been developed jointly with local teachers.

Museums with good school loan service collections can also include oral history tapes and transcripts in addition to their normal material. Rochdale Museum Service, for example, has included a tape of the sound of textile machines as well as reminiscences about cotton manufacturing.

7) RADIO BROADCASTING

In the early days of BBC local radio broadcasting there were many programmes which had oral history at their core. Oral history on commercial radio is not commonplace but certainly not unknown. One early series based on the memories and reminiscences of people who once lived and worked in Trafford Park, Manchester, was recorded and transmitted by Piccadilly Radio, Manchester, and still remains important and useful source material. In the USA, Vermont Historical Society and Woodsmoke Productions produced Green Mountain Chronicles and managed, with some difficulties, to get their oral history material transmitted on commercial stations. As in the UK, the problem was that few broadcasters wanted to transmit anything longer than a few minutes. This must have been frustrating for the original oral historians but it does, and can, provide good publicity for the project as well as generating income.

8) ORAL HISTORY AND ART

Although little is written on this subject, oral history – whether formally recorded on tape or by direct conversation – must have provided inspiration over the years for artists and sculptors. One such community-based project is the Salford Quays sculpture on the old docksite near the Manchester Ship Canal. The area is under considerable redevelopment, with multiplex cinemas, leisure facilities, high-quality housing, hotels, and the Lowry Centre – in honour of the Salford artist L.S. Lowry.

Salford Docks was the inland end of the Manchester Ship Canal and in its heyday was Britain's third busiest port employing over 3,000 people. Since the closure of the docks in the early 1970s, there was a feeling of loss among the local communities who had provided the labour force for the docks since the building of the Ship Canal in the 1890s.

The Salford Quays sculpture used oral history material partly to inspire the shape as a whole, and also as a basis for the illustrations and text on each of the steel panels. (Author)

Salford Quays Heritage Centre, who have long experience of recording oral history material relating to the docks, became involved in coordinating an art project undertaken by Ordsall Community Arts. The commission in 1996 by the Beefeater Restaurant and Pub situated at Salford Quays was 'to create a community-involved artwork which would stand as a tribute to the men and women who had worked on the docks'.

The designs for the sculpture were produced by a group of former dock workers. The sculpture by Noah Rose has four curved fins reminiscent of the shape of propellers and ship's hulls. Each of the steel panels carries 'snapshots from each contributor's life story on the docks'. For example, on the south-facing panel one docker recalls working down a hole shovelling sulphur:

. . . a horrible job . . . no breathing masks or goggles, tears in the eyes, everyone was crying, red faces . . . every time there was a spark below there was a fire. I got my hair burnt like a lot of others, and we used to lie on the floor until the fumes went.

Sketches, drawings and even poems are included on the panels. The basic concept, though, for the sculpture was to use the memories of those who had given so much of their lives to working on the docks.[4]

Artists have experimented directly using oral history in their work. Alison Marchant was commissioned to produce a new artwork called Time and Motion. The exhibition space was the disused area of a local cotton mill where she projected stark confrontational images of mill women on to a large roll of cotton fabric hung from a central beam.

A recording was made with a relative, Alice Slater, a former weaver, and her reminiscences were inter-cut with the sound of mill looms. Surrounding the screen was a collection of objects – remnants of former activity in the mill – shuttles, bobbins, oily rags, etc. In the words of the artist chalked on the floor, 'Drawing attention to a conventional, detrimental process (whereby history is made and perceived as novelty/nostalgia, and emptied of substance) objects and experiences undergo a movement, counteracting the stasis of a museum, to create a web of interacting forces'.

The work was further expanded in 1992 at Oldham Museum and Art Gallery when sixteen interviews with women workers were recorded for a similar installation inside a gallery space, entitled Tying the Threads.[5]

9) ORAL HISTORY ON THE INTERNET

The potential for publishing and exchanging information on the Internet is huge. In the USA, where access in many ways is easier, innumerable projects are making their results known across the world. Universities and other academic bodies have tended to lead the way, but now museums, archives, libraries and similar organizations, including, of course, individuals, have websites on all sorts of oral history work.

One way to use the Internet is as an effective publishing medium which costs relatively little to set up. Another way is information exchange, using e-mail and user groups which provide platforms for questions and open discussion. The creation of a website also acts as an international noticeboard for the activities of organizations and individuals. Slightly less obvious applications for oral history websites include research, publicity, public relations and advertising.

Some oral history projects have established websites which are basically information pages about their institutions or work in hand, while others have details or selections from interview transcriptions. More ambitious projects have combined both image and oral history, but the reception computer requires a sound card to be installed in order to hear the material.

The difficulty with oral history on the Net, especially if it is selective, is therefore its accuracy and trustworthiness. Many organizations present stories in the way they wish the information to be perceived for a variety of reasons including political objects and persuasiveness.

How is it possible to know the accuracy of material without access to the original? The value of access to complete interviews and transcripts along with other relevant background information cannot be emphasized enough. The Net allows almost anything into cyberspace whether it is pornography or propaganda. Certainly there have been pages purporting to be oral history which, on closer examination, have been there simply for political propaganda purposes. It may be a valid way of allowing the voice of a depressed minority to be heard, but it comes back to the same observation – how can its accuracy and authenticity be verified? Websites should therefore be regarded with some caution, as should all other sources of information.

Having questioned authenticity and accuracy of oral history material on the Net it would not seem unreasonable to question what controls exist, if any, on such things as copyright, moral rights, and the observation of closures or restrictions applied by informants. The lack of censorship on the Net and the possibility of exploitation of material retrieved from the Net has been the subject of considerable discussion in the United States. The Annual Conference of the Oral History Society of the United States in 1996 looked at the issue of oral history on the Net and in the words of the reviewer: 'It opens an ethical can of worms. . . . Can there be informed consent when interviewers and interviewees can barely imagine how their words may be taken up and used by a vast anonymous audience? How can archivists maintain copyright restrictions . . . and how will people obtain legal recourse if their stories are exploited?' (The obvious answer to which might be to not put anything other than basic project information and say a sound bite on the Net, with an invitation to contact the website address by e-mail, fax, telephone or letter.)[6]

A recent straightforward search for the keyword 'Oral History' brought a staggering return of thousands of references to the term. An examination of the pages soon reveals a preponderance of projects based in the United States. Page after page lists oral history programmes set up by universities, community education groups and societies. A few examples will suffice:

Community Development Corporation Oral History project, the rural African-American communities of Mississippi.
http://www.picced.org/advocacy/mace.htm

Skylighters. An Oral History of the 225th AAA Searchlight Battalion.
http://www.strandlab.com/225ths/belmont2.html

Oral history centers. Homepage at http://www.indiana.edu/~ohrc/centers.htm

Alaska and Polar regions Department of the Elmer E Rusmuson Library at the University of Alaska Fairbanks. Details of the extensive Oral History programme relating to Alaska.
http://www.uaf.edu/library/libweb/oralhist/home.html

National Library of Australia – Oral History interviews. Publications. 1144 bytes.
http://www.nla/gov.au/l/oh/conduct.html

National Library of Australia – Coming Oral History events towards Federation 2001.
http://www.nla.gov.au/l/oh/coming.html 1308 bytes.

Oral history of modern architecture. Interviews with the greatest architects of the twentieth century.
http://www.bookwire.com./Bookinfo.Title%24T000001217. 2473 bytes.

Institute of American Indian Studies – South Dakota Oral History Center

Oral history on science, space and technology. On-line catalogue.

Stirling speaks: Theodore Brandley Library Oral History of Stirling, USA

Preliminary list of presidential records & historical materials in the Ronald Reagan Library. White House staff exit interviews. http://gopher:nara.gov.70/0/inform/library/reagan/nlspart4.txt

Smithsonian oral and video history collections

Elvis Presley on-line. Contribute to 'the King's' Oral History (!)

As the Internet develops its potential as a contact medium for oral historians, it could be extremely useful. At the moment there are so many entries on the net that it is almost impossible to read them all and so it has become self-defeating. If other countries, such as developing nations, are to get a look in then there has to be some way of navigating through the current log-jam of information.

CD-ROMS

The use of CD-ROMS in home computer systems is now widespread and some organizations have developed interactive CD-ROMS primarily for use in the classroom or home situation. It is now technically possible to access inter-active CD-ROMS directly on the Internet and several institutions have gone down this road. However, the development cost of CD-ROM is still extremely high although, without doubt, it is an effective way to publish results and information.

The CD-ROM audio and visual approach has limitations for the serious oral historian and researcher and should be seen as an exciting way of discovering initial information about obscure projects across the world. Even if complete interviews and transcripts are included on the CD-ROMS or Website pages, they should be regarded with the same degree of suspicion as any other publication or information source. CD-ROMs are not a substitute for original recordings and transcripts, although extremely useful.

A number of organizations have started to publish Oral History on CD-ROM despite the cost. In Australia a CD-ROM has been published by Firmware Publishing and includes sixty-three stories in 450 pages of text. Ninety photographs illustrate the transcripts and in total there is about six hours of sound. The CD-ROM tells the story of how aboriginal people came to terms with white settlers and their alien culture. There are also photographs of the interviewees as well as maps and name search capability.[7]

ORAL HISTORY IN THE FUTURE

The usefulness of oral history as part of the heritage preservation process is obvious. Outside the UK the potential is even greater and the use of oral history is expanding rapidly. In countries where the oral culture is strong but under threat, oral history will come into its own not just as an information retrieval tool but also as an educational resource. What impact the Internet will have on oral history across the world remains to be seen. It may do much to remove conventional taboos about history and challenge established ideas about minorities. This is a global view, and it is important not to lose perspective that oral history is about personal memories and experience. The retrieval process is in many ways a natural but methodical extension of what we all do naturally anyway – talk.

ORAL HISTORY AS A PROFESSION

The explosion of interest in oral history will have other consequences as yet unseen. What has become obvious over the many months of research for this publication is the need to establish a regulatory body representing the interests of practising professional fee-charging oral historians, much as the Law Society or Institute of Chartered Surveyors represents the interests of their members. At present oral history is heavily biased towards social history research and certainly the Oral History Society in the UK was not conceived as any kind of regulatory or professional body.

It is not my intention to diminish in any way the opportunities oral history has presented to people to be heard. However, the next generation of practising professional oral historians should be professionally trained and accredited before offering skills and services to others.

Across the world new uses for oral history are being created all the time. In many cases these new uses are far from having a purely academic role. A new breed of professional oral historian is emerging to exploit these roles and there is evidence that this is already occurring.

Oral historians are already available for hire, my own successful consultancy being an indisputable testament to that fact. It is also beginning to happen in the United States and it will be only a matter of time before an Oral History Practice is established somewhere. The need for a regulatory body with a professional register is clear and unequivocal. What is less clear is which body will have the courage and enlightenment to pick up the gauntlet either here in the UK, in the United States or in some other part of the world.

USEFUL ADDRESSES

Age Exchange, The Reminiscence Centre, 11, Blackheath Village, London SE3 9LA 0181–318–9105

British Empire & Commonwealth Museum, Clock Tower Yard, Temple Meads, Bristol BS1 6QH 0117–9254980

Heritage Recording Services, 8 Trem Arfon, Llanrwst, Conwy CB, North Wales Tel/fax 01492 640005. (The author's own consultancy and contract service on all aspects of oral history, including training, interviewing, post editing and sound track preparation for exhibitions, indexing, cataloguing and transcription, collection management and care, etc. Free brochure available on services.)

Imperial War Museum, Department of Sound Records, Imperial War Museum, London 0171–416–5000

Kirklees Sound Archive, Tolson Memorial Museum, Ravensknowle Park, Huddersfield HD5 8DJ 01484–223830

Living History Unit, Leisure Services Department,
New Walk Centre, Welford Place,
Leicester LE1 6ZG 0116 2527334

Museum of Welsh Life, St Fagan's, Cardiff CF5 6XB 01222–569441

National Sound Archive, The British Library, 96, Euston Road, London NW1 2DB Tel 0171–412–7440

North West Sound Archive, Clitheroe Castle, Ribble Valley, Lancashire BB7 1AZ Tel/Fax 01200–427897

Oral History Association Box 97234, Baylor University, Waco, Texas 76798–7234

Oral History Society. Contact: Department of Sociology, University of Essex, Colchester CO4 3SQ

RTS Audio Services, 5, Malvern Avenue, Atherton, Manchester M29 9LP 01942–892193 (Specialist audio/oral history replay systems for museums, exhibitions, etc.)

School of Scottish Studies, University of Edinburgh, 27 George Square, Edinburgh EH8 9LD 0131–650–1000

Southampton Oral History Archive, Tower House, Town Quay, Southampton SO1 1DX 01703–635904

Wessex Film & Sound Archive, Sussex Street, Winchester SO23 8TH 01962–847742

Zonal Ltd., Holmethorpe Avenue, Redhill, Surrey, RH1 2NX tel 01737–767171 (Manufacturers of high quality reel-to-reel tape, cassettes & R-DAT. Recommended product for use on the UHER reel-to-reel portable is the 846 series 5" reel 12RL (1200 feet or 38 minutes 40 seconds per side at 3.75 inches per second recording speed.)

SAMPLE QUESTIONS

Each question sheet should start off in roughly the same way. A useful reminder of the basic but effective interrogative key words is presented across the top – namely WHY WHEN WHAT WHERE WHO WHICH HOW or simply WWWWWWH. The approach adopted by the author is not the only approach; some oral historians work purely on keywords as *aide-mémoires*. The first sheet is straightforwardly on childhood: school-days has been missed out quite deliberately and can be found in Appendix 2b. Childhood is one of the most popular of all subjects for oral history recording. The questions can also be used as a basis for reminiscence work with the elderly.

A) CHILDHOOD

Where were you born? When?
What is your earliest memory?
Where were you living? (home)

Family

Tell me something about your early childhood.
How many brothers and sisters did you have?
What did your father do for a living?
Other than being a housewife, did your mother ever work?
What did she do? For how long? Where?

Health

Childbirth
Can you recall any of your brothers and sisters being born?
Where were they born?
    If they were born at home then ask questions on –
Who delivered the baby?
How long did the delivery take?
What complications were there?
(If they do not have brothers or sisters ask if they can recall any other people in the area giving birth at home)
What happened if the child was stillborn?
What happened to the child? (e.g., Was there a burial?)

Diseases and illness

If any member of your family became ill whom did you approach for help?
Tell me about doctors. Were they ever paid? How?
What diseases and illnesses did you have as a child?
Can you recall things like rickets, ringworm, etc.?

Housing

What kind of house were you brought up in?
How many rooms were there?
Describe the layout of the house to me. Start at the front door and take me through the house. (Draw a plan if necessary)
How were rooms lit? (Candle, oil, electricity)
How was it paid for?
Where were candles/oil bought from?
What was on the floors? (Sand, flagstones, linoleum, peg-work rugs, coconut matting, carpets, etc.)

How were floors cleaned? By whom?

What was on the walls? (Wallpaper, pictures, dampness)

How was the house heated?

Who actually did the housework? Were domestic staff ever employed? How were they engaged? Where did they live/come from? What were they paid? When?

Where was the nearest telephone? When did you first use a telephone?

Can you recall seeing rats and mice?

Can you recall seeing cockroaches?

How were they dealt with?

Who owned the property you lived in?

To whom did you pay the rent? (If it was rented)

How much was it?

How did you light a fire? Describe it to me. (Firewood, logs, kindling, coal, blowers, etc. Where was fuel kept?)

What kind of fireplace was there in the living room/kitchen, etc.?

How was it cleaned?

Who emptied the ashes? Where were they put?

What memories have you of the chimney being swept?

Did it ever go wrong?

How did the chimney sweep know the brushes were at the top?

What happened to the soot? (It was sometimes used as a fertiliser)

How was water heated?

What water supply was there?

Tell me something about the toilet facilities.

Was there an inside toilet? When did that arrive?

If the toilet was outside what kind was it? (Flush, bucket, long-drop, tippler, channel-type, etc.)

How elaborate was it?

What happened in the winter when you wanted to use the outside toilet?

Who cleaned the toilet? How?

Who cleaned the rooms? How?

Who cleaned the front-door step? How was it cleaned? (Hint at finding out about scrubbing, in the north using donkey stones (sanding) and red leading.)

Social life

Where did you go in the evening as a teenager?

What can you recall of street entertainers? dancing bears, hurdy-gurdy, etc.

Tell me about your friends. Where did you meet? What sorts of things did you do together?

Can you ever recall seeing fighting in the street or in public?

Tell me about some of the games that children used to play in the street.

What can you recall of election time?

Traditions and customs

Going roughly through the year, remind me of some the traditions and customs. (New Year, Shrovetide, Easter, Morris Dancing, Bonfire Night, Christmas, etc.)

Religion

Religious life and church, Sunday school outings

How important was religion to you?

Which faith/church did you belong to? Why?

How often would you go to church?

How closely were you involved in the activities of the church? What sorts of things did you do? (Church of England might include May Queens, Whitsuntide processions in northern England, Sale of Work, Flower festivals, Church Army, Sidesmen duties, etc.)

Holidays

When did you first go on holiday? Where to?

How much did it cost?
Whom did you go with?
How did you get there?
Where did you stay when you got there?
What did you do?
When did you first go abroad?
Where to?

Television

When did you first see television?
What was on?
What was your favourite programme? Why?
What are your favourite programmes today?

Cinema and theatre

How often did you go out to the cinema?
Whom did you go with?
What did you watch?
How did you get there?
Tell me about going into the cinema.
How often did you go to the theatre/pantomime?
Where did you go? Whom did you go to see?
How did you get there?

Circuses and fairgrounds

Tell me something about your memories of the circus. (Big Top travelling circuses, animals, high wire, etc. Blackpool Tower Circus.)
What can you recall of travelling fairgrounds?
When did they come?
What kind of things were there?
Can you recall eating candy-floss for the first time?
What sort of prizes could you win?
Tell me about the dodgems.

Shops

Tell me about street traders (fish, bread, groceries, knife-sharpeners, gypsies with pegs, hot peas, etc.).
What did they sell and when did they come?
What did they cry?
Was there a local Co-op shop? Tell me about the Co-op. What can you recall about collecting the 'Divi'?
Where would your mother take shoes/boots/clogs to be repaired? Who would repair them and how?
Where was the nearest market? Tell me about it.
What stalls were there? To what extent did your mother buy from there? What did she buy?
Where would you buy fresh fruit?

Food and meals

On a typical morning what did you eat before going to school?
Did you ever go hungry?
Did you ever see any of your friends hungry?
What did you eat around mid-day?
What did you eat at tea-time?
What meals did you have on Saturday and Sunday?
How were they different?
What meats did you eat?
How was it prepared?
Who prepared it and how?

Can you recall eating bacon?
Where were eggs obtained from?
How was food kept? (Cold cellar, meat-safe, refrigerator, salted, pickling, etc.)
In season did your mother ever make jams? (If yes, what kind and where did the fruit come from?)
What food did you eat at Christmas? (Christmas dinner, mince pies, trifle, drink, etc.)
Can you recall being ill after eating any particular foods?
What was your favourite food?
Did your mother have a baking-day? Which day?
What did she make?
Did she make her own bread? (If Yes. How? Who kneaded the dough? Where was it baked?)
What other things did she bake?
Where did she store the baked food?
How often was fish eaten? What kind? Where was it bought from? How was it prepared?

Wash-day

Did your mother have a wash-day? (If yes, which day?)
How did she organize the clothes/linen to be washed?
Go through the wash-day with me. What time did she start?
What time did she finish?
How were clothes washed? With what? (Soap, scrubbing, Dolly Blue, etc.)
How were they dried out of doors?
Can you recall how they were dried indoors?

Money matters

Who was/were the wage earner/s?
Who looked after the money?
Can you recall families going to the pawnbrokers? What happened at the pawnbrokers? How were things redeemed?
How often was money drunk away?
How was money saved up? Where?
What can you recall of burial clubs, insurance collection, etc.?
When did you first have a bank account?

Personal matters (This section is included for completeness but a great deal of discretion is required before asking intimate questions. The questions can be drip fed in much the same way as a solicitor builds up the case by asking smaller less relevant questions which in total prove the point. This kind of interviewing must have the clearest and highest standards of interviewing possible. The feelings of the interviewee must be taken into account at every stage. The objective, for purposes of example, is to discover information about domestic violence.)

How long were you married before the separation?
How long have you lived in this house?
How on earth did you manage to raise five children in such a small house? (Inviting an answer which illustrates the problems of privacy in the home.)
How on earth did you get a minute to yourself? (The question is now directly more personal.)
It must have been a bit embarrassing sometimes at night. How did you get around that? (Invites personal response.)
There has been a great deal of talk in the papers about the difficulties of family life, married life – wife beating, drunkenness and all the rest of it. Can you recall any of that in the area where you lived? (This question deliberately depersonalizes it, but invites a response which may indirectly refer to their own private experiences.)
When did your own marriage finally break up? (The interviewee will probably offer a date or a period of years as an answer. What has actually happened is that the person is now aware that the next question may well very personal.)
Can I ask you – I know this is very personal, but can I ask you why your marriage broke down? (The final stage has been reached and will either continue to be personal or will end at that point.)

B) PRIMARY SCHOOL DAYS

An assumption has been made for the purposes of this question sheet that the informant actually went to a typical British state or church school. The question sheet forms a basis for use with children on project work in a school situation. Separate question are likely to be needed to cover, for example, secondary education, Grammar Schools, private tuition, public school education, etc.

WHY WHEN WHAT WHERE WHO WHICH HOW

First steps
Tell me about any basic education (e.g., reading, writing, arithmetic) you received before going to school.
What experience did you have of nursery education?
How old were you when you first went to school?
Where did you go to school?
Tell me about your first day at school.
How did you feel on your first day?
Can you recall having a sleep at school?
Who took you? How did you get there?
How far was it from home?

Organization in the school
Tell me about some of your teachers.
Whom did you like and why?
Whom did you dislike and why?
Go through a typical day at school.
How did teachers deal with breaches of discipline?
Tell me about teachers using the cane/slipper/board duster, etc.
Can you recall any particularly violent teachers?
Who rang the bell at playtime?
Tell me about the headmaster's/mistress's room.
How important was religion at school?
Who taught you religious studies? (Vicar, Father, Nuns, Special teacher, etc.)
What religious occasions did you celebrate?
Can you recall any children who were not of your faith? (i.e., not corresponding to the principal faith in the school.)
What happened to them during religious instruction?
Can you recall morning assembly? What religious content was there?

Lessons
Tell me about drill practice. (The very elderly may recall this.)
Tell about gym and games classes. What did you wear?
Describe one of the classrooms to me. (*Aide-mémoire:*blackboard, long desks, slates, books, chalk, windows, school milk, lighting, heating, floor covering, colour of the walls, smell, etc.)
Tell me about your lessons.
How were you taught to write, read, etc? Who taught you?
Can you remember your times tables? (Usually older people have an instant response to this question.)
What happened at Christmas-time?
What happened in the summer? (Some schools had lessons out of doors, grew flowers, went for nature walks in country places, etc.)

General
What friends did you make? Who were they?
Are you still in touch with any of them?
What enemies were there?
Tell me about bullying. Were you ever bullied? If so, how?
How common was it to have lice in your hair?
How did you get rid of lice from your hair?

Who did it for you?
What games did you play at school, say, in the playground? Tell me about .... How did you play that?
(*Aide-mémoire*: Girls – skipping games, ball games, chanting. Boys – football, horseplay, fighting, cricket, etc.)

Health

What childhood diseases can you recall from school? (Scarlet fever, impetigo, diphtheria, measles, German measles, etc.)
How were they treated? Were any of them ever fatal?
If you cut yourself while at school who cleaned and dressed the wound?
What did you eat for lunch?
Where did you eat?
Tell me about school dinners.
What can you recall of very poor children. How were they dressed? What happened at lunch time?
Can you recall school milk on a cold winter's day? (This is a lead or encouragement question mainly for older people but should give a response that the milk was often frozen in the bottles and had to be defrosted on radiators.)

C) WARTIME MEMORIES

The recording of wartime memories is extremely important. Effective self-censorship of newspapers and other media during the Second World War has meant that large areas of Home Front activity has not been adequately recorded.

Secret developments have remained largely secret, while plans and drawings were often systematically destroyed to ensure they never fell into enemy hands. The location of wartime installations and activities is the subject of several surveys currently under way in which oral history plays a major role. The samples have, therefore, been divided into two areas – tried and tested sample questions and subject headings.

Second World War: the Home Front – sample subjects

Ack-ack units
Adolf Hitler
Air crashes
Air Training Corps
Air-raid shelters
Air-raid warning posts (ARP)
Air-raids
Aircraft
Aircraft recognition
Airfields and airfield construction
Ambulance drivers
American troops
Anderson shelters
Anti-aircraft guns
Armament production
Armament storage
Army camps
Army training
Atlantic convoys
Barrage balloons
Bevin Boys
Black market
Black-out curtains
Bodies
Bombing – direct hits
Cargoes
Casualties
Censorship
Christmas celebrations
Cinema and films

Civil Defence
Collieries – air raid precautions
Command centres
Conscientious objectors
D-Day
Dances
Declaration of War
Decoys – aerodromes, mock-up ships, etc.
Delousing
Diseases
Disruption in cities caused by bombing
Emergency water supplies (EWS)
Engineering – secret work, war work, etc.
Entertainment
Evacuees
Explosives – transportation
Famous people visiting local area
Farming
Firefighting
Fire-watching
First Aid
Fishing industry
Foil dropped from the sky
Food – distribution and control
Food and cooking
Fund raising
Gas decontamination centres
Gas masks
Gas-powered vehicles
Graffiti and drawings
Home Guard (LDV)
Houses – protection against air-raid damage
Ice-breaking ships
Identity cards
Incendiary bombs
Internment camps
Land Army
Local Defence Volunteers, *see* Home Guard (LDV)
Lord Haw-Haw
Marriage in wartime (Clothing, dress, food, etc.)
MI5
Military police
Newspapers
Observer Corps
Petrol supplies
Pill-boxes
Poaching
Police
Posters and signs
Prisoners of war – on farms, etc.
Propaganda
Radar
Radio – as a source of information
Railway working
Rationing and ration books
Red Cross

Refugees
Reservoirs – protection
Road blocks
Royal Naval Air Stations
Royal Ordnance factories
Royalty
Searchlights
Seaside during the war
Secrecy
Shift work
Ships
Shrapnel
Sign posts – removal, etc.
Sirens
Spies
Spitfire Week
Submarines
Tank traps
Telegrams
Textile manufacture – importance to war effort
Theatres
U-boats
Underground bunkers
Unexploded bombs
US air-bases
Utility clothing
Victory in Europe
Victory in Japan
Wages
Weather
Winston Churchill
Women workers
WVS
Z-batteries

Second World War: the Home Front – sample questions

Tell me something about the kind of community you lived in before the war.
How did it change?
How did you know that war had been declared?
How did you feel about it?
Tell me about men going to war. (Call-up papers, trains, etc.)
What can you tell me about rationing? (Ration books, Black Market, queues, petrol rationing, etc.)
Can you recall anything about the Land Army?
What kind of things were made in the local factories during the war?
Who made them?
What war work were you involved in?
Tell me something about the ARP.
Tell me something about the formation of the Home Guard.
Who was in it?
Where did they practise?
What did they do?
In many places pill-boxes were constructed. Can you recall where they were locally? (Have plan if necessary)
Tell me about road blocks.
What happened if you showed a light at night? (Leads into black-out stories, etc.)
Can you recall any local gun positions?
Where were the local air-raid shelters?

Did you personally ever use them?

Tell me about your experiences in an air-raid.

Was your home ever damaged? (If it was destroyed ask what happened then)

In the event of a fire where did the fire brigade get their water from? (Concrete tanks, streams, etc.)

Can you recall ever seeing an enemy plane?

Did you ever actually see the enemy? (This leads into PoW camps, prison trains, etc.)

How did people locally cooperate during the war?

Tell me about the American service men coming into the war.

What correspondence was there with men who were fighting?

Tell me about Churchill.

How did you feel on hearing about Dunkirk? (Leads into discussion about small boats being used in the evacuation)

Do you recall anything about Digging for Victory?

How on earth did a young person getting married manage to obtain all the things necessary for a wedding with everything being on ration?

Tell me about searchlights.

D) COUNTRY HOUSES AND ESTATE MANAGEMENT

The use of a base plan for the location of buildings and other structures and for the recording of information is essential in this kind of recording. A camera is also an advantage. Rather than giving specific 'tried and tested' questions in this section subject headings are listed to illustrate the wide range of possibilities.

Historical

Estate management in the past.

Gardens and gardening – former methods. Location of greenhouses, rose gardens, heated walls, bothies, wells, etc.

Ground maintenance generally. Trees, ponds, fences, walls.

Horses. Uses, types of horse, shoeing, stables, riding, working horses, etc.

Kitchen produce and food production generally. Market garden.

Land tenancy and rent collection. Evictions.

Mining subsidence.

Poaching and game. Shoots.

Power generation – former gas works, water turbines, water wheels, windmills, electricity generators, etc.

Research into people and their work.

The House and Family

The House – exterior. Maintenance problems – guttering and down spouts, roof leakage, etc.

The House – interpretation of individual rooms.

The interpretation of existing structures, interior and exterior. Cottages, houses, barns, saw mills, etc.

The interpretation of old photographs.

Vehicles and their usage. Early cars, carts, carriages, etc.

Visitors – local families, tradesmen, etc.

Workers – house staff, ground staff, tenant farmers, etc.

Contemporary Estate and Country House Management

Boundary – disputes.

Boundary – identification and location of boundary markers.

Boundary – location of estate records and plans.

Building – sources of stone, etc.

Buildings – structural alterations.

Building – structural problems, etc.

Buildings – usage identification (standing or otherwise).

Conservation of artefacts.*

Drainage – identification of problem areas.
Drainage – location of pipes and land drains, etc.
Drainage – location of voids and cavities (e.g., old cellars).
Estate organization – where it has a direct relevance to modern estate management.
Infill sites – old rubbish tips, back fill sites, etc.
Mining and quarrying – identification of old sites, tunnels, voids, drainage courses carrying polluted material.
Mining subsidence.
Power generation – former gas works, water turbines, water wheels, windmills, electricity generators, etc.
Rights of Way
Road repairs – sources of stone, organization, etc.
Storm damage.
Tree and coppice management.
Water supply, feeder courses, ponds, cisterns, pumps, etc.
Wells – identification and location.

* Information about the location, storage and use of artefacts of all kinds. Their origins, original location or movement within the house, damage and how it was repaired, cleaning regime, cleaning statuary and paintings, lights, chandeliers, carpets, etc. Other objects might include farm machinery and equipment, vehicles, iron gates, pond and garden statuary, sun dials, etc.

E) MARITIME HISTORY

This is a vast subject. Again, rather than offering specific questions, the approach has been to offer possible subject areas.

Air support services
Boat-building
Buoys
Cargoes – handling
Cargoes – types
'Cod Wars'
Collisions at sea
Coral reefs
Cranes
Customs and Excise
Disaster experiences
Diving
Dock Labour
Docks and harbours – warehousing
Dredging
Ferries
Fish-weirs
Fishing – deep sea
Fishing – drift net
Fishing – inshore
Fog
Icebergs and pack ice
Launching ships
Lighthouses
Merchant seamen
Navigation
Navy and Marines
Oil and gas platforms
Oil tankers
Passenger liners
Pollution – from land

Pollution – from wrecks
Rescue services – coast guard
Rescue services – helicopters, etc.
Rescue services – lifeboats
Sailing ships
Salmon fishing
Seasickness
Second World War
Shellfish industry
Ship-building
Smuggling – animals
Smuggling – drugs
Smuggling – goods generally
Storms at sea
Submarine operation
Superstitions
Weather
Whaling
Wrecks
Wrecks and hulks

Coastal survey work is more orientated towards the identification of maritime archaeological features such as wrecks or Bronze Age fish weirs. At the time of writing a great deal of work, particularly in Scotland, Wales and the north east of England, was under way recording information.
    Subject areas include:

Active erosion of land
Aircraft navigation beacons (Berry Head, Torbay, Calf of Man, etc.)
Archaeological sites – e.g. Jarlshof in Shetland
Ballast banks
Boat yards (including very small one-boat yards)
Bridges (Forth, Menai, Conwy, Tower Bridge, etc.)
Buoys and bells
Burial sites
Castles and similar fortifications
Causeways
Caves
Channel Tunnel
Churches
Coastal and sea movement (raised beaches, etc.)
Container ports
Cranes
Customs and Excise Buildings
Deposit of land
Desalination plants
Detritus deposits (discarded shells, etc.)
Dredgers
Dry docks
Electricity and underwater telegraphy cables
Ferries
Fish weirs
Floating docks and pontoons
Flood barriers (e.g. the Thames Barrier)
Gunnery and missile ranges
Haaf-net fishing
Herring smoking sheds

Holiday camps
Iron works
Jetties
Land reinforcement
Land speed test areas (South Wales)
Leisure facilities – holiday camps, resorts
Lifeboat stations
Lighthouses
Martello Towers
Mining – tin mining in Cornwall, coal-mining in north-east England, copper mining at Great Orme, North Wales, etc.)
Natural oil seepages
Nuclear power stations
Oil refineries
Piers
Public houses and inns
Quarries
Religious sites
Roads – low water access to islands, etc.
Sail lofts
Salterns
Sand dune migration (May cover early marine sites or buildings such as St Enodoc's church, Cornwall)
Sewage outfalls
Ship canals
Ship-yards
Shore-line peat beds
Slipways
Submerged forests
Transmitting stations
Tunnels under estuaries (Tyne, Mersey, Thames, etc.)
Villages and fishing communities
Warehouses
Wrecks and hulks

Second World War
Aeroplane wrecks
Air fields
Air-raid shelters
Ammunition deep sea dumps
Army camps
D-Day landing practice areas
Forts (e.g. in Bristol Channel)
Gun emplacements
Gunnery and bomb aiming practice sites
Landing craft concrete barriers
Mine emplacements
Prisoner of War camps
Radar installations
Sea plane bases
Shipwrecks – specific wartime wrecks
Tank defences
Transmitting stations
Underground installations in cliffs, etc. – hospitals, control centres, ammunition dumps, etc.

F) DIALECT AND LANGUAGE

Emphasis has been placed in the text on the importance of not influencing or unintentionally supplying dialect words during survey interviewing. By using photograph/s or drawing/s, a series of questions can then be asked without supplying the word.

Example 1 Coal-mining

What name do you give to the area in a mine opposite to the floor? (Suggestions could include roof, top, upper, etc.)
What name do you give to the vertical column supporting the upper part? (Post, pit prop, stanchion, etc.)
What do you call the process whereby you need to lie on your side to work or swing in a confined space to work (Hewing, holing-out, etc.)
What name do you give to the area of coal left in to support the roof? (Pillar, stack, column, etc.)
What name do you give to the worked-out area of a coal-mine? (Gob, goaf, worked out area, etc.)
Who was responsible for actually getting the coal? (Collier, coal-hewer, etc.)
What name was given to the person who assisted? (Waggoner, dateler, runner, etc.)
What name was given to the material removed from under the coal? (Seat earth, dirt, muck, etc.)
What name was given to hard rock? (Warrant, bullion, sandstone, etc.)

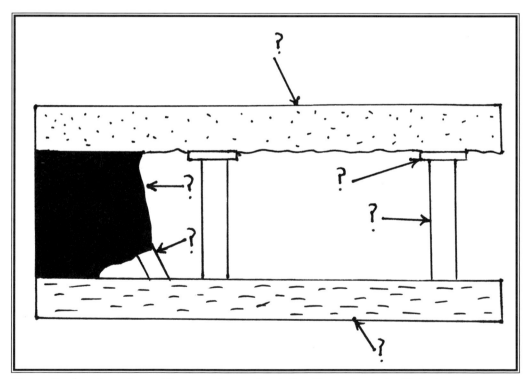

Cross-section through a coal-seam. The parts to be named are indicated by question marks. (Author)

PHOTOGRAPHS AND PHOTOGRAPHY

It has been suggested throughout this book that photography is particularly useful to oral historians. Old photographs can act as a catalyst in encouraging people to talk. Many photographs preserved in public collections are interesting but preserved with little contextual information and deserve, where possible, to be explained or interpreted by informants.

Sometimes, for example in a village survey, photographs need to be taken to complement the memories of people – buildings, street furniture, signs, etc. – so that future generations know exactly what is being talked about. Finally there is the possibility of photographing the informant him- or herself to accompany the final interview.

Professional practice will sensibly dictate that original photographs never leave the protective care of public collections. Today there is so much good copying technology around that photographs and indeed documents can be easily copied. Modern copiers also enlarge and 'laser' or colour copiers can give almost photographic quality to black and white originals. There is a counter-argument that certain photocopiers produce ozone and other gases that can affect prints, especially colour prints, but the hazard is small compared with the gains. A clean flatbed photocopier glass is a prerequisite to any copying.

There are some very high quality digital scanning systems available which produce full-colour almost perfect photographic copies. However, the process is expensive per unit print and the colour tends to fade in time.

There are a number of good practical reasons for not using original photographs on location, apart from any preventative conservation policy in force. For example, the enlargement of picture detail or the direct annotation on to the surface of copies. If two copies are made of an image, leaving one behind as a 'thank you' is often greatly appreciated.

All images need to be numbered in a prominent place making them readily identifiable during an interview. Complicated photographs of industrial processes or technical machinery may need dividing up into squares – rather like an Ordnance Survey map – so that a grid reference can be given. The top of the picture from left to right should be marked A to Z and the left-hand side from the top left 1 to 20 or whatever is appropriate. The grid can be drawn directly on to the photocopy or if that is inappropriate, then a transparent cell of the type used for overhead projectors can be placed over the photocopy and hinged on the left, appropriately marked with a navigational location grid.

Sequences of photographs, such as a craft process, need putting into chronological order. One of the problems that arises is that the order might not be correct. This only comes to light during the course of the interview. The informant might vary the process, or text books in which initial research has been undertaken might simply be wrong. Numbering the sequence 1 – ? whatever, is the simplest way. As long as the prints are numbered and tied into the interview conversation then the information is useful.

Build the identification into the interview structure. For example:

Q: Now what is that large round object on the right at C5?
A: C5, C5 – yes that's a drying tin for drying paper, etc.

Not all informants will allow their photograph to be taken. The nature of their reminiscences may be such that identification would be inappropriate and undesirable. However, most people will allow a photo to be taken and it is a most useful adjunct to the interview.

Taking the photograph on an occasion other than the interview session is far better if it can be achieved. It allows concentration on photography rather than audio recording. The picture should capture something of the character of the person and his or her environment, and should be taken with the minimum of fuss.

My own approach is to use the oral history interview techniques described elsewhere as a warm-up session for the sitter. Ask about something he or she will remember and chat freely about. There may even be a little further reminiscence, something he or she has forgotten to tell me on the previous occasion.

Take the photo when the sitter is least expecting it. You can, of course, direct the sitter to look at certain things or sit in a certain way, but keep chatting, keep communicating. The difference between great portraits and poor portraits is not technical or sophisticated cameras – it is timing. Never be frightened of taking four or five or more pictures. About two pictures into the sequence say something like 'What is your happiest memory' or 'Tell me something about your

This photograph was taken using a basic 35 mm camera on a monopod and natural window light. (Author)

wedding day', and be ready to fire the shutter. There is a moment as people begin to recall when their faces will change and reflect their innermost thoughts. Press the shutter. The equipment need not be sophisticated for such a simple record; a modern compact camera (set at its widest angle) with flash or one of the older 35mm single lens reflex cameras with a flash gun is ideal.

On warmer summer days, I usually ask informants to stand just outside the doorway and photograph them from the outside using natural daylight. Photographing informants in their garden or greenhouse is also a good idea and will guarantee some useful light as well as more relaxed manner.

In the winter, an exterior shot may well not be an option. If the interviewee is bedridden or has a mobility problem then photographs will need to be taken indoors. Indoor photography requires a little more time and effort to get right. One of the easiest ways to light the subject for record purposes is to use window light, especially if the window is south-facing. Turn the subject towards the window so he or she is in effect looking out. Use a monopod to steady the shot. Take several pictures with or without flash; also switch on any tungsten lamps such as reading lamps. They will come out reddish brown on daylight colour film but will help raise the light level. (You can purchase filters to correct daylight film to tungsten light film or simply buy tungsten-balanced film, but a certain amount of colour mix – tungsten and daylight – is acceptable.) Strip lighting is, however, greenish and unacceptable.

Check the background to ensure that there are no bright reflective surfaces to throw the light back. Use a 100 or 200 ISO film speed, colour negative. Faster film speeds such as 200 ISO to 400 ISO, even with a modest in-built flash gun, will allow you to take the whole room with the subject seated in the centre. Again look for reflections from objects such as mirrors, TV screens, vases, etc. Avoid room clutter especially close to the camera.

If more than one person is to be photographed ask them to stand or position themselves very close together and to look over your left shoulder rather than right into the camera lens. The reason for this is that one reflective surface is the human eye and the flash can be reflected in what is known as red-eye. By looking slightly to one side or by positioning the camera and subject slightly off central axis will avoid the effect. Occupying the subject or subjects with a prop is another useful ploy. A pet such as dog is another way to obtain a good informal portrait.

With more sophisticated cameras and flash guns it is often possible to bounce the flash off a light-coloured ceiling giving good general overall light distribution. This technique is described in detail in most good books on photography.

Films should be processed as soon as possible after exposure. This is particularly true in hot humid climates. In the UK photo processing is widely available although you get what you pay for. Many people welcome a copy of the picture you have taken. The easiest and cheapest way is to have duplicates made at the processing stage.

Archival processing is highly specialized and outside the scope of this book. Colour prints can, however, be screened into digital systems and on to Photo-CD and its clones, and be re-photographed via filters into its primary colours on black and white film for permanence.

Modern prints are coated on a plastic base. Most colour prints fade or change with time and should be stored with great care. Refer to one of the many good guides available to storing and conserving photographs for technical advice.

At least one copy of the print/s should be stored in association with the recording. The photographs will need labelling on the reverse in permanent black and relating in some way to the recording. (Name, place, date of photograph, photographer, accession number of interview, etc.)

If it is ever intended that the photograph might be used for publication – and that includes exhibitions – permission will need to be obtained from the sitter for that purpose. This permission could be included on the normal clearance sheet or in a separate document giving permission to use the photograph for specific purposes.

CLEARANCE, DEPOSIT AND COPYRIGHT NOTES: AUDIO AND VIDEO

Smalltown Museum & Art Gallery, Smalltown, Anywhere (UK) Tel 01234–5678910

Clearance Instructions for Oral History on Audio and Video

Smalltown Borough Museum is grateful for your kind help and co-operation in its oral history recording programme. As you know, the recordings, audio/video, will be preserved for posterity and used in accordance with the Museum's Constitution.

However, under the 1988 Copyright Act, it is now necessary to seek your written permission to use the recordings for our purposes. This in no way restricts any use you may wish to make of the information you so kindly supplied, but it does allow us to ensure that your contribution is preserved for posterity and used in accordance with our Constitution, and your wishes.

Brief description of interview.

Closures
1) Have you any objections to Smalltown Museum using your contribution for the following non-commercial uses:
Instruction
a) Public reference/performance Yes/No
b) Educational use (in schools, etc.) Yes/No
c) Broadcasting on radio or television Yes/No
d) As a source that may be published Yes/No
e) Distribution on the Internet Yes/No

2) Do you have any objection to your name being mentioned? Yes/No

3) Do you wish to apply a time restriction before your contribution is released? Yes/No

Copyright
Would you be willing to give your literary copyright to Smalltown Museum? Yes/No

Commercial use
Is your permission required before entering into any commercial arrangements for using the recording? Yes/No

Signed
Address
Tel number
Date of birth
Place of birth
Date of recording

Any notes and additional information

ORAL HISTORY SOCIETY ETHICAL GUIDELINES

For interviewers and custodians of oral history recordings and related materials

1. Interviewers have the following responsibilities before an interview takes place:

1.1 To consider the purpose of the interview and the possible range of future uses to which it might be put.

1.2 To carry out research and acquire sufficient technical knowledge to conduct an interview of the best possible standard.

1.3 To inform the interviewee of the purpose for which the interview is to be carried out, with background information where appropriate.

1.4 To determine the preferences of the interviewee as to the location and conduct of the interview (for example, the presence of other persons; subject matter or personal references to be avoided).

2. The interviewer has the following responsibilities during the conduct of an interview:

2.1 To ensure that the interviewee's preferences as to location and conduct of the interview are abided by.

2.2 To treat interviewees with respect and courtesy.

3. The interviewer has the following responsibilities after an interview has taken place:

3.1 To inform the interviewee of the arrangements to be made for the custody and preservation of the interview and accompanying material, both immediately and in the future, and to indicate *any* use to which the interview is likely to be put (for example, research, education use, transcription, publication, broadcasting). To record in writing (and later carry out or convey to others) any restrictions use or other conditions which the interviewee may require.

3.2 To inform the interviewee of his or her rights under copyright law,[1] and to obtain a statement in writing of the interviewee's wishes concerning future copyright ownership. Even where the interviewee agrees to transfer copyright to the interviewer or to an institution, copies of substantial portions of interviews should not be passed to others without the knowledge of the interviewee.

3.3 To ensure that the interviewee is informed (preferably in writing) when arrangements made under 3.1–3.2 above are carried out. If these responsibilities are transferred to others (for example an archive or other place of deposit), this should be with the knowledge and consent of the interviewee and should be recorded in writing.

3.4 To inform the interviewee of any new circumstances or changes to provisions made under 3.1–3.2 above.

3.5 To ensure that the interview is documented, indexed, catalogued and made available as agreed with the interviewee, and that a copy of the recording or transcript is given to the interviewee if an undertaking to do so has been given.

3.6 To ensure that all possible measures are taken to preserve interview recordings and related materials.

4. Sponsoring institutions or places of deposit such as archives, libraries, museums, or university departments have the following responsibilities:

4.1 To select interviewers of sufficient competence and skill, and to give sufficient guidance or training to ensure that these guidelines are carried out.

4.2 To ensure that recordings and documentation are carried out to the best possible, and at least to a sufficient standard.

4.3 To ensure that information on copyright ownership and other restrictions and conditions is recorded in writing and preserved. To document fully in writing all transfers of interview recordings and related material from individuals or others and ensure that 3.3 is fully carried out.

4.4 To ensure that responsibilities under 3.4–3.6 are understood and carried out.

4.5 To avoid the acquisition of interviews which are not accompanied by documentation indicating provenance, availability for use, and copyright status, except where there is a realistic prospect that 4.6 can be carried out successfully.

4.6 If interviews as described in 4.5 are acquired, to ensure that all possible steps are taken to contact interviewees or their heirs in order to obtain written statements concerning copyright and access.

4.7 To restrict access to interviews (even where this has not been required by the interviewee) in appropriate cases.[2]

4.8 To ensure that names and personal details of interviewees are not passed on to third parties (for example broadcasters) without the consent of interviewees. Institutions should not become involved in any business arrangements which may result from such contacts.

4.9 To decide whether to charge for services and to fix a standard scale of charges which will apply to all users.[3]

Notes:
1 Interviewees own the copyright in their words, which may not be published, broadcast or otherwise exploited without their permission. See *Copyright and Oral History* above.
2 Access might need to be restricted if circumstances exist or arise in which the interests or social and professional standing of the interviewee, or of others involved with the interviewee or mentioned in the interview, could be harmed by providing access. Such restrictions should only be applied if considered essential, but should apply to all potential users. The value of retaining recordings to which access is restricted should be considered before they are acquired. It is recommended that restrictions should last for a maximum of thirty years from the date of recording, and that interviews are not acquired to which access has to be restricted beyond the death of the interviewee.
3 The purpose of charging should be to cover the costs of providing access and to further the work of the institution. A 'sliding scale' of charges should be drawn up, relating to use. Typically, academic researchers and local users or societies would not be charged for access or time involved in routine supervision, but should pay for photo- and audio-copying, etc. at cost. Commercial users such as broadcasters or publishers may be charged for any services provided, at current commercial rates. It is recommended that additional charges for the use of extracts from recordings and transcripts are kept low, or not imposed at all. It should be made clear to interviewees that charges are being made, and that such income will be put to good use.

RIO DE JANEIRO EARTH SUMMIT, 1992: AGENDA 21

The UK Government's support of 'Agenda 21', an action plan for now and the next millennium for both environment and people, unwittingly created a ready-made role for oral historians. There are significant economic, social and environmental implications under Agenda 21, including the control of emissions and pollution, and the sustainability or otherwise of many current practices. Some local authorities have adopted new approaches including greater local community involvement, the creation of partnerships and local action groups, the encouragement of 'sustainable' activities, awareness of quality items in the local environment, and general equality – health, freedom from persecution, freedom from poverty, and a greater input into the decision-making process.

It will be apparent from the main text of this book that oral history is a realistic and practical way of exploring many of the issues under Agenda 21, especially as a tool for local empowerment. The use of oral history allows the creation of a resource for community or educational use, as well as providing a major source of original information on which to base decisions. Some of the areas where oral history could be used constructively include:

archaeology and industrial archaeology research
education generally, including life-long learning programmes
environmental impact assessments
erosion pattern changes
ethnicity
Health & Safety at Work, identification of dangerous practices, encouragement of sustainable practices
health care
heritage audits
language and dialects; culture retention
management decision-making relative to Agenda 21
meteorology, changes in weather patterns, extreme events, etc.
national parks, interpretation, planning, heritage audits
peace-maker role
pollution identification and control
race relations
reminiscence work
road transport: alternative strategies
site research, location of hazards, former factories, etc.
skill loss recording and mentoring
soundscape reconstruction and sense-of-place research
tourism development and impact
town and country planning, conservation areas, estate management, etc.
vegetation changes
water quality and water-power
wind power, etc.

NOTES

Abbreviation: *OHJ, Oral History Journal*

INTRODUCTION

1. Internet: http://www.ampas.org/academy/oral.html In the United States the Academy Oral History Programme has been documenting the lives of those working in the film industry including film editors, screenwriters, directors and producers (Motion Picture Academy).
2. For a fuller discussion see John Kotre, *White Gloves: How We Create Ourselves Through Memory* (Simon & Schuster, New York, 1995).

CHAPTER 1: WHAT IS ORAL HISTORY?

1. *The World Book Encyclopedia* – 'The origins of language' (USA, nd).
2. 'News from abroad', *OHJ* 19 (1991), no. 1, pp. 13–14.
3. 'Current British Work', *OHJ* 19 (1991), no 1, p. 9.
4. Dearling, Robert, Dearling, Celia and Rust, B. *Guinness Book of Recorded Sound* (Guinness Superlatives 1984), pp. 21–2.
5. As an example, see Roos, J.P. & B. 'Upper class life over three generations: the case of the Swedish Finns', *OHJ* 12 (19??), no 1.
6. 'News from abroad', *OHJ* 19 (1991), no 1, p. 14.
7. Ibid.

CHAPTER 2: ORAL HISTORY FOR THE ARCHIVE, LIBRARY AND MUSEUM PROFESSIONAL

1. Included for convenience under this heading is field archaeology. It is recognized that the subject is not exclusive to the museum world.
2. The recording reference number 1979.0031 is available on loan from the NW Sound Archive UK.
3. Graham, Stanley. 'The Lancashire Textile Industry: a description of the work and some of the techniques involved', *OHJ* 2 (1980), no. 2. The recordings and photographs are available at the Pendle Heritage Centre, Barrowford, Nelson. The massive mill engine still operates and is open to the public during the summer.
4. This recording was part of series made for the British Wool Marketing Board's Visitor Centre and is an example of oral history being used for public relations purposes. See Chapter Three for further information on oral history for business, management and environmental planning.
5. Brough, Joseph. *Wrought Iron – the end of an era at Atlas Forge, Bolton* (Bolton Metropolitan Borough Arts Department, nd). There are good colour photographs of iron puddling. The recordings are housed at the North West Sound Archive.
6. The relationship between industrial archaeology and the needs of businesses and planners is closer than might at first be appreciated. The accurate recording of drainage systems or the extent of extraction could well yield important information to planners and quarry companies. The extent of underground working is not always accurately represented on plans. Not only is such information of economic importance but it is also of potential use to rescue services and the police attempting to trace a missing child or similar. Chapter three deals more fully with the potential of oral history, business and planning.
7. Perks, R. 'The Ellis Island Immigration Museum, New York', *OHJ* 19 (1991), no. 1, pp. 79–80.

8. Hyslop, Donald and Jemima, Sheila. 'The *Titanic* and Southampton: The Oral Evidence', *OHJ* 19 (1991), no. 1 pp. 37–43.
9. Howarth, Ken. 'Why are all the curtains rotten? Oral History and the Interpretation of Brodsworth Hall', *Interpretation Journal (UK)*, July 1997, pp. 8–11.
10. Included for convenience under this heading is Fine Art in its wider sense. It is recognized that the subject is not exclusive to the museum world.
11. 'Current British Work, Artists' Lives', *OHJ* 24 (199?), no. 1, p. 8.
12. 'Telling Tales with Technology', *OHJ* 25 (1997), no. 1, p. 28.
13. Frostick, Elizabeth. 'The use of oral evidence in the reconstruction of dental history at Beamish Museum', *OHJ* 14 (1986), no. 2.
14. Jenkins, Geraint J. 'The collection of ethnological material', *Museums Journal*, 74 (1974), no. 2, pp. 7–11.
15. The uneasy relationship between professional archivists and oral history has been explored in some depth in an excellent article entitled 'Archival Science and Oral Sources' by Jean-Pierre Wallot and Normand Fortier, reproduced in the *Oral History Reader* section 30, published by Routledge in 1998.
16. Kakar, S. 'Leprosy in India: the intervention of Oral History' *OHJ* 23 (1995), no. 1, pp. 37–45.
17. Interview with Humphrey Spender held by both Bolton Museum and North West Sound Archive. Photographs copyright Bolton Museum.

CHAPTER 3: ORAL HISTORY FOR BUSINESS, MANAGEMENT AND ENVIRONMENTAL PLANNING

1. Thomson, A. 'Oral History and Ethics: A Brazilian Experience', *OHJ* 21 (1996), no. 1, pp. 23–5.
2. Internet: various search engines under 'Terra Firma Design'.
3. Internet: HistoryEnterprise http://www.historyenterprises.com/history.htm.
4. The work at London Transport Museum is a good example of what can be achieved using oral history. The Museum is situated at Covent Garden Piazza in London. Tel 0181–318–9105 or 0171–379–6344 for further information.
5. Conti, K.D. 'Oral Histories: the overlooked PR tool'. http://www.iabc.com./cw/conti.htm.
6. Internet http://www.law.unc.edu/oralhist.html.
7. Internet http://gopher:nara.gov.70/0/inform/library/reagan/nlspart4.txt.
8. Internet http://www.unc.edu/depts/sohp/04007I.html.
9. Thomson, A. 'Memory and a sense of place', *OHJ* 25 (1997), no. 1, pp. 23–4.
10. Gant, R. 'Oral History and local meteorology', *OHJ* 14 (1968), no. 2, pp. 67–9. The Royal Meteorological Society Specialist Group for History of Meteorology & Physical Oceanography have recorded interviews with eminent meteorologists and oceanographers. The British Antarctic Survey has also recorded former employees.
11. Both from Yahoo! search engine on the Internet. No addresses given.
12. Waller, Prue. 'Spinning Room: the making of a documentary film', *OHJ* 17 (1989), no. 2, pp. 60–1.

CHAPTER 4: ORAL HISTORY IN THE COMMUNITY

1. Howarth, Ken. *Dark Days: Memories of the Lancashire & Cheshire Coalmining Industry* (1978), pp. 98–107.
2. McKinlay, Alan & Hampton, John. 'Making Ships, Making Men: working for John Brown's between the wars', *OHJ* 19 (1991), no. 1, pp. 21–8.
3. Perks, Robert. 'By train to Samarkand: A view of Oral History in the Soviet Union', *OHJ* 19 (1991), no. 1, pp. 64–7.
4. Adams, Caroline. 'Across seven seas and thirteen rivers', *OHJ* 19 (1991), no. 1, pp. 29–33.
5. Kakar, S. 'Leprosy in India: The intervention of Oral History', *OHJ* 23 (1995), no. 1, pp. 37–45.
6. See also the paper by Fido, R. & Potts, M. '"It's not true what was written down!" Experiences of life in a mental handicap institution', *OHJ* 17 (1989), no. 2, pp. 31–4.
7. Walmsley, Jan. 'Life History Interviews with people with learning disabilities', *OHJ* 23 (1995), no. 1, pp. 71–7.
8. 'News from abroad', *OHJ* 25 (1997), no. 1, p. 17.
9. 'A personal experience of polio.' Tom Atkins interviewed by Rob Wilkinson, *OHJ* 23 (1995), pp 82–4.
10. Adams, John. 'I am still here: A life with encephalitis lethargica', *OHJ* 23 (1995), no. 1, pp. 78–81.

11. *OHJ* (1989) vol. 17, no. 2 Reminiscence. The issue covers oral history and reminiscence as a social movement, etc.
12. Osborn, Caroline. *A practical guide to reminiscence work* (Age Exchange, 1990).
13. Mere, Rosie. 'Travelling on – Life Story Telling in a psychiatric day hospital', *OHJ* 20 (1992), no. 1, p. 75.
14. 'Report on Oral History Association in Cambridge, Massachusetts', *OHJ* 19 (1991), no. 1, p. 19.

CHAPTER 5: ORAL HISTORY IN THE CLASSROOM

1.   Children's Employment Commission Report 1842 p 163 item 102.
2.   Howarth, Ken. *Dark Days*, pp. 15–17.
3.   Redfern, Allan. *Talking in Class. Oral History and the National Curriculum* (Oral History Society, Colchester, 1996).
4.   Hewitt, Maggie. 'History is everything that's behind you': uses of Oral History in schools' *OHJ* 22 (1994), no. 2, pp. 85–7.
5.   Lomas, Tim. 'Oral History and the National Curriculum', *OHJ* 20 (1992), no. 1, p. 35.
6.   Orchard, Irene. 'Oral History and teenagers: Cross curricular applications', *OHJ* 20 (1992), no. 1, pp. 58–62.
7.   The example is based on a real event and place near Little Lever, Bolton, known as Nob End. The grid reference is SH109/753064.
8.   NW Sound Archive (UK) recording 1980.0003. Loan copy available.
9.   BBC Radio Manchester – canals, railways. Recordings now held at North West Sound Archive.
10. 'News from abroad – Australia', *OHJ* 22 (1994), no. 2, pp. 14–17.

CHAPTER 6: RECORDING ORAL HISTORY: PLANNING

1.   Bob Blauner. 'Black Lives, White Lives: Three Decades of Race Relations in America', *OHJ* 19 (1991), no. 1, pp. 74–5.
2.   Perks, Robert. 'By train to Samarkand: A view of Oral History in the Soviet Union Oral History', *OHJ* 19 (1991), no. 1.
3.   In section ten entitled 'Ways of listening', in Perks, R. & Thomson, A. *The Oral History Reader* (Routledge, 1998), there is useful discussion about the relevance of group approach. Some examples are cited where the western style of interview is generally unknown and where targeted and focused responses derived from within the group are far more usual.
4.   Ibid; it is reported that individual contributions in some non-western societies are considered 'dangerous encounters'. 'Ways of Listening', is a useful introduction to oral tradition and oral history in a non-western context.
5.   Cross, N. and Barker, Rhiannon. *At the Desert's Edge* (Panos 1991), p. 1 and rear cover.
6.   Ibid, p. 1.
7.   'Current British Work' *OHJ* (1996), vol. 24, no. 1, pp. 4–5.
8.   Fussell, Angela. 'Politics with a small P: Collecting with that personal touch', nd. Copy of unpublished paper in possession of author. Also Fussell, Angela. *Make 'em Laugh, Make 'em cry! Collecting for Lifetimes – The Interactive Museum about Croydon people* (Nordisk Museologi, 1997).
9.   Howarth, Ken. 'The Strangeways Oral History project', *OHJ* 20 (1992), no. 1, pp. 76–7.
10. Perks, R. and Thomson, A. 'Ways of Listening', p. 117.

CHAPTER 7: RECORDING ORAL HISTORY: THE INTERVIEW

1.   'Ethics and Method', *OHJ* 22 (1994), no. 2, pp. 21–2.
2.   Walmsley, Jan. 'Life History Interviews with people with learning disabilities', *OHJ* 23 (1995), pp. 71–7.
3.   Refer to Clayton, Joan. *Interviewing for Journalists* (Piatkus, London 1994) for a fuller account on WWWWWWH questions.
4.   Perks, R. and Thomson, A. 'Ways of Listening', pp. 120–1.

5. Morris, Desmond. *Manwatching* (Triad/Panther Books 1977) pp. 86–101 for detailed description of tie-signs, etc.
6. Oral History Association, Cambridge, Massachusetts (1990) annual meeting report OH (1991), vol. 19, no. 1, p. 19.

CHAPTER 9: ORAL HISTORY ON VIDEO

1. Dan Snipe, in an article reproduced in Perks, R. and Thomson, A. *The Oral History Reader* (Routledge 1998), section 31 makes out an excellent case for the inclusion of image – whether film or video – for recording aspects of history generally and oral history specifically. However, unfortunately, he makes no reference to editing and the devaluation of the interview as a primary source. It is nevertheless recommended reading for anyone interested in image and oral history.
2. For a fuller description of television lighting for interviews refer to Millerson, G. *The Technique of Television Production* (Focal Press 1990), chapter 9. While the multiple lamp technique used by television is not necessarily appropriate to oral history interviews, the chapter is a good basic guide to lighting and how it works.

CHAPTER 10: USING ORAL HISTORY

1. Thomson, A. 'People's History & Community Publishing: The Federation of Worker Writers and Community Publishers', *OHJ* 19 (1991), no. 1, pp. 60–1.
2. Oral History Association (1990) Annual Meeting, Cambridge, Massachusetts *OHJ* 19 (1991), no 1, p. 20.
3. 'Current British Work. Blowing a Lapwing's Egg'. *OHJ* 25 (1997), no. 1, p. 14.
4. Four Corners. Salford Quays Sculpture. Pamphlet, 1997.
5. Marchant, Alison. 'Treading the traces of discarded history: Oral History installations', *OHJ* 20 (1992), no. 2, p. 48.
6. Annual Conference of the Oral History Association (USA) 'From Memory Maps to Cyberspace', *OHJ* 25 (1997), no. 1, pp. 21–4.
7. 'News from abroad', *OHJ* 22 (1994), no. 2, pp. 16–17.

BIBLIOGRAPHY

Aldred, John. *Manual of Sound Recording* (Fountain Press, 1978) (Good technical manual on the techniques of sound recording)

Clayton, Joan. *Interviewing for Journalists* (Piatkus, 1994) (The best publication seen so far dealing with interviewing skills)

Cross, Nigel and Baker, Rhiannon (eds). *At the Desert's Edge – Oral Histories from the Sahel* (Panos, 1992) (Excellent book on oral history in North Africa)

Finnegan, Ruth. *Oral Traditions & Verbal Arts* (Routledge, 1992) (Places oral history into an anthropological framework. Essential reading for fieldworkers)

Humphries, Stephen. *The Handbook of Oral History – Recording Life Stories* (Inter-action Imprint, 1984) (Long regarded as the standard textbook for community-based oral history work)

Jones, Graham. *How to use the Internet* (How to Books, 1996)

Lawrence, Jane and Mace, Jane. *Remembering in groups. Ideas from reminiscence and literacy work* (Oral History Society)

Millerson, Gerald. *Television Production* (Focal Press, 1990) (Details of basic and advanced lighting set-ups for video work)

Nisbett, Alec. *The Technique of the Sound Studio* (Focal Press, 1972) (Good technical manual on the techniques of sound recording.)

Oral History. *The Journal of the Oral History Society* (1969)

   The *Journal* is the main publication in the UK giving details of current oral history work. There are literally thousands of different projects outlined both at home and abroad. It's essential reading for anyone interested in oral history.

Osborn, Caroline. *A Practical Guide to Reminiscence Work* (Age Exchange, 1990)

Perks, Rob. *Oral History – an annotated bibliography* (British Library, National Sound Archive, 1990)

Perks, Rob. *Oral History – talking about the past* (Historical Association & Oral History Society, 1995)

Perks, Rob and Thomson, Alistair. *The Oral History Reader* (Routledge, 1998). The work contains thirty-nine published extracts on oral history from around the world. It includes references to the development of oral history, interviewing, advocacy and empowerment, interpreting memories and making histories. Specifically, it has sections on Black History, Life History interviews with people with learning disabilities, Women's history, Reminiscence, Lesbian History, and Children and oral history. It forms a good basis for understanding current thinking in oral history at an international level.

Redfern, Allan. *Talking in Class – Oral History and the National Curriculum* (Oral History Society, Colchester, 1996) (Essential reading)

Slim, Hugo and Thompson, Paul. *Listening for Change* (Panos, 1993). (Essential reading on the techniques and approaches used by those in the 'aid world'. It is a companion volume to *At the Desert's Edge* listed above.)

Thompson, Paul. *The Voice of the Past – Oral History* (OUP, 1990) (Essential reading)

Thompson, Paul and Perks, Rob. *Telling how it was. A guide to recording Oral History* (BBC Education, nd)

Ward, Alan. *Copyright, Ethics & Oral History* (Oral History Society)

INDEX